1– 2– &
3–Section Sewings

NON-ADHESIVE BINDING VOLUME II

First Edition May 1995
First Edition Second Printing August 1995

Published by keith a smith BOOKS
22 Cayuga Street
Rochester, New York 14620-2153

Distributed by Keith A. Smith
22 Cayuga Street
Rochester, New York 14620-2153
Telephone or FAX: 716-473-6776

Library of Congress Card Catalogue Number: 95-92079

ISBN: 0-9637682-2-0

1– 2– &
3–Section Sewings

NON-ADHESIVE BINDING VOLUME II

Keith A. Smith

Decorative Sewing Patterns

BOOK NUMBER 169

KE TH

KEITH A. SMITH BOOKS • ROCHESTER NY

TABLE of CONTENTS

Part 3 3-SECTION SEWINGS

Part 4 REFERENCE

ACKNOWLEDGMENTS

Scott McCarney, my partner, for his constant loving support.

Fred Jordan, my binding teacher, for the past fourteen years.

Betsy Palmer Eldridge, for her instructions on stitches and sewing structures. Her dedication to the field is generously evident in her massive undertaking to see that my terminology is not conflicting, and that my stitches and sewing structures are not in error.

My gratitude for all those who allowed me to photo-reproduce their work in this volume. Special thanks to Steven Clay, for all the photographs of books that have been published by Granary Books, 568 Broadway, Suite 403, New York, NY 10012.

※

The photographs of bindings by various contemporary binders are not meant to illustrate the sewings presented here, but to augment. They cannot illustrate, as the decorative sewings were designed *as* I wrote the book. —All but a half dozen of the 122 spine patterns in this book were devised by me since 1993. However, it is mainly the *path of the sewings* which is mine; the sewings are based on standard stitches.

Some of the stitches were learned from a workshop, *Sewing Variations,* taught by Betsy Palmer Eldridge.

Others are inspired by embroidery. Stitches conceived for the single plane sewing of embroidery were translated to a binding sewing path, in and out of sections, through a continuous support of a paper cover.

In Part 2, the *2–Section Running Stitch Sewing* was sent to me by Bert Borch of Calgary, who learned it from Betty Lou Chaika at Penland School. The sewing was also popularized by Hedi Kyle.

TO BETSY PALMER ELDRIDGE

INTRODUCTION

1– 2– & 3–Section Sewings is the second of three books I have written on *Non-Adhesive Binding*.

VOLUME I

Non-Adhesive Binding, sub-titled *Books Without Paste Or Glue*, was written in 1990. It was my 128th book, and my first on the subject of binding. It is now referred to as Volume I. It was conceived as a general textbook.

Volume I has a lengthy introduction to set an aesthetic tone of *why* binding, before it illustrates *how-to*. Part 1 continues with an introduction of terms and supplies. Properties of paper are discussed—grain direction, folding, scoring, cutting and tearing. This is followed by assembled and folded down sections, and their proportion and size from the origin of the sheet. Imposition concludes this chapter.

The following chapter is on sewing stations, needles, thread and knots. General reference on covers completes the preparation prior to binding.

Part 2 presents thirty-two simple to elaborate bindings. Part 3 describes covers requiring no paste or glue. Part 4 has several references. One is the source section. This is a list of several hundred sources for bookstores and dealers; distributors; guilds and organizations; periodicals; binding tools, equipment and materials; paper; services; and workshops and apprenticeships.

Obviously, no one book can present but a small part of what should be said. In time, with others writing, a more rounded profile of the subject shall emerge.

Methods of sewing on raised supports were only touched upon in Volume I. Before the book went to press, I had a desire to explore this area. Little did I realize it would become a book in itself—which is now published as Volume III, titled *Exposed Spine Sewings*.

Volume I, *Non-Adhesive Binding, Books Without Paste Or Glue.*

VOLUMES II & III

In 1993, I started my second book on non-adhesive binding. It was written *as* I devised each of the sewings, inspired largely by a workshop titled "Sewing Variations" offered by Betsy Palmer Eldridge. Utilizing a plethora of stitches which she presents to students, I started devising exposed spine sewings which could employ one or more of these stitches. Each prototype sewing was followed immediately with computer text and drawings.

The project started right off with sewings, without an introduction of equipment and procedures. The novice could begin with Volume I. However, since this second book begins with 1–section sewings and proceeds to 2, it is fairly easy to follow without prior sewing experience. Any jargon can be looked up in the *Glossary* in the back of this book.

The second part of the project was variations on raised supports. These sewings are complicated, and not for the beginner. They offer a challenge for the bookbinder to consider unorthodox procedures. All have exposed spine sewings. The *kettle stitch* was eliminated for its lack of beauty. Although the ultimate in function, it was replaced by a variety of methods I explored as *changes-over*.

My second binding book project grew to an enormous amount of pages. It was not practical to publish as a single paperback book with a two inch wide, Smythe sewn spine. I had to split it in half. This proved to be logical, as well as practical:

Volume III contains all the elaborate, multi-section sewings *along,* as well as *across* the spine. Those who are enthused by the possibilities in Volumes I and II can elect to explore the more intricate involvement, and satisfaction, of sewing the structures presented in Volume III.

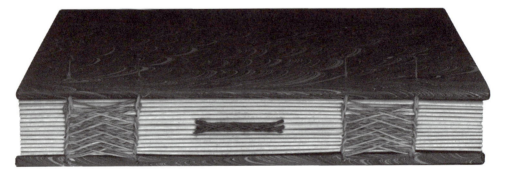

Each separate sewing *across* the spine is accomplished with a thread having a needle on each end. Sewing is at paired stations. I have named this the Celtic Weave. It is described in Volume III, *Exposed Spine Sewings.*

Booklets: The first half of the project became the book you are now holding, which I refer to as Volume II.

The bookbinder deals with a multi-section sewing out of necessity. Rounding and backing, and attaching the boards are functional, but also presents the opportunity of decoration. These are explored in Volume III.

Variation on The Icicle, described in Volume III, *Exposed Spine Sewings*. This raised support sewing climbs by packing, eliminating the need for a kettle stitch. The spine is rounded section by section, without a hammer or moisture which would mar the paper and the exposed spine sewing. The spine is never pasted. Supports are laced on and tied to the boards.

However, the calligrapher and visual artist creating bookworks, generally require a structure of fewer pages. This demand for simple binding structures with a limited number of pages is addressed in Volume II.

I have pondered and played with permutational possibilities of sewing a booklet with a limited number of pages.—No paucity of presentation here. This volume describes 122 sewings which can be used for as little as four, or as many as perhaps a hundred pages. These formats are imposed as one, two, or three sections, presenting a veritable encyclopedia for the reader to browse through, and from which to choose. I wanted to present a rich array of possibilities affording the reader room in which to dream. I am sure this comes from memories as a little boy, browsing the Sears & Roebuck catalogue for things I would never acquire.

In this volume, paper limp covers are used instead of boards. The one-piece paper cover is not attached separately, but sewn on, along with the section(s). This is known as a *continuous support sewing.*

Instead of a single fold on the spine-cover, two hinge-folds give a depth to the spine, even on the 1–section sewings. The spine is "decorated" by the process of sewing. Patterning is created using traditional bookbinding stitches and sewing, as well as adapting embroidery stitches.

REINFORCE the SPINE: A word of warning: Since the only support is the cover itself, the paper spine should be reinforced. Although discussed in Volume I, it should be at least noted here. Use cover-weight paper for the jacket. A second spine can be cut and glued on the inside of the spine-cover. Volume I discusses spines, folding the cover paper to form 2– and 3–ply spines. No glue is used. The sewing holds the layers together.

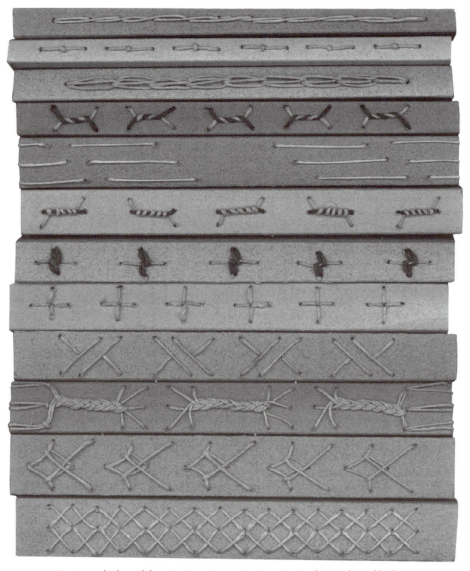

Preview of a few of the 1– 2– & 3–section sewings. Have fun, and good luck.

INCREMENTAL WRITING

There was no running manuscript, after the fact, poured to flow into the pages of this book. Layouts in all my published books are composed *as* the text is written. Text, drawn and photographic illustrations are designed to fit the page. I see the page as a unit of punctuation, extending from spaces between words, clustering of words into phrases and clauses, which are denoted by periods, commas and other points of punctuation into sentences. The textual structure then extends to verses or paragraphs. I wish to extend these to the page unit.

Since the invention of moveable type, the writer has not had control of *the page,* which was necessarily relinquished to the printer/publisher. Not until the home computer changed from a word processor to typesetting capabilities did the writer have the means to reclaim command of the printed page. The writer can now compose the book, the page, as well as the contents. These are ideas I have written about in Book Number 120, *Text in the Book Format.*

With the addition of Volumes II and III to the binding book series, I have paid attention to *the section* as a unit of composition. In these two volumes, each section is a completed unit; no sewing description extends from one section to the next. This gives limited autonomy to the section.

Having each section as a completed unit comes out of my concern for those who purchase the books in sheets, unbound, as folded and gathered sections. This allows each reader to bind all, or however many sections desired into a book. The remainder of Volume II or III can be sewn utilizing one or more sections, of one or more sewings described.

Volume II presents 1– 2– and 3–section sewings. Each section, or any two or three successive sections can be sewn as samples of bindings described in this book.

It is appropriate for a book on binding to be offered in sheets. This not only affords the binder opportunity to sew, but the end result is a manual far easier to follow, since the hand-sewn book stays opened to whatever page it is turned. Sewings which are through the fold permit the book to open and to lie flat.

Sewing across, rather than along the spine is an ideal way to bind this volume. The 2–needle Coptic Sewing or the Greek Sewing are recommended for sewing a multi-section manual. They use paired sewing stations across the spine. The result is a manual that lies flat. The binder has both hands free to sew, without the wandering of self-turning pages of the opened book.

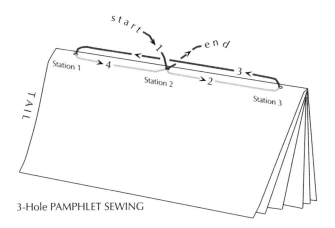

3-Hole PAMPHLET SEWING

HOMAGE TO THE PAMPHLET SEWING

The most common 1–section sewing is the Pamphlet Sewing. 3–, 4– and 5–Hole Pamphlet Sewings are described in Volume I of *Non-Adhesive Binding*. In addition, a Single-Sheet Pamphlet, as well as a 2–Section Pamphlet Sewing are described. Therefore, I will not duplicate the information in this Volume. But in writing a text on *1– 2– & 3–Section Sewings,* I would be amiss not to repeat one of the diagrams of this sewing.

PART 1
1–SECTION SEWINGS

BOOKLETS with a two hinge-fold spine

1–SECTION SEWINGS: Volume I describes six versions of the pamphlet sewing. They are quick, but offer little decorative possibility for showing off a nice sewing.

The pamphlet sewing generally has a paper cover. The spine is reduced to a single hinge-fold. All sewings of a single section in Volume II will expand the spine to a narrow width, requiring two hinge-folds. This permits the side-covers to lie flat against the book block. It also allows for a better presentation of the sewing on the spine-cover.

It is important to measure the thickness of the section. If the spine-cover is too wide for the section, the cover can be easily crushed, especially if stored on a bookshelf

Presentation of a Brief Text: A 1–section booklet might require only four pages of text. This could appear on pages 5 through 8 of a sexto constructed of three folios. The middle folio contains pages 3 and 4, as well as 9 and 10. Page 3 could be the title with page 4 blank. Page 9 could be blank, with page 10 as the colophon. The first folio, pages 1, 2 and 11, 12 could be a colored laid paper as endsheets. The briefest text can be sewn with an imposing presentation. See diagram below and on page 19.

2–SECTION SEWINGS: The 2–section pamphlet sewing, delineated in Volume I, only adds the possibility of more pages. The spine remains nothing more than the fold of a single hinge.

Volume II presents thirty-two 2–section sewings sewn through a paper cover. The pattern visible on the spine is expanded from that of the single section sewing. Still, spine design remains quite limited compared to the permutation of the 3–section sewings.

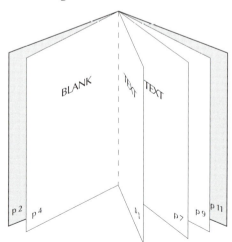

Imposition of a twelve page booklet with a four page text.

ENDSHEET	ENDSHEET
page 12	page 1

COLOPHON	TITLE
page 10	page 3

TEXT	TEXT
page 8	page 5

ENDSHEET	ENDSHEET
page 2	page 11

BLANK	BLANK
page 4	page 9

TEXT	TEXT
page 6	page 7

Imposition of a 1–section, twelve page booklet with a four page text.

3–SECTION SEWINGS: The 3–section booklet permits a rich range of patterns visible on the spine-cover. I have devised seventy-five 3–section sewings and described them for this binding book.

This presents an encyclopedia of booklets to browse through or peruse, and from which to choose to sew. I have been especially aware of the needs of book artists and calligraphers who need a format of a few pages, as opposed to multi-section sewings.

Number of Pages: Often, even with the briefest of texts, I will impose a 3–section sewing. Sewing three folios separately allows for the least number of pages—twelve. The same four page text imposed as 1–section, on the previous page, could be sewn as a 3–section sewing.

The number of possible pages containing text or pictures as a 3–section sewing can be as few as four or five, as just described.

The 3–section sewing offers a wide range of number of possible pages:
- The quarto allows for twenty-four pages.
- A sexto at twelve pages, times three sections gives thirty-six pages.
- Octavos sewn result in a forty-eight page book.
- The duodecimo, a twenty-four page section, would give a 3–section sewing containing seventy-two pages.

DASH SEWING

Running stitch is a binding *and* an embroidery term. Binders also call it a *running slip stitch,* because it slips, and does not lock. It presents a simple, attractive sewing. Stitches can be uniform or varied for sake of design. Utilizing spaces between the stitches offers further possibilities of patterning.

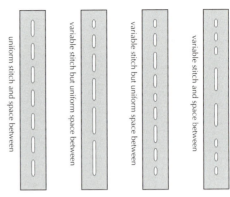

uniform stitch and space between

variable stitch but uniform space between

variable stitch but uniform space between

variable stitch and space between

Four spine-covers with variations in stations

HEAD

tie-off

tie-off

TAIL

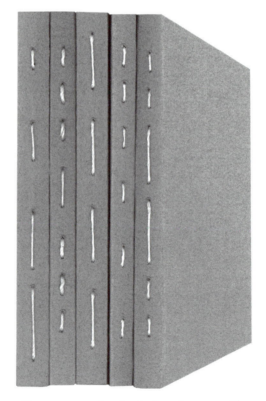

Above are examples of a single section sewn with straight running stitches, referred to as the DASH SEWING. On the far left, the gradual progression of the increasing length of the stitch is counterpointed by the inversely proportional spaces between.

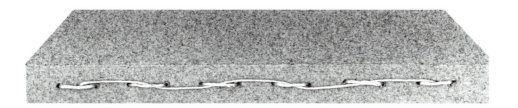

THE LACED DASH

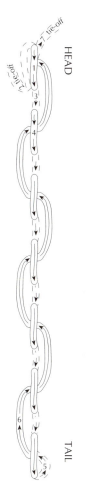

The *inter-laced running stitch* is an embroidery term. The stitch is easily transposed to become a sewing on the spine for a single section.

SEWING PROCEDURE

Steps 1-4. As with the straight running stitch sewing, stations are placed along the spine keeping in mind the length of the stitches and the spaces between. The Inter-Laced Running Stitch Sewing requires two additional stations.

5. One station is added prior to the one at the tail. This permits an exit after the Straight Running Stitch is completed.

6. The thread then slips under each segment of the running stitch, alternating from one side to the other.

7. Another station is needed beyond the first one at the head. This permits entry so that the thread can be tied-off.

Books on embroidery are a rich resource of functional ideas for bindings, as well as an aesthetic means of drawing with thread and needle on the side-covers.

NOTE: The diagram shows a tie-off at step 2, and another at step 7. Rather than tying two knots, you might omit step two. Tie both loose threads together at the end of the sewing.

FIGURE *8*

A running stitch sewing gives a dash or dotted line pattern; a *Figure 8* gives a solid line of tangent stitches. These can be made by sewing either the Saddler's Harness *Figure 8,* or, by the Lacing *Figure 8.* The Saddler's Harness is done with care, since the tension may cause it to rip the paper:

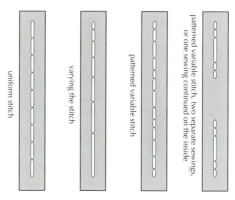

Four spine-covers with variations in patterning

HEAD   TAIL

SADDLER'S HARNESS *Figure 8*
sewn with one needle, initially places uneven stress on the paper

Sewing with two needles, one on each end of a single thread creates a lacing stitch. This is not to be confused with an embroidery lacing stitch, which is only for sake of design (see: *Laced Dash,* on the previous page). The bookbinder's lacing stitch is functional; it weaves in and out, attaching the section to the spine-cover.

Start at the head. With the needle in your right hand, enter the station closest to the head. Take the needle in your left hand to the next station and enter. Take the needle assigned to your right hand and exit this second station. Proceed to the third station, exit with the left needle, then enter with the right. Continue this figure 8 pattern to the final station and tie-off on the inside:

HEAD   TAIL

L = the needle in your left hand; *R* = needle in your right.

LACING *Figure 8*
sewn with two needles, less stressful on the paper

The only variables for the sewing of the Lacing *Figure 8* is the size(s) of the stitch and the number of separate sewings along the spine to attach the single section to the spine-cover:

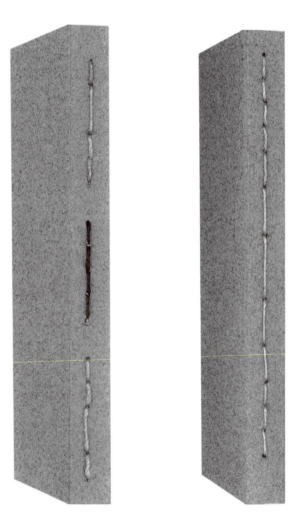

Examples of the Lacing FIGURE *8* SEWING. On the left, the 1–section booklet has three separate FIGURE *8* SEWIGNGS, with the middle sewing in a different color thread. On the right is a single sewing of the FIGURE *8*.

DOT-DASH SEWING *(the machine stitch)*

This step stitch sewing is the same construction as the stitch on your sewing machine. The bobbin is pulled to the surface to lock in place the on-going thread on the surface.

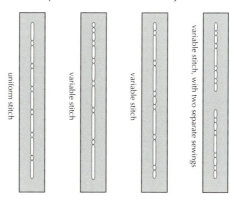

As any seamstress or seamster will tell you, this familiar sewing is as pleasing as violets in a garden of less commonplace blooms.

When I "draw" with my sewing machine on my paper prints and collages, I invariably use a different color bobbin than the other thread. Loosening the tension allows the bobbin to be pulled up even more, showing a dotting of color interrupting the dashes of the thread on the surface.

FAUX MACHINE SEWING: Two colors of thread can be tied together, creating one long thread, half of which is one color, the other half the "bobbin" color. Thread the former with a needle and exit the first station. Pull until the knot is up against the station on the inside. Enter each successive station and loop under the bobbin thread. Exit. The second color (bobbin thread) will pop at every station, except at the head and the tail.

SEWING PROCEDURE

For the Dot-Dash Sewing, start on the inside at the tail. Exit. Lay the thread across the spine. Enter at the head. Change colors at this point if you wish a different color "bobbin". Proceed towards the tail to the next station. Exit, loop around the top thread and enter the same station. Proceed to the following station. Exit, loop around top thread and re-enter. Continue in this manner to the tail. Pull on the top stitch to tighten. Tie-off:

HEAD   Step 1: Start by exiting at the tail; enter at the head.   TAIL

DOT-DASH SEWING *(Machine Stitch)*
This step stitch sewing is sewn with one needle.

ALTERNATIVE PROCEDURE

When you pull on the top stitch to tighten, you will notice it pulls easily. It is not locked.

The step stitch sewing on the previous page does not alternate sides, as it does with the running slip stitch, used with the *Figure 8* stitch. Therefore the Dot-Dash Sewing is not even as secure as a running slip stitch sewing. To strengthen the machine stitch, I add a locking stitch:

HEAD

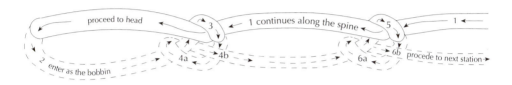

DOT-DASH SEWING *(Machine Stitch)*
DETAIL with lock stitches

The top thread (step 1) enters at the head to become the bobbin and proceeds to the next station. The bobbin exits (3) and loops over the top stitch and enters. The bobbin loops around itself (4a), then slips under to lock (4b). It then proceeds to next station on the inside. Steps 3 and 4 are repeated at each successive station.

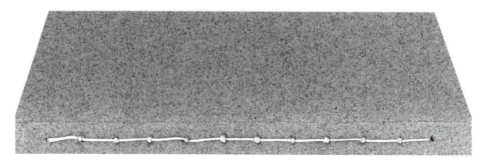

This is an example of the DOT-DASH SEWING.

THE TWIST *Exit Backward*

Back Stitch is embroidery term. It describes the route of the sewing. To begin, exit station 1, enter 2, proceed to 1 and tie-off. Then the pattern begins:

> Exit station 1, enter 3. Exit 2, enter 4.
>
> Exit station 3, enter 5. Exit 4, enter 6.
>
> Exit station 5, enter 7. Exit 6, enter 8, et cetera.

The permutation of this sewing is more than merely design. The previous sewings were illustrated with variations of length of stitch or space between stitches. Variations on this sewing result in sub-categories of the basic stitch sewing:

- The TWIST, *Exit Backward*
- The TWIST, *Exit Forward* page 28
- DOUBLE DASH, *Alternating Exits* page 29
- The TWIST, *Exit Backward and Link* page 30
- PEARL DASH page 34
- The HITCH, *Exit Backward and Loop* page 36
- ALTERNATING HITCH page 38

The list of variations could go on. Each variation gives a different look to the spine sewing.

NOTE: Betsy Palmer Eldridge says that some sewing manuals refer to the *back stitch* as the *half-back stitch*—which "more accurately describes what happens".

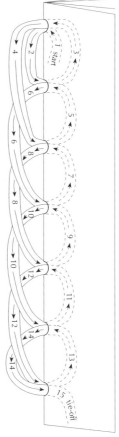

Side view of
THE TWIST *Exit Backward*

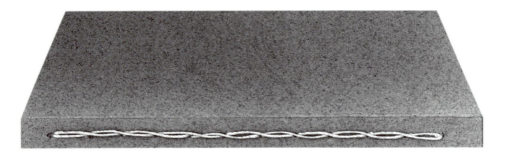

THE TWIST *Exit Backward* is one of many variations of back stitch sewing.

Since the sewing path of the thread from station to station is identical in all the variations, the sewing only differs in exiting, backward or forward, and if you link. Inside, the fold pattern is continuous for all the sewings:

Inside view of all variations of the Back Stitch Sewings.
referred to as THE TWIST

SEWING PROCEDURE

The first description will be for The Twist, *Exit Backward*

NOTE: The procedure is described sewn on the bench. If you hand-hold your book to sew, standing the book on the tail, the terms *exit backward* would be interpreted as *exit right*.

Start on the inside. Exit the first station. Enter station 2. Tie-off at station 1. Exit station 1 making sure you are back of the previous stitch. Enter station 3. Exit station 2 back of the other thread. Enter station 4. Exit station 3 back of the other thread. Enter station 5. Exit 4 back of the stitch. Enter station 6.

Continue in this manner until you enter the final station for the first time. Then exit backward the next to last station, and, again enter the final station. Tie-off.

The odd-numbered steps in the illustration at the right are performed on the inside of the section. They create a row of tangent stitches characteristic of all variations of this sewing (see illustration at the top of this page).

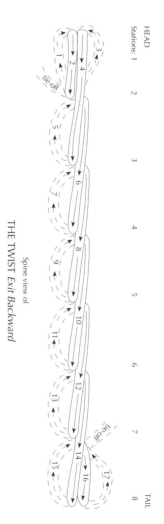

Spine view of
THE TWIST *Exit Backward*

HEAD
Stations: 1

2

3

4

5

6

7

TAIL
8

THE TWIST *Exit Forward*

SEWING PROCEDURE

Sew in the same manner as for The Twist *Exit Backward* as described on the previous page, except always exit forward, rather than backward.

Both sewings give a corkscrew effect. *Exit Forward* seems to be twisting clockwise, *Exit Backward* appears to be a counter-clockwise corkscrew:

HEAD   TAIL

THE TWIST *Exit Backward*
the appearance of a counter clockwise twist

THE TWIST *Exit Forward*
the appearance of a clockwise corkscrew

Compare the sewing below with the diagram of *Exit Backward* on the previous page.

Spine view of
THE TWIST *Exit Forward*

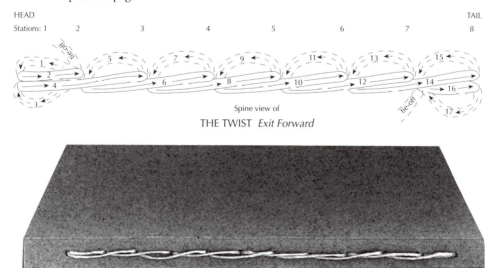

Example of the back stitch sewing referred to as THE TWIST *Exit Forward.*

DOUBLE DASH *Alternating Exits*

The final variation of the back stitch sewing created by a change *only in the exiting procedure,* is called the Double Dash, because there is no twist. Twists are caused by always exiting to the left, or always to the right. In this sewing, the twist is eliminated by altering the exiting procedure. This gives two parallel lines of stitching:

HEAD   TAIL

DOUBLE DASH *Alternating Exits*
View of the spine-cover

SEWING PROCEDURE

1   Start on the inside. Exit the first station at the head. Enter station 2. Tie-off at station 1.

2. Exit station 1 making sure you are on the left side of the first stitch on the spine.

3. Enter station 3.

4. Exit station 2, this time to the right of the other thread.

5. Enter station 4.

6. Exit station 3 on the left of the thread.

7. Enter station 5.

8. Exit 4 on the right Enter station 6.

Remaining Stations:

Continue in this manner until you enter the final station for the first time. Then exit the next to last station on the proper side, and, again enter the final station. Tie-off.

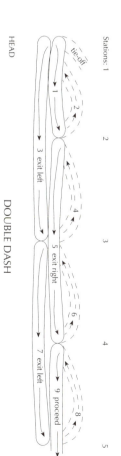

THE TWIST   *Exit Backward and Link*

SEWING PROCEDURE

1. Start on the inside at the head. Exit station 1.
2. Enter station 2. Tie-off.
3. Exit station 1 backward of the stitch 2. (That is, exit towards the head.)
4. Enter station 3.
5. Exit backward at station 2.
6a. Slip behind both threads, labeled as steps 2 and 4, in a counter-clockwise, semi-circular motion.
6b. Proceed to station 4. Enter.
7. Exit station 3. to the right.
8a. Slip behind both threads, labeled as steps 4 and 6, in a counter-clockwise motion.
8b. Proceed to station 5. Enter.

On the right, this Back Stitch Sewing is referred to as THE TWIST *Exit Backward and Link*.

Holding this book in hand, the three-quarter from the left will emphasize the twist of the thread of the lengthy stitches on the spine.

Turning the spine, the three-quarter view from the right punctuates the "beads", created by slipping under the two threads after exiting in a semi-circular movement.

HEAD   TAIL

THE TWIST *Exit Backward and Link*

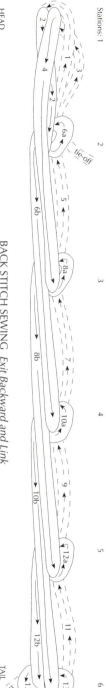

Sewing the Remaining Stations: Continue with the pattern—Retreat on the inside to the previous station. Exit backward of the previous stitches. Slip behind both threads and proceed two stations. Enter.

Upon entering the station at the tail, retreat to the next to last station. Exit back of the stitches. Slip behind both threads, enter the station at the tail.

13a. (Not shown in the diagram below.) Slip under at thread on the inside (step number 11) before exiting the station 6. This will anchor the stitch (step number 12b).

13b. Exit to the right. Slip behind both threads (steps 10 and 12) to form the final "bead".

13c. Enter the station at the tail. Tie-off.

Gallery installation of books by Hedi Kyle, Center for Book Arts, New York, NY, 1993. Various hand-held as well as wall-displayed, and ceiling-to-wall books.

"Group of late 18th century children's books, 1785-1809, that have undergone home preservation and repair; from the Benjamin Vaughan Collection at the American Philosophical Society, Philadelphia, PA.

All were traditional bindings, mostly sewn on cords. Now are home sewing repairs, mostly over sewn. Average size is 11 X 8 cm." —Hedi Kyle.

PEARL DASH

The addition of the dotting thread, punctuating the common Dash Sewing is a gem. More such dotting will follow in other sewings in Volumes II and III.

Sewing Stations: This sewing, referred to as the Pearl Dash, requires an odd number of sewing stations. Example two, above, is an exception, requiring an even number of stations.

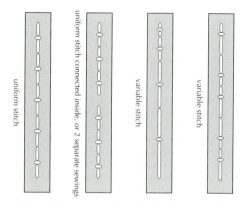

Four spine-covers with variations in patterning

uniform stitch

uniform stitch connected inside, or 2 separate sewings

variable stitch

variable stitch

SEWING PROCEDURE

1a-1d. Start inside. Exit station 1. Enter station 3. Tie-off at station 2.

2. Exit station 2. Lap over the stitch. Re-enter station 2.

3a-3d. Exit station 3. Enter station 5.

4. Exit station 4. Lap over the stitch. Re-enter station 4.

5a-5d. Exit station 5. Enter station 7.

6. Exit station 6. Lap over the stitch. Re-enter station 6.

7. Exit station 7. Enter station 9.

8. Exit station 8. Lap over the stitch. Re-enter station 8.

Sew the remaining stations in this manner. After making the final pearl, tie-off on the inside.

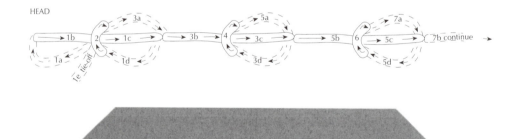

Example of the PEARL DASH

BOW TIE   *Running Stitch Sewing with Pearl*

Units of the Bow Tie Sewing, spaced along the spine, is more pleasing to me than the continuous thread of the sewing, the Pearl Dash, page 34.

Sewing Stations: The number of sewing stations for the Bow Tie Sewing must be in increments of three.

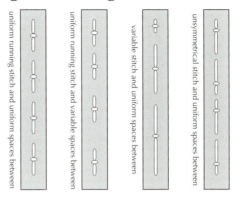

Four spine-covers with variations in patterning

SEWING PROCEDURE

1. Start on the inside at the head. Make a running stitch to the tail, using only the odd-numbered stations:

HEAD

2. Retreat back to the head, exiting at the even-numbered stations to lap over the stitch and re-entering the same station to form the pearl. Tie-off both loose threads at station 2:

TAIL

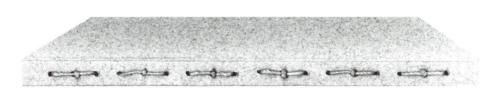

Example of the BOW TIE

THE HITCH *Exit Backward and Loop*

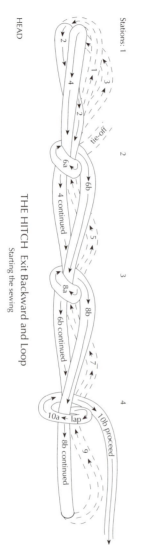

The sewing pattern for the Hitch *Exit Backward and Loop* is the same as for the previous sewing, except for the linking process. As you exit back of the two threads, lap the stitch. Then, in a clockwise motion, slip behind both threads. Proceed two stations and enter.

SEWING PROCEDURE

1. Start on the inside at the head. Exit station 1
2. Enter station 2. Tie-off.
3. Exit station 1 back of the thread labeled step 2.
4. Enter station 3.
5. Exit backward at station 2.
6a. Lap the stitch (4b). Slip behind both threads (steps 2 and 4) in a counter-clockwise motion.
6b. Proceed to station 4. Enter.
7. Exit backward at station 3.
8a. Lap the stitch (6b). Slip behind both threads (steps 4 and 6) in a counter-clockwise motion.
8b. Proceed to station 5. Enter.

The remaining stations are explained on the following page.

HEAD   TAIL

THE HITCH *Exit Backward and Loop*

Sewing the Remaining Stations: Continue with the pattern: Retreat on the inside to the previous station. Exit the threads. Lap the stitch, slip behind both threads and proceed two stations. Enter.

Upon entering the station at the tail, retreat to the next to last station. Exit back of the two threads. Lap the stitch, slip behind both threads and enter the station at the tail. Tie-off.

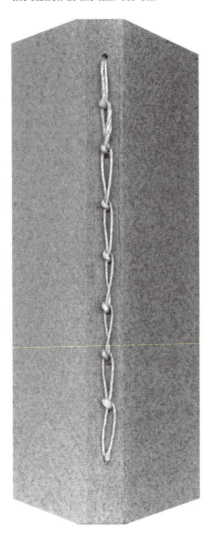

Example of the sewing referred to as
THE HITCH *Exit Backward and Loop*

THE HITCH Exit Backward and Loop
Ending the sewing

ALTERNATING HITCH

SEWING PROCEDURE

1. Exit station 1.
2. Enter station 2. Tie-off.
3. Exit station 1 forward of the stitch labeled as step 2.
4. Enter station 3.
5. Exit station 2 to the right of the thread.
6a. Lap the stitch (step 4). Slip behind the threads labeled as steps 2 and 4 in a counter-clockwise motion. 6b. Proceed to station 4. Enter.
7. Exit station 3 to the left of the threads.
8a. Lap and slip behind the threads labeled as steps 4 and 6 in a clockwise motion.
8b. Proceed to station 5. Enter.

Sewing the Remaining Stations: Continue with the pattern, repeating steps 5 through 8: Retreat on the inside to the previous station. Exits alternate, first coming to the outside of the spine to the right of the threads, the next time, to the left. The lap the stitch and the slip behind both threads also alternate. When you exit to the right, use a clockwise motion to lap. Exiting left requires a counter-clockwise lap. Proceed on the spine two stations. Enter.

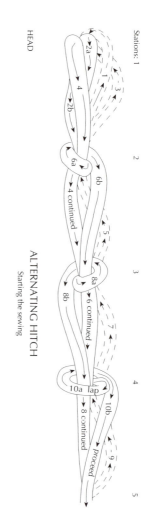

ALTERNATING HITCH

Upon entering the station at the tail, retreat to the next to last station. Exit and lap the stitch, slip behind both threads and enter the station at the tail. Tie-off.

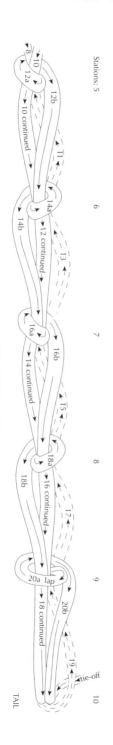

ALTERNATING HITCH
Ending the sewing

Example of the sewing referred to as the
ALTERNATING HITCH

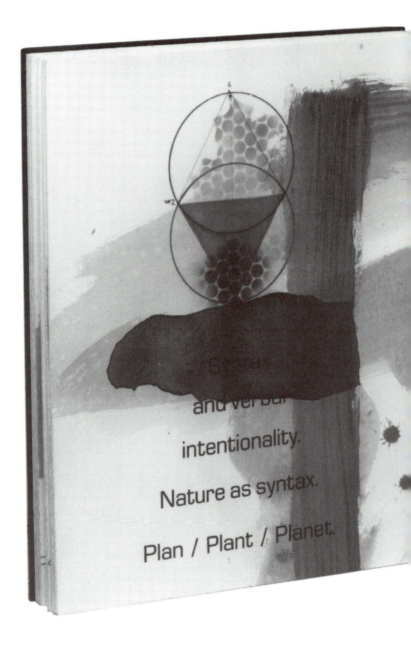

Above and right: *Synesthesia,* original painting and drawing by Timothy Ely with text by Terence McKenna, Granary Books, 1992. Typography and letterpress by Philip Gallo, The Hermetic Press; binding is by Daniel Kelm, The Wide Awake Garage. 75 copies made; 20 lettered G-Z hors commerce; 55 numbered 1-55 for sale. 24.1 x 17.7 cm.

Traders. The Art assists Nature's work. Man is the measure. What is old is holy. Ideology and material culture are kinds of virtual reality. Decadence is sophistication severed from genuine feeling. Innocence—The Unexpected. Singularities & the forces that mold them. The felt presence of the Other means that History is the harbinger of singularity. History is an undigested understanding of time. From Big Bang to Big Surprise. The singularity confronted, your life & everybody's. Vacuum fluctuation/Asteroid impact. Political imperative:

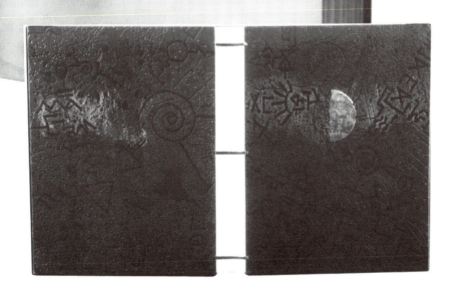

SEWN CHAINS

Linking to form a chain is an extraordinarily beautiful sewing pattern. I use it in many sewings.

SEWING PROCEDURE

1. Start on the inside. Exit station 1, enter station 2 and tie-off. This forms the (single) anchor to start the linking. A double anchor between station 1 and 2 would imitate the chain between the other stations. For a double anchor, repeat step 1, exiting station 1 and entering station 2 before continuing with step 3. A double anchor is illustrated on page 274.

2. Proceed to station 3. Exit and link under the thread at station 2. Enter station 3.

3. Proceed to the next station (4). Exit and link under the thread at the previous station (3). Use the same clockwise or counter-clockwise movement as for the previous linking. Enter the same station which you exited (4).

Sewing the Remaining Stations: Repeat step 3 for each of the remaining stations. After forming the link at the tail, enter and tie-off with a half hitch.

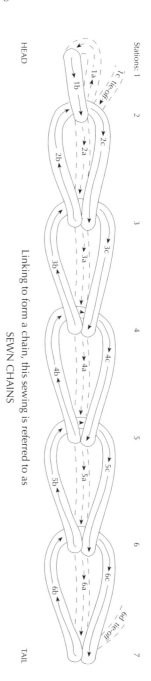

HEAD

Linking to form a chain, this sewing is referred to as SEWN CHAINS

TAIL

Stations: 1 2 3 4 5 6 7

ANCHOR STITCH for the LINK STITCH SEWING: The drawn illustration on the lower left is how the anchor almost always appears. Stations 1 and 2 are placed closely together for a very small anchor, rather than as appears in the drawn illustration on the facing page.

In the drawing on the lower right, I have repeated steps 1a and 1b to form two threads on the spine between stations 1 and 2. With all stations spaced equidistantly, the two threads appear as a link, suggesting no anchor stitch.

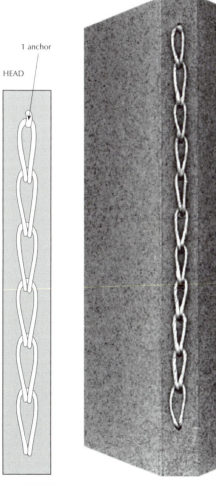

1 anchor

HEAD

2 anchors

HEAD

SEWN CHAINS
View of the spine-cover

Example of SEWN CHAINS
A chain pattern is formed by link stitch sewing

SEWN CHAINS
With double anchor as fake link

Vogel Trek / Bird Migration,
Jeroen van Westen. 1987.
Edition of 3. In the collection
of the Museum Meermanno
Westreenianum, The Hague,
The Netherlands.

Closed:
250 x 250 x 300 mm.
Stretched:
250 x 250 x 4500 mm.

Horen, Zien, Spreken / To Hear, To See, To Speak, Jeroen van Westen. 1986-88. Edition of 3. Cardboard print. Imaged fold book, bound at three points. Partially opened, it closes to a wooden shaft. Collection of Samsom Publishers, Alphen a/d Rijn, The Netherlands. 200 x 200 x 1000 mm. Extended ground plan equally-sided triangle 1000 x 1000 x 1000 mm.

Horen, Zien, Spreken / To Hear, To See, To Speak, Jeroen van Westen. Free-standing, the book requires three "page turners" to open and fully extend the book for viewing.

nu / now, Jeroen van Westen, 1987. Edition of 7. In several collections, including The Royal Library, The Hague, The Netherlands. Two separate fold books
for two people are slotted to fit when together in a single complex. Lino cut,
cardboard print, pencil and acrylic paint. 120 X 80 X 20 mm. each. Extended,
120 x 80 x 500 mm.

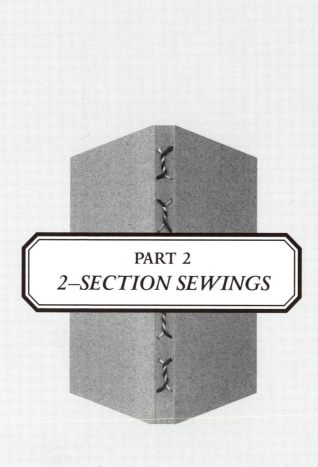

PART 2
2–SECTION SEWINGS

2–SECTION SEWINGS

Sewing patterns on the spine are greatly expanded with two sections. In a matter of minutes, with a pencil, I map out the sewing pathway of as many patterns that come to mind. Exploring 2–section sewings is exciting after binding and writing for 1–section sewings.

Certain designs prove too difficult, requiring a convoluted sewing path to get all the stitches in the design upon the spine. I like Gertrude Stein. I like patterns which are simple, repetitive, easy to learn, and more important, easy to explain and for others to learn.

The "FIRST" SECTION: In the sewing procedures, *first* does not necessarily mean the beginning of the book. On the bench, you may start sewing from the back, towards the front of the book.

GAP between SECTIONS: With two sections sewn to a paper cover, the inevitable gap between sections is seen when turning pages. If it is seen as offensive, some tight sewings will eliminate this gap. For those sewings which set the sections slightly apart, there are other solutions:

•A liner of the same paper used for the sections can be placed inside the paper cover. It does not have to be glued down. Sew the cover and liner as a single unit. The gap between sections will be less noticeable with the same color and texture seen in the gap.

•Use a concertina guard (book block pleat). See Volume I, page 271.

•The paper cover can have foredge turn-ins. The liner or guard is placed, or even tabbed, underneath the turn-in.

At the top, the spine-cover shows in the gap between sections. On the bottom, a less obtrussive book block pleat of the same type paper protrudes between the sections.

2–Needle Sewing: Sections can be sewn separately with the same or different colors of thread. Better sewing pathways come from sewing the sections simultaneously via an alternating path. Many sewings are designed more efficiently by sewing with two needles rather than one.

THREAD COLORS: If two colors of thread are desired, tie the ends of the thread. Clip the dangling threads close to the knot. The knot will be hidden in the gap between the sections. Thread the extremes of both colored threads with a needle. If a single color of thread is used, place a needle on each end.

BEGINNING THE SEWING: Start without the cover. Enter the mountain peak of station 1 of the first section with one color. Let the needle dangle on the inside of the section.

Enter the mountain peak of station 1 of the second section with the remaining color thread. Let the needle dangle on the inside of the section. Station 1 exists only for the sections. The beginning station for the spine-cover is labeled station 2.

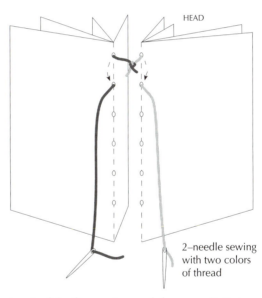

HEAD

2–needle sewing
with two colors
of thread

Adjust the tension, pulling the sections tightly together. The knot will be on the mountain peaks of the tangent sections.

Set on the cover. Exit station 2 of the first section, and the cover. Exit station 2 of the second section, and through the paper cover. Proceed with the directions for sewing that particular binding.

This starting procedure can be used for all 2–section sewings which use only a single color of thread, with a needle attached at each end. This will result in only one knot tied at the head, and it will be in the gap between the sections, rather than in the valley(s) of the section(s).

NOTE: No extra stations need be added to the sections. Existing stations can accommodate starting and ending a sewing. This more direct approach is described on page 113.

PARALLEL BARS

The patterns of the spines for the 2–section sewings will start off with the simplest, straight line horizontal and vertical designs. It will then progress to spines designed with diagonals. Finally, the more complex sewing paths and designs will be described.

The first 2–section sewing which will be described is referred to as Parallel Bars.

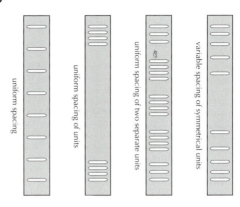

Four spine-covers with variations in stations

Above, Two examples of PARALLEL BARS; the sewing spans the sections

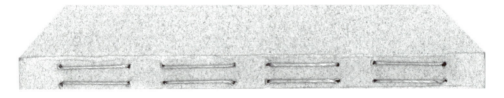

THE DASH, shown directly above, is diagrammed on page 54. The sewing is straight stitches in the valleys.

SEWING PROCEDURE

1. Start at the head on the inside of the first section (to be sewn). Exit station 1.
2. Span and enter the second section at station 1.
3. Exit station 2.
4. Span and enter the first section at station 2. Tie-off, but do not clip the thread which holds the needle.
5. Exit station 3.
6. Span and enter the second section at station 3. Maintain even pressure in the sewing for uniform stitches on the spine, as well as in the valleys of the sections.
7. Exit station 4 of the second section.
8. Span and enter the first section at station 4.
9. Exit station 5.
10. Span and enter the second section at station 5.
11. Exit station 6.
12. Span and enter the first section at station 6.
13. Proceed to station 5 on the inside. Tie-off with a half hitch.

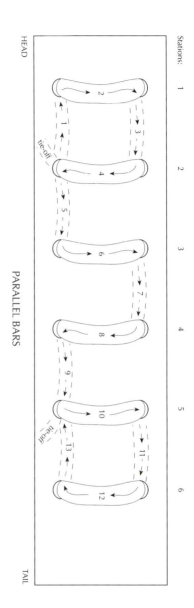

PARALLEL BARS

THE DASH

The two sections of the Dash could be sewn separately. However, this would result in four knots—one at each head and tail of both sections. The sewing path described below requires only one knot, tied-off discreetly in the gap between the sections. It is sewn with two needles.

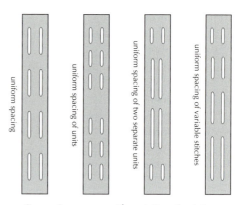

Four spine-covers with variations in stations

SEWING STATIONS

The start of the sewing is similar to that described on page 51. Instead of entering the mountain peaks of both sections in station 2, You will start in station 1, which only exists for the sections. Sewing begins with the cover at station 2.

At the tail, sewing with the cover ends with station 7. Station 8 is placed only in the sections as a means to tie-off.

Design the look of the straight stitches on the spine-cover. This will require six stations for three paired stitches. Pierce the cover. Align the sections to the cover to mark those six stations on the sections.

Add a station near the head and the tail for the sections, only, to begin and end the sewing. These will be referred to as stations 1 and 8.

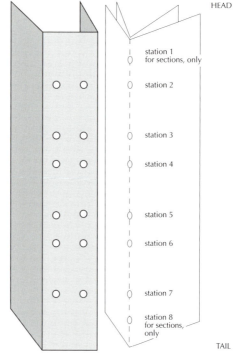

Sewing stations for cover and sections for

THE DASH

SEWING PROCEDURE

This is a 2-needle sewing. Thread a needle on each end. One will be referred to as the left, the other the right. Sewing steps are numbered as well as designated *L* for the path of the left needle, and *R* for the other needle.

1. With one needle, enter the left section, but not the cover, at station 1 from the mountain peak to the valley. With the other needle, enter station 1 of the remaining section. Adjust the tension so that the two sections are pulled tightly together, and the length of the thread is equal in both sections.

2L. Exit station 2 of the first section.

2R. Exit station 2 of the second section.

3L. Enter station 3 of the first section.

4L. Exit station 4.

3R. Enter station 3 of the second section.

4R. Exit station 4.

5L. Enter station 5.

6L. Exit station 6.

5R. Enter station 5.

6R. Exit station 6.

7L. Enter station 7.

8L. Exit station 8 of the section, but not the cover.

7R. Enter station 7.

8R. Exit station 8 of the section, but not the cover.

9L and 9R. Tie-off with the two threads with a square knot in the gap between the sections on the inside of the spine-cover.

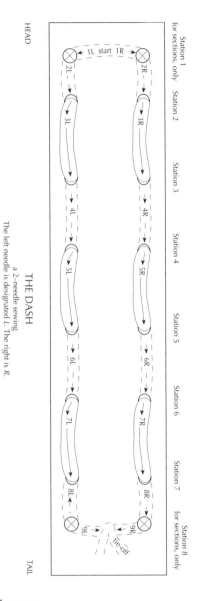

THE DASH

a 2-needle sewing

The left needle is designated *L*. The right is *R*.

DOT-DASH

The Dot-Dash is a variation of the previous sewing. Like the Dash, there is an extra station at the head and tail, for the sections, only, to begin and end the sewing.

The remaining sewing stations vary depending upon your design for the straight stitches on the spine-cover.

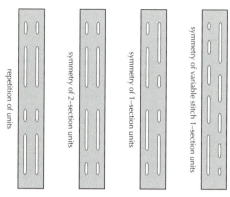

Four spine-covers with variations in stations

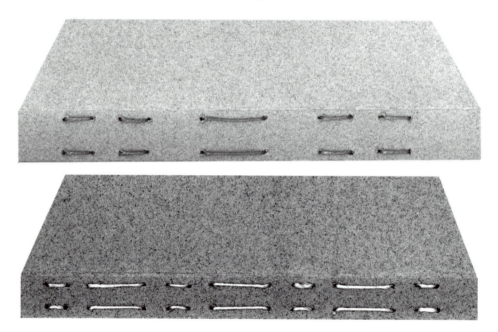

Two examples of the sewing DOT-DASH

HEAD   TAIL

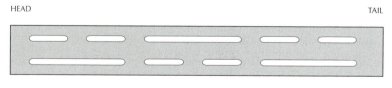

DOT-DASH

DASH & BARS

The Dash & Bars is sewn with one needle. Number of stations depends on the height of the book. This would be ten stations: | | ⁼ | | ⁼ | | The diagram is for ten stations each section. The photographic illustration is fourteen stations for each section: | | ⁼ | | ⁼ | | ⁼ | |

SEWING PROCEDURE

1. Exit the first section through station 1.
2. Set on the second section. Span and enter the second section into station 1.
3. Exit station 2.
4. Span and enter the first section into station 2.
5. Exit station 3.
6. Enter station 4. Tie-off.
7. Exit station 5.
8. Span and enter the second section into station 5.
9. Exit station 4.
10. Enter station 3.
11. Exit station 6.
12. Span and enter the second section into station 6.
13. Exit station 7.
14. Enter station 8.
15. Exit station 9.
16. Span and enter the second section into station 9.
17. Exit station 8.
18. Enter station 7.
19. Exit station 10.
20. Span and enter the first section into station 10.
21. Tie-off at station 9 with a half hitch.

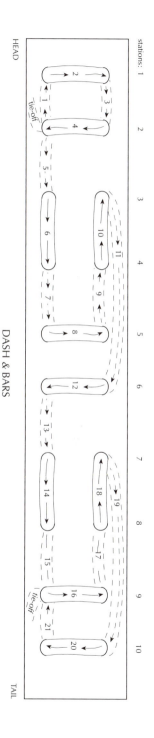

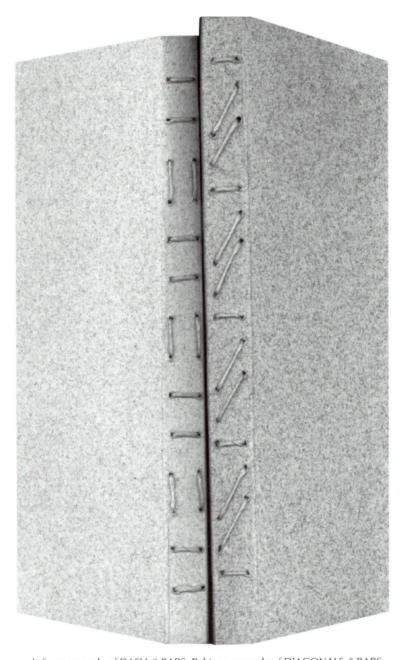

Left, an example of DASH & BARS. Rght, an example of DIAGONALS & BARS.

DIAGONALS & BARS

SEWING PROCEDURE

1. Exit the first section (to be sewn) through station 1.
2. Span and enter the second section into station 1.
3. Exit station 2.
4. Angle and enter the first section into station 3. Tie-off.
5. Exit station 4.
6. Angle and enter the second section into station 3.
7. Exit station 5.
8. Span and enter the first section into station 5.
9. Exit station 7.
10. Angle and enter the second section into station 6.
11. Exit station 7.
12. Angle and enter the first section into station 8.
13. Exit station 9.
14. Span and enter the second section into station 9.
15. Exit station 10.
16. Angle and enter the first section into station 11.
17. Exit station 12.
18. Angle and enter the second section into station 11.
19. Exit station 13.
20. Span and enter the first section into station 13.
21. Tie-off at station 12 on the inside with a half hitch.

HEAD

DIAGONALS & BARS

DIAGONALS & BARS

ALTERNATING DIAGONALS & BARS

SEWING PROCEDURE

1. Exit the first section through station 1.
2. Set on the second section. Span and enter the second section into station 1.
3. Exit station 2.
4. Span and enter station 2 of the first section. Tie-off.
5. Exit station 3.
6. Angle and enter the second section into station 3.
7. Exit station 4.
8. Span and enter the first section into station 4.
9. Exit station 5.
10. Span and enter the second section into station 5.
11. Exit station 6.
12. Angle and enter the first section into station 6.
13. Exit station 7.
14. Span and enter the second section into station 7.
15. Exit station 8 .
16. Span and enter the first section into station 8.
17. Exit station 9.

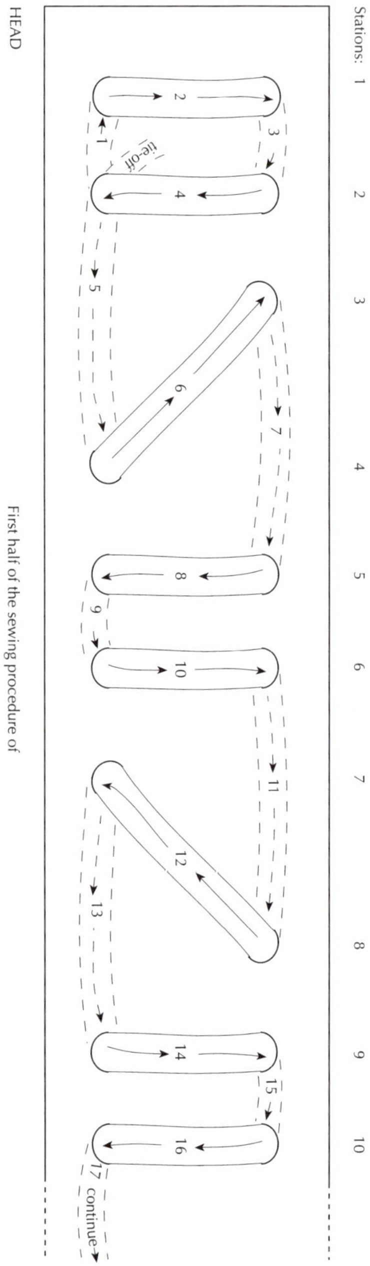

HEAD

Stations: 1 2 3 4 5 6 7 8 9 10

ALTERNATING DIADONALS & BARS

First half of the sewing procedure of

continue

18. Angle and enter the second section into station 9.
19. Exit station 10.
20. Span and enter the first section station 10.
21. Exit station 11.
22. Span and enter the second section into station 11.
23. Exit station 12.
24. Angle and enter the first section into station 12.
25. Exit station 13.
26. Span and enter the second section into station 13.
27. Exit station 14.
28. Span and enter the first section into station 14.
29. Tie-off on the inside at station 13 with a half hitch.

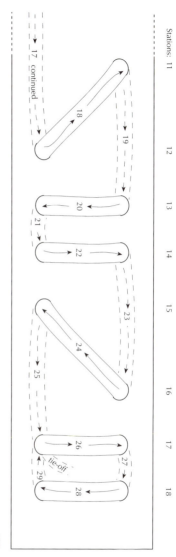

Completing the sewing of
ALTERNATING DIAGONALS & BARS

HEAD   TAIL

ALTERNATING DIAGONALS & BARS

BARS & ARROWS

SEWING PROCEDURE

1. Exit the first section (to be sewn) through station 1.
2. Set on the second section. Span and enter at station 1 of the second section.
3. Exit station 2.
4. Span and enter the first section at station 2. Tie-off.
5. Exit station 3.
6. Span and enter the second section at station 3.
7. Exit station 5.
8. Angle and enter the first section at station 4.
9. Exit station 5.
10. Span and enter the second section at station 5.
11. Exit station 6.
12. Span and enter the first section at station 6.
13. Exit station 7.
14. Angle and enter the second section at station 6.
15. Exit station 9.
16. Angle and enter the first section at station 8.
17. Exit station 9.
18. Span and enter the second section at station 8.
19. Proceed on the inside to station 10. Exit.

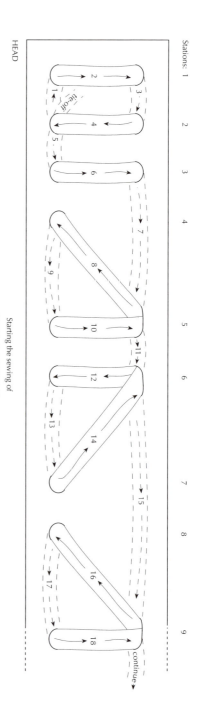

HEAD

Starting the sewing of
BARS & ARROWS

Stations: 1   2   3   4   5   6   7   8   9

tie-off

continue

20. Span and enter the first section at station 10.
21. Exit station 11.
22. Angle, enter the second section at station 10.
23. Exit station 13.
24. Angle and enter the first section at station 12.
25. Exit station 13.
26. Span, enter the second section at station 13.
27. Exit station 14.
28. Span and enter the first section at station 14.
29. Exit station 15.
30. Angle, enter the second section at station 14.
31. Exit station 16.
32. Span and enter the first section at station 16.
33. Exit station 17.
34. Span, enter the second section at station 17.
35. Exit station 18.
36. Span and enter the first section at station 18.
37. Tie-off on the inside at station 17 with a half hitch.

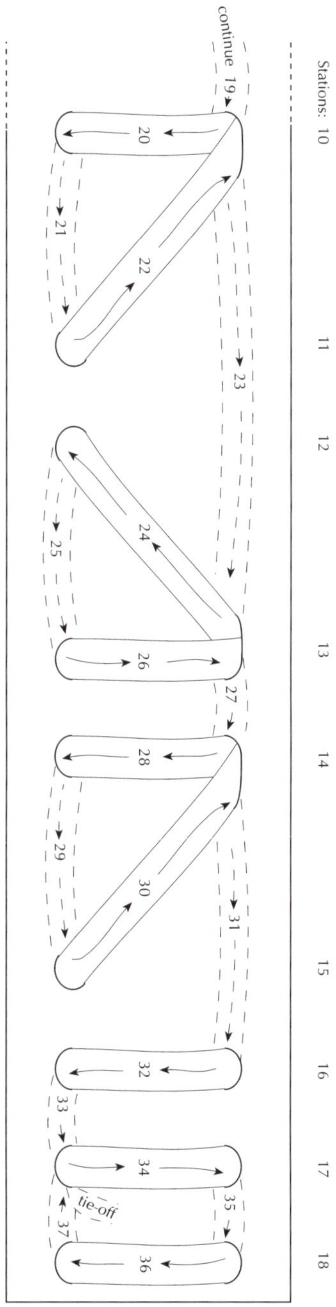

Completing the sewing of
BARS & ARROWS

Stations: 10

continue

19

20

21

22

23

11

24

25

12

26

27

13

28

29

30

31

14

32

33

15

34

35

16

tie-off

37

36

17

18

TAIL

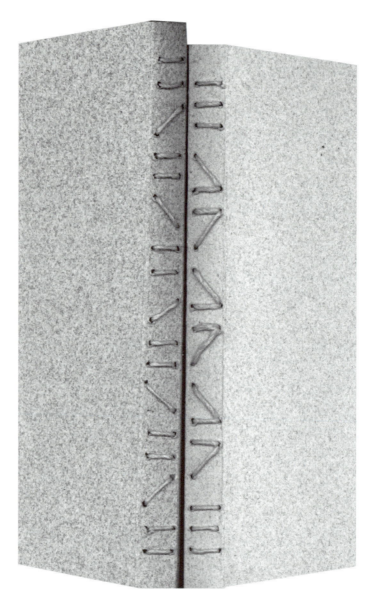

On the left is an example of ALTERNATING DIAGONALS & BARS, shown on page 60. On the right is BARS & ARROWS, described on page 62.

STANDING Z's OR LYING N's

This sewing is dedicated to K. Noël Philips, Philip Zimmermann and the Zimmerboys—Nicholas Philips and Martin Grumman. When Philip and Noël named their first child, I presumed the name starting with an *N* was a play on the first letter of her first name and his last, since they are very conscious of typography. At about that time *No-Doze*™ was running an ad on television where two of their tablets with an embossed *N* rolled 90° to form two *Z's,* suggesting sawing logs of sleep. This sewing is not titled Standing *N's* and Lying *Z's* in honor of said brand of sleeping pill.

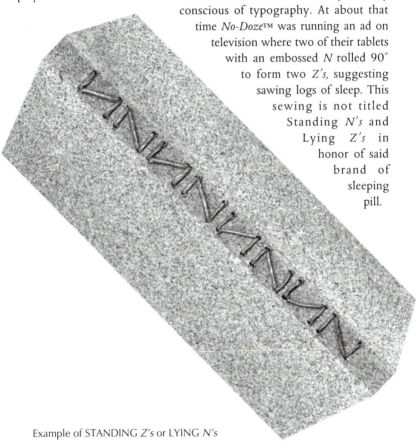

Example of STANDING *Z's* or LYING *N's*

HEAD   TAIL

Standing *Z's* or Lying *N's*

SEWING PROCEDURE

The Standing *Z's* or Lying *N's* is sewn with a single needle. The pattern of sewing is completed by sewing the first four stations. The remaining stations, in units of four, are sewn in the same manner.

1. Start on the inside of the first section at the head. Exit station 1.
2. Enter the second section into station 2. The diagonal is always the first stitch of the letter form which is sewn.
3. Exit station 1.
4. Enter the first section into station 1. Tie-off.
5. Exit station 2.
6. Enter the second section into station 2.

This completes the letter form. The pattern is then reversed:

7. Exit station 3.
8. Enter the first section into station 4.
9. Exit station 3.
10. Enter the second section into station 3.
11. Exit station 4.
12. Enter the first section into station 4.

Remaining Stations: Repeat steps 1-6 and 7-12 to create each additional letter form. Tie-off on the inside.

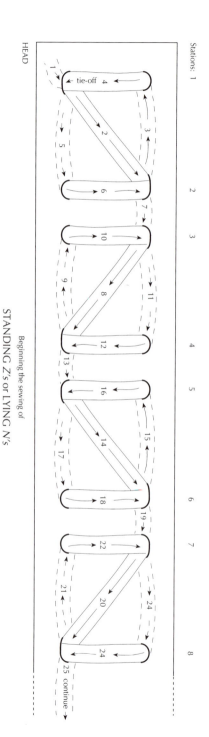

HEAD

Beginning the sewing of
STANDING *Z's* or LYING *N's*

Stations: 1　2　3　4　5　6　7　8

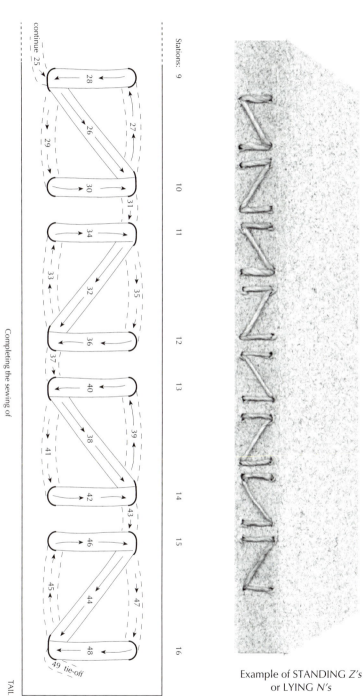

Completing the sewing of
STANDING Z's or LYING N's

Example of STANDING Z's
or LYING N's

BROKEN Z's

Sewing Stations: The first section pierces stations 1, 3, 4, 6, 7, 9, 10, 12 and 13. The second section pierces stations 1, 2, 4, 5, 7, 8, 10 and 11.

SEWING PROCEDURE

1. Start on the inside of the first section at the head. Exit station 1.
2. Set on the second section. Span and enter the second section into station 1.
3. Exit station 2.
4. Angle and enter the first section into station 3. Tie-off.
5. Exit station 4.
6. Span and enter the second section into station 6.
7. Exit station 5.
8. Angle and enter the first section into station 6.
9. Exit station 7.
10. Span and enter the second section into station 7.
11. Exit station 8.
12. Angle and enter the first section into station 9.
13. Exit station 10.
14. Span and enter the second section into station 10.
15. Exit station 11.
16. Angle and enter the first section into station 12.
17. Exit station 13.
18. Span and enter the second section into station 13.
19. Tie-off on the inside at station 11 with a half hitch.

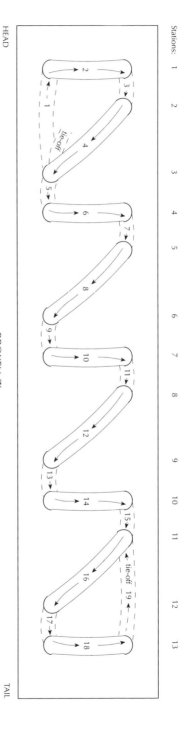

On the left is an example of BROKEN Z's, page 68. On the right is the ZIGZAG, which is diagrammed on the following page.

ZIGZAG

SEWING PROCEDURE

1. Start on the inside of the second section at the head. Exit station 1.
2. Enter the first section into station 2.
3. Exit station 1.
4. Enter the second section into station 1. Tie-off.
5. Exit station 2.
6. Enter the first section into station 2.
7. Exit station 3.
8. Enter the second section into station 2.
9. Exit station 3.
10. Enter the first section into station 3.
11. Exit station 4.
12. Enter the second section into station 3.
13. Exit station 4.
14. Enter the first section into station 4.
15. Exit station 5.
16. Enter the second section into station 4.
17. Exit station 5.
18. Enter the first section into station 5
19. Exit station 6.
20. Enter the second section into station 5.
21. Exit station 6.
22. Enter the first section at station 6. Tie-off.

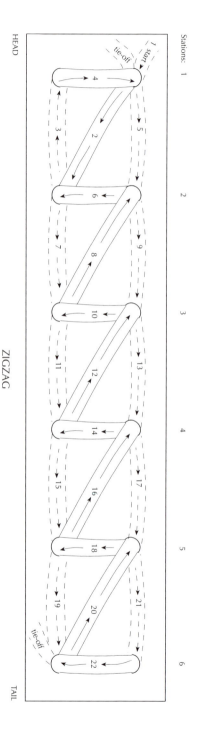

HEAD

ZIGZAG

TAIL

Stations: 1 2 3 4 5 6

LIGHTNING BOLT

Sewing Stations: The first section pierces stations 3, 5, 7 and 9. The second section pierces stations number 1, 2, 4, 6 and 8.

SEWING PROCEDURE

1. Start on the inside of the first section. Exit station 3.
2. Set on the second section. Angle and enter the second section at station 1.
3. Exit station 2.
4. Angle and enter the first section at station 3. Tie-off.
5. Exit station 5.
6. Angle and enter the second section at station 2.
7. Exit station 4.
8. Angle and enter the first section at station 5.
9. Exit station 7.
10. Angle and enter the second section at station 4.
11. Exit station 6.
12. Angle and enter the first section at station 7.
13. Exit station 9.
14. Angle and enter the second section at station 6.
15. Exit station 8.
16. Angle and enter the first section at station 9.
17. Exit station 10.
18. Angle and enter the second section at station 8. Tie-off on the inside with a half hitch.

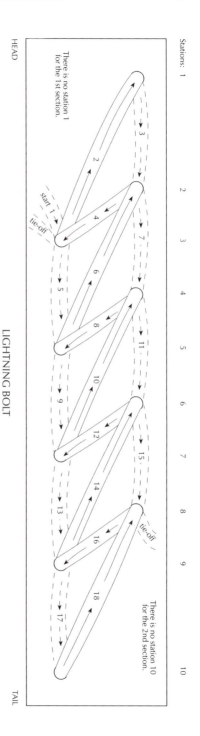

HEAD

Stations: 1   2   3   4   5   6   7   8   9   10

There is no station 1 for the 1st section.

LIGHTNING BOLT

There is no station 10 for the 2nd section.

TAIL

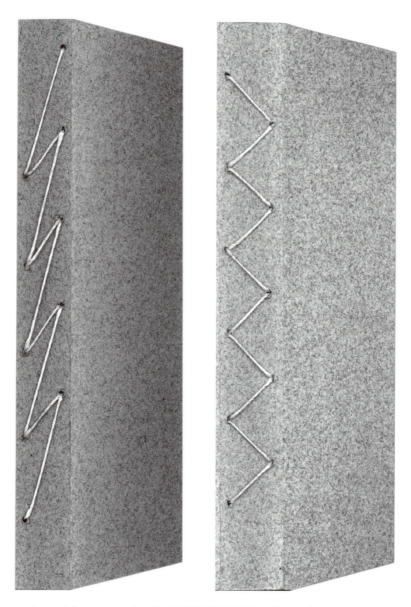

On the left is an example of the LIGHTNING BOLT, which is diagrammed on the previous page. On the right is PINKING SHEARS, diagrammed on page 73.

PINKING SHEARS

Sewing Stations: The first section to be sewn pierces the odd-numbered stations. The second section pierces the even-numbered stations.

SEWING PROCEDURE

1. Start on the inside of the second section. Exit station 2.
2. Set on the first section. Angle and enter the first section at station 3.
3. Exit station 1.
4. Angle and enter the second section at station 2. Tie-off.
5. Exit station 4.
6. Angle and enter the first section at station 3.
7. Exit station 5.
8. Angle and enter the second section at station 4.
9. Exit station 6.
10. Angle and enter the first section at station 5.
11. Exit station 7.
12. Angle and enter the second section at station 6.
13. Exit station 8.
14. Angle and enter the first section at station 7
15. Exit station 9.
16. Angle and enter the second section at station 8.
17. Exit station 10.
18. Angle and enter the first section at station 9.
19. Exit station 11.
20. Angle and enter the second section at station 10. Tie-off.

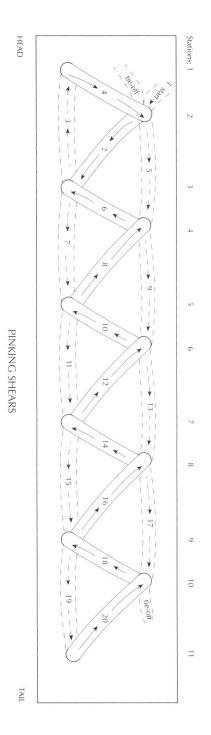

PINKING SHEARS WITH BARS

The two bars, horizontal parallel stitches at the head and tail, are more than design. I prefer to border many of these diagonal sewings with a bar to attach the sections close to the head and tail.

Sewing Stations: The first section to be sewn pierces stations 1, 2, 4, 6, 8, 10 and 12. The second section pierces stations 1, 3, 5, 7, 9, 11 and 12.

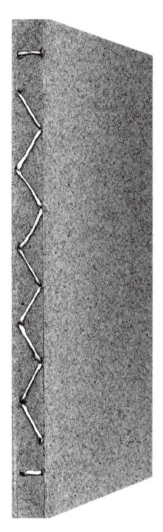

An example of PINKING
SHEARS WITH BARS

HEAD   TAIL

PINKING SHEARS WITH BARS

SEWING PROCEDURE

1. Start on the inside of the first section. Exit station number 1.
2. Span and enter the second section at station 1.
3. Exit station 3.
4. Angle and enter the first section at station 2. Tie-off.
5. Exit station 4.
6. Angle and enter the second section at station 3.
7. Exit station 5.
8. Angle and enter the first section at station 4.
9. Exit station 6.
10. Angle, enter the second section at station 5.
11. Exit station 7.
12. Angle and enter the first section at station 6.
13. Exit station 8.
14. Angle, enter the second section at station 7.
15. Exit station 9.
16. Angle and enter the first section at station 8.
17. Exit station 10.
18. Angle, enter the second section at station 9.
19. Exit station 11.
20. Angle and enter the first section at station 10.
21. Exit station 12.
22. Span and enter the second section at station 12.
23. Tie-off at station 11.

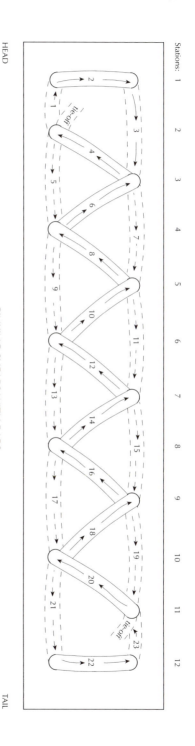

CARETS

This alternating *V* motif might be referred to as Carets.

This might be translated into two sewings. Every other caret could be one color, alternating with a second color.

Two carets could be seen as a unit. The first two, and the final two carets would be one color. The middle two carets would be sewn separately as a second color.

Sewing Stations: The first section to be sewn pierces stations 1, 3, 4, 5, 7, 8, 9, 11 and 12. The second section pierces stations 2, 3, 5, 6, 7, 9, 10, 11 and 13.

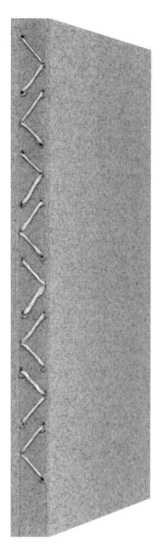

An example of the sewing referred to as CARETS

HEAD   TAIL

CARETS

SEWING PROCEDURE

1. Start on the inside of the first section to be sewn. Exit station 1.
2. Angle and enter the second section at station 2.
3. Exit station 3.
4. Angle and enter the first section at station 4. Tie-off at station 3.
5. Exit station 3.
6. Angle and enter the second section at station 2.
7. Exit station 5.
8. Angle and enter the first section at station 4.
9. Exit station 5.
10. Angle and enter the second section at station 6.
11. Exit station 7.
12. Angle and enter the first section at station 8.
13. Exit station 7.
14. Angle and enter the second section at station 6.
15. Exit station 9.
16. Angle and enter the first section at station 8.
17. Exit station 9.
18. Angle and enter the second section at station 10.
19. Exit station 11.
20. Angle and enter the first section at station 12.
21. Exit station 11.
22. Angle and enter the second section at station 10.
23. Exit station 13.
24. Angle and enter the first section at station 12. Tie-off.

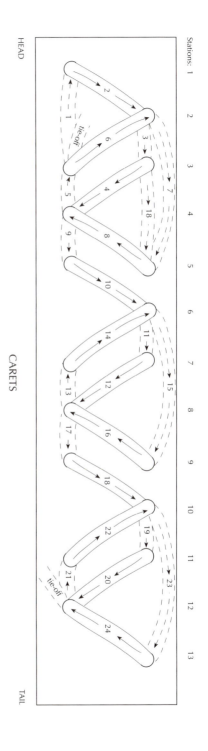

SETS OF DIAGONAL BARS

The photographic illustrations and drawn diagram of the sewing procedure of Sets of Diagonal Bars all have six sewing stations for each section.

The procedure is identical to the sewing of Parallel Bars, which is described on page 52.

Sewing Stations: The sewing stations vary, depending upon the pattern designed for the spine. For the pattern on

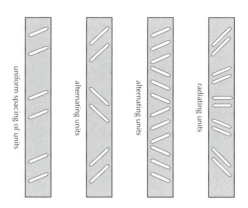

Four spine-covers with variations in stations

the facing page, the first section to be sewn pierces stations 1, 2, 5, 6, 7 and 8. The second section pierces stations 2, 3, 4, 5, 8 and 9.

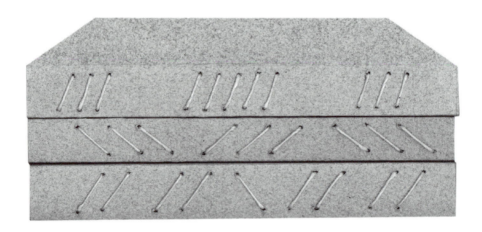

These three examples are the sewing referred to as SETS OF DIAGONAL BARS.

SEWING PROCEDURE

1. Start on the inside of the first section at the head. Exit station 1.
2. Set on the second section. Angle and enter the second section at station 2.
3. Exit station 3.
4. Angle and enter the first section at station 2. Tie-off.
5. Exit station 5.
6. Angle and enter the second section at station 4.
7. Exit station 5.
8. Angle and enter the first section at station 6.
9. Exit station 7.
10. Angle and enter the second section at station 8.
11. Exit station 9.
12. Angle and enter the first section at station 8.
13. Proceed to station 7 on the inside. Tie-off with a half hitch.

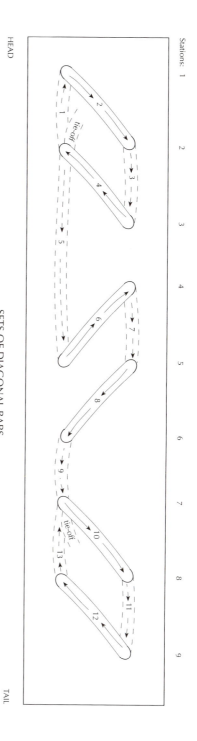

LATTICE

Sewing Stations: The first section to be sewn pierces stations 1, 3, 4, 5 and 6. The second section pierces stations 2, 3, 4, 5, 6 and 7.

SEWING PROCEDURE

1. Start on the inside of the first section at the head. Exit station 1.
2. Set on the second section. Angle and enter the second section at station 3.
3. Exit station 2.
4. Angle and enter the first section at station 4.
5. Tie-off. Exit station 3.
6. Angle and enter the second section at station 5.
7. Exit station 4.
8. Angle and enter the first section at station 6.
9. Exit station 5.
10. Angle and enter the second section at station 7.
11. Proceed to station 5 on the inside. Tie-off with a half hitch.

Below is an example of the LATTICE.

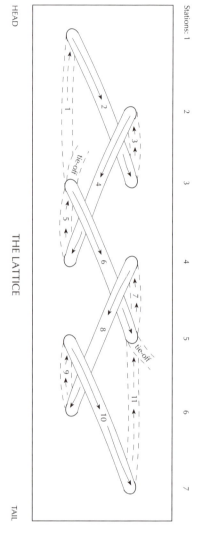

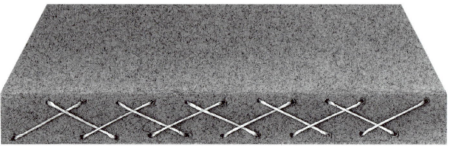

X SERIES

Several of the 2–section sewings were devised around the letter form *X*. They tend to be some of my favorites. I think they remind me of ribbon which ties a wrapped present. Indeed, some of the sewings in the *X* series even resemble tied bows.

The first four *X* sewings are designed with the motif on the oblique:
If you wish, line up the sewing stations so that the intersecting legs of the *X* are at a right angle:

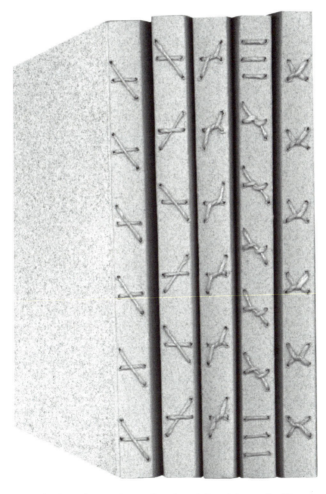

Some examples from the *X* series sewings from left to right are the *X's*, described on page 82; ALTERNATING *X's*, as described on page 83; TWISTED *X*, described on page 84; TWISTED *X* WITH BARS, as described on page 86; and LINKED *X*, page 88.

X's

SEWING PROCEDURE

1. Start on the inside of the first section. Exit station 1.
2. Set on the second section. Angle and enter the second section at station 3.
3. Exit station 2.
4. Span and enter the first section at station 2. Tie-off.
5. Exit station 4.
6. Angle and enter the second section at station 6.
7. Exit station 5.
8. Span and enter the first section at station 5.
9. Exit station 7.
10. Angle and enter the second section at station 9.
11. Exit station 8.
12. Span and enter the first section at station 8.
13. Exit station 10.
14. Angle and enter the second section at station 12.
15. Exit station 11.
16. Span and enter the first section at station 11.
17. Exit station 13.
18. Angle and enter the second section at station 15.
19. Exit station 14.
20. Span and enter the first section at station 14.
21. Tie-off on the inside at station 13 with a half hitch.

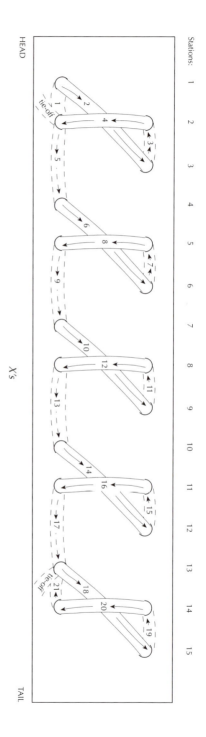

ALTERNATING *X's*

SEWING PROCEDURE

1. Start on the inside of the first section. Exit station 1.
2. Set on the second section. Angle and enter the second section at station 3.
3. Exit station 2.
4. Span and enter the first section at station 2. Tie-off.
5. Exit station 5.
6. Span and enter the second section at station 5.
7. Exit station 4.
8. Angle and enter the first section at station 6.
9. Exit station 7.
10. Angle and enter the second section at station 9.
11. Exit station 8.
12. Span and enter the first section at station 8.
13. Exit station 11.
14. Span and enter the second section at station 11.
15. Exit station 10.
16. Angle and enter the first section at station 12.
17. Exit station 13.
18. Angle and enter the second section at station 15.
19. Exit station 14.
20. Span and enter the first section at station 14.
21. Tie-off on the inside at station 13 with a half hitch.

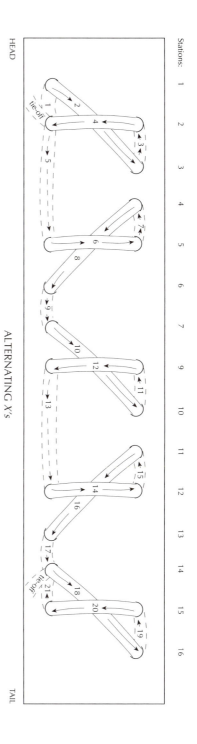

2–SECTION TWISTED *X*

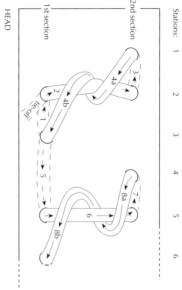

Sewing procedure of the Twisted *X* is identical to the previous sewing, with the addition of the twist, which is accomplished in 2 steps:

- Step 4a angles forward, passes under the stitch (step 2). Tension is applied towards the head.
- Step 4b maintains that tension, then angles and enters station 3. Enter with slight tension, carefully monitoring the formation on the spine to create an *X*.

Creating the tension in sewing of the
TWISTED *X*

In this illustration, the first twisted *X*, created by steps 1 through 4b, is drawn as the sewing will appear with proper tension in creating the twist.

The second twisted *X*, created by steps 6 through 8b, is illustrated with very loose tension. This is to clearly show the path of creating the twist *X*.

SEWING PROCEDURE

1. Start on the inside of the first section. Exit station 2.
2. Set on the second section. Span, enter the second section at station 2.
3. Exit station 1.
4a. Drop, angle forward of the thread (step 2), and then pass under. Pull the tension towards the head.
4b. Proceed across the thread (2). Keep the tension; enter the first section at station 2a. Tie-off.

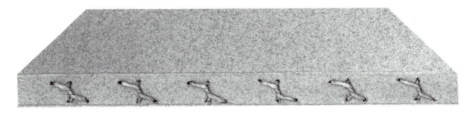

This is an example of the 2–section sewing referred to as the TWISTED *X*.

5. Exit station 5.

6. Span and enter the second section at station 6.

7. Exit station 4.

8a, b. Angle forward of the thread (step 6) and pass under. Pull the tension towards the head. Proceed across the thread (6). Keep the tension; enter the first section at station 6.

9. Exit station 8.

10. Span and enter the second section at station 8.

11. Exit station 7.

12a, b. Angle forward of the thread (10). Pass under. Pull towards the head. Proceed across the thread (10). Keeping tension, enter the first section at 9.

13. Exit station 11.

14. Span and enter the second section at station 11.

15. Exit station 10.

16a, b. Angle forward of the thread (14). Pass under. Pull towards the head. Proceed across the thread (14). Keeping tension, enter the first section at 12.

17. Exit station 14.

18. Span and enter the second section at station14.

19. Exit station 13.

20a, b. Angle forward of the thread (18). Pass under. Pull towards the head. Proceed across the thread (18). Keeping tension, enter the first section at station 15.

21. Tie-off on the inside at station 14 with a half hitch.

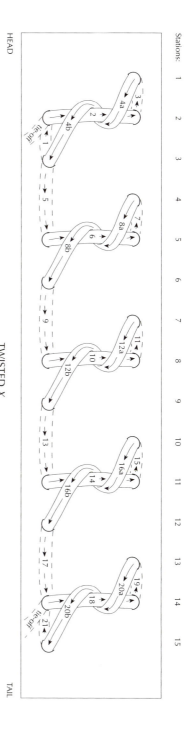

HEAD

TWISTED X

TAIL

Stations: 1   2   3   4   5   6   7   8   9   10   11   12   13   14   15

TWISTED X WITH BARS

SEWING PROCEDURE

1. Start inside of the first section. Exit station 1.
2. Span and enter the second section at station 1.
3. Exit station 2.
4. Span, enter the first section at station 2. Tie-off.
5. Exit station 3.
6. Span and enter the second section at station 3.
7. Exit station 5.
8. Span and enter the first section at station 5.
9. Exit station 4.
10a. Climb at an angle, lap over the thread (step 8).
10b. Backtrack under the thread (8). Pull tension towards the head. Angle and enter the second section at station 6.
11. Exit station 8.
12. Span and enter the first section at station 8.
13. Exit station 7.
14a, b. Angle, lap over the thread (step 12). Backtrack under the thread (12). Pull tension towards the head. Angle and enter the second section at station 9.

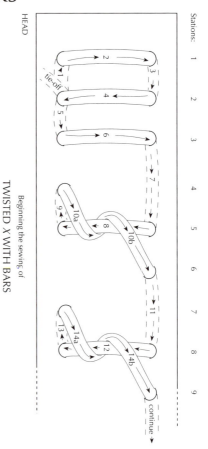

Above is an example of the TWISTED X WITH BARS.

15. Exit station 11.
16. Span and enter the first section at station 11.
17. Exit station 10.
18a. Angle, lap over the thread (16). Backtrack under the thread (16). Pull tension towards the head.
18b. Angle, enter the second section at 12.
19. Exit station 14.
20. Span and enter the first section at station 14.
21. Exit station 13.
22a. Angle, lap over the thread (20). Backtrack under the thread (20). Pull tension towards the head.
22b. Angle, enter the second section at 15.
23. Exit station 17.
24. Span and enter the first section at station 17.
25. Exit station 16.
26a. Angle, lap over the thread (24). Backtrack under the thread (24). Pull tension towards the head.
26b. Angle, enter the second section at 18.
27. Exit station 19.
28. Span and enter the first section at station 19.
29. Exit station 20.
30. Span, enter the second section at station 20.
31. Exit station 21.
32. Span and enter the first section at station 21.
33. Tie-off on the inside at station 20 with a half hitch.

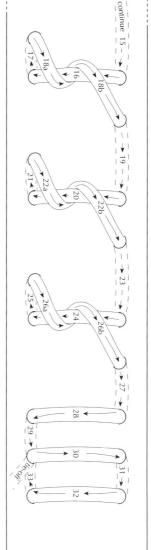

Completing the sewing of
TWISTED X WITH BARS

LINKED *X*

The Linked *X* is similar to the Twisted *X*, described on page 84. In that sewing, the *X* is formed by pulling the tension towards the head, then pulling towards the tail to maintain tension. In this sewing, the procedure is more simple. The needle passes under the thread, tension is adjusted towards the tail as you angle and enter the other section.

- Step 4a angles backward, passes under the thread (step 2).
- Step 4b reverses direction, angles toward station 2. Tension is applied to pull the threads into an *X*.

Enter station 2, carefully monitoring the formation on the spine to create an *X* which is uniform with all the other *X's* on the spine.

- The first twisted *X*, in this illustration, created by steps 1 through 4b, is drawn as the sewing will appear with proper tension in forming the *X*.

- The second twisted *X*, steps 6 through 8b, is illustrated with no tension to clearly show the path of the sewing procedure.

Tension is carefully applied just prior to entering the even-numbered stations in the first section.

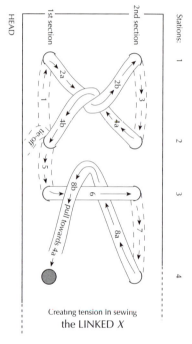

Creating tension in sewing
the LINKED *X*

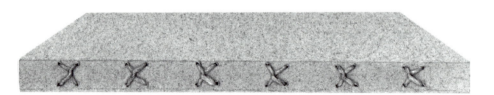

Above is an example of the sewing LINKED *X*.

SEWING PROCEDURE

1. Start on the inside of the first section. Exit station 1.
2. Span and enter the second section at station 1.
3. Exit station 2.
4a. Angle backward, pass under the thread (step 2).
4b. Reverse direction, angle towards station 2. Pull to adjust tension before proceeding. Enter the first section at station number 2. Tie-off.
5. Exit the next station towards the tail (3).
6. Span and enter the second section at the same numbered station (3).
7. Exit the next station towards the tail (4).
8a. Angle backward, pass under the last thread (step 6).
8b. Reverse direction. Pull towards tail to adjust tension. Be careful to keep the tension uniform, so that the *X* resembles the previous. Enter the next station in the first section (4).

Remaining stations:

Repeat steps 5 through 8b to form each additional *X* stitch. After finishing the final *X*, retreat on the inside to the previous station. Tie-off with a half hitch.

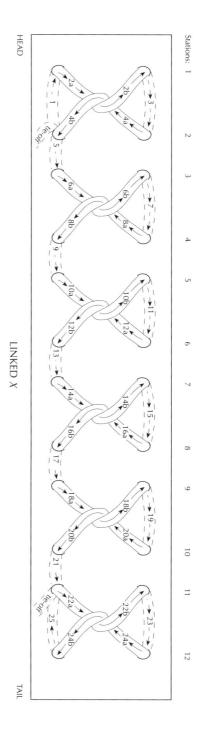

SOFT *K*

The Soft *K* is the identical sewing as that for the Linked *X*. The difference is only in the amount of tension during step 4, and, every step divisible by 4:

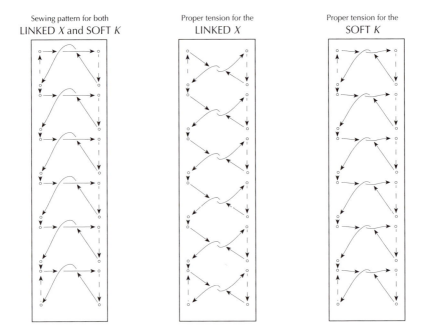

Sewing pattern for both
LINKED *X* and SOFT *K*

Proper tension for the
LINKED *X*

Proper tension for the
SOFT *K*

On the left is the sewing procedure for both the Linked *X* and the Soft *K*.

In the Center is how the Linked *X* will appear, by applying tension to pull the horizontal stitch to become an *X*.

On the right, the Soft *K* is sewn with almost no tension to the arcing thread.

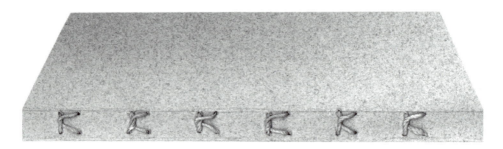

Above is an example of the sewing the SOFT *K*.

SEWING PROCEDURE

1. Start on the inside of the first section. Exit station 1.
2. Span and enter the second section at station 1.
3. Exit station 2.
4a. Angle backward, pass under the thread (step 2).
4b. Reverse direction, angle towards station 2. Carefully adjust tension before proceeding. Enter the first section at station number 2. Tie-off.
5. Exit station the next station towards the tail (3).
6. Span and enter the second section at the same numbered station (3).
7. Exit the next station towards the tail (4).
8a. Angle backward, pass under the last thread (step 6).
8b. Reverse direction. Apply very little tension. Be careful to keep the tension uniform, so that the *K* resembles the previous. Enter the next station for the first section (4).

Remaining stations:

Repeat steps 5 through 8b to form each additional *K* thread. After finishing the final *K*, retreat on the inside to the previous station. Tie-off with a half hitch.

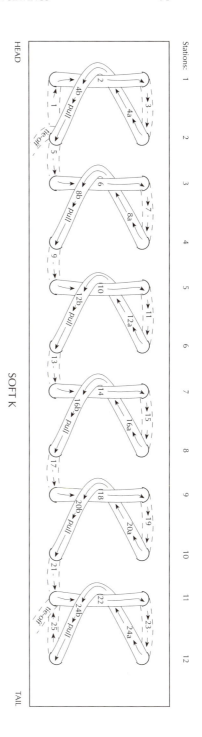

TIED BOW

Tension on this double *K* sewing pulls and bows the vertical stroke of the *K*. Therefore, I do not refer to it as a *K*; it reminds me of a ribboned knot.

The spine in this sewing should be reinforced. If a paper cover is used, the spine could be folded to become two or three ply (see: *Flat Back with Foredge Turn-Ins*, page 236 in Volume I). Another method is to cut a strip of paper the dimensions of the spine and glue it on the inside of the spine-cover.

SEWING PROCEDURE

1. Start on the inside of the first section. Exit station 1.
2. Span and enter the second section at station 1.
3. Exit station 2.
4a. Angle backward, lap the thread (step 2).
4b. Reverse direction, slip under the thread (2). Angle towards station 2. Carefully adjust tension before proceeding. Enter the first section at station 2. Tie-off.
5. Exit the next station towards the tail (3).
6a. Angle backward, lap the thread (step 2).
6b. Reverse direction, slip under the thread (2). Carefully adjust the tension. Angle forward towards the next station (3). Enter the second section.

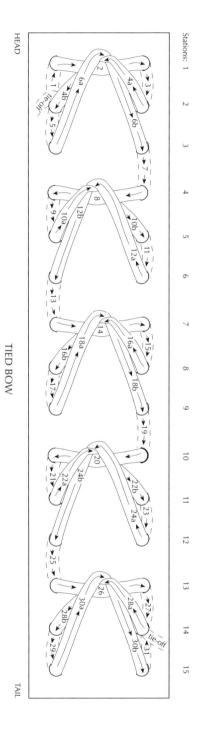

HEAD

Stations: 1 2 3 4 5 6 7 8 9 10 11 12 13 14 15

TIED BOW

TAIL

7. Exit the next station towards the tail (4).
8. Span and enter the first section (station 4).
9. Exit the next station (5).
10a. Angle backward, lap the last thread (step 8).
10b. Reverse direction; slip under the thread (8). Apply very little tension. Be careful to keep the tension uniform, so that the sewn unit resembles the previous. Angle forward towards the next station (5). Enter the second section.
11. Exit the next station (6).
12a. Angle backward, lap the last thread (step 8).
12b. Reverse direction; slip under the thread (8). Adjust the tension to keep the sewn units uniform. Angle forward towards the next station (6). Enter the first section.
13. Exit the next station (7).
14. Span and enter the second section (7).
15. Exit the next station (8).
16a. Angle backward, lap the thread (14).
16b. Reverse direction slip under the thread (14). Angle towards the next station (8). Adjust the tension. Enter the first section.
17. Exit the next station (9).
18a. Angle backward, lap the thread (14).
18b. Reverse direction, slip under the thread (14). Adjust the tension. Angle forward towards the next station (9). Enter the second section.
19. Exit the next station (10).

Remaining stations: Repeat steps 8 through 18b to form the following two alternating sewn units. After finishing the final unit, retreat on the inside to the previous station. Tie-off with a half hitch.

Example of
the TIED BOW

BARBER POLE

Sewing Stations: Each section, and the spine-cover, will need two stations for each intertwined unit. The sections will need two extra stations: Station 1 is not pierced on the cover. It is for the sections, only, to start the sewing. Station 8 is pierced in the sections, only, to be used to tie-off in the gap between the sections, rather than inside one of the sections.

HEAD   TAIL

Sewing stations for the sections
For the cover, pierce all stations, except 2 and 8

The Barber Pole is an *X* sewing. It requires two needles. I suggest using two colors of thread to bring out the intertwined pattern.

The other variable is the number of twists in forming the unit. An even number of twists allows the lighter color starting in the first section at station 2 to enter station 3, back in the first section:

HEAD   TAIL

BARBER POLE with an even number of twists

An odd number of twists allows the lighter color starting in the first section at station 2a to enter station 3 of the second section. This seems preferable, as the arms and legs of the *X* are diagonally opposed:

HEAD   TAIL

BARBER POLE with an odd number of twists

SEWING PROCEDURE

Starting the sewing with two needles is explained on page 51.

1. Lay cover aside. Start on the outside of the sections. A needle enters each section from the mountain peak to the valley at station 1. Center the thread dangling from each section. Pull the sections tightly together. The needle and thread which, for now, is inside the first section, will be referred to as the *x* needle. The thread and needle inside the second section will be the *y* needle. They cannot be called *1ˢᵗ* and *2ⁿᵈ* because for an odd number of twists, each needle will alternate sewing one section, then the other. Place on the cover.

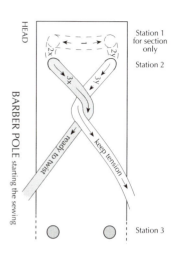

2x. Exit the first section at station 2 to outside of the spine-cover with thread *x*.

2y. Exit the second section through station 2 with thread *y*.

3. Grasp thread color *x* with right hand and color *y* with your left. Pull the threads laterally until they intersect close to station 2. This forms the arms of the *X*.

Reposition your grip if necessary, so that it is close to station 2. Rotate the *x* color thread in a clockwise motion. At the same time, rotate the *y* color thread counter-clockwise to form the first twist. Repeat until the desired number of evenly shaped twists is achieved.

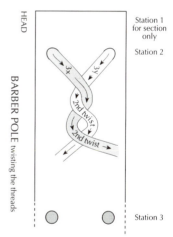

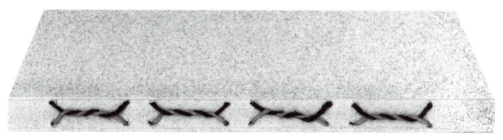

Example of the BARBER POLE, with an even number of twists. An even number of twists keeps the color in the same section; an odd number allows the color to alternate from one section to the other.

4x. Maintain the tension as you take thread *x* and enter the proper station 3. You will enter the first section if you have made an even number of twists. Thread *x* will enter the second section at station 3 if an odd number of twists.

4y. Maintain the tension as you take thread *y* and enter the remaining station 3. This forms the legs of the *X*.

5x. Exit the next station (4).

5y. Exit the next station (4).

6.   Create the next unit on the spine: Cross the two threads to form the arms of the *X*. Twist to shape the desired number of twists.

7x. The *x* color of thread enters the next station (5) of the second section, if an even number of twists. Enter the next station in the first section if an odd number of twists.

7y. The *y* color enters the other station.

Remaining Stations:

Continue in this manner sewing the remaining units. After the last unit is completed, enter the sections. Exit the final stations (8) pierced only in the sections. Tie-off in the gap between the sections.

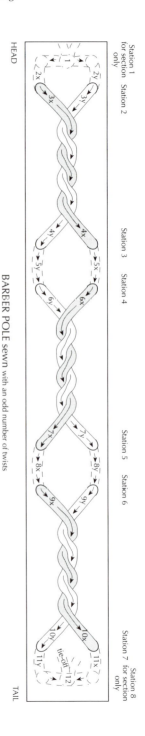

BARBER POLE sewn with an odd number of twists

DESCENDING *X's*

The Descending *X* is sewn with two needles.

Sewing Stations: The spine-cover has 9 stations, equally spaced. The sections have an additional 2 stations: Station 2, for the sections, only, is to start the sewing. Station 10, for the sections, only, is to tie-off on the inside of the spine-cover in the gap between the sections.

The sewing procedure at each station will always start with the needle coming from the first section. At times this will be the needle labeled *x*, and at other times, the *y* needle will be extending from the first section.

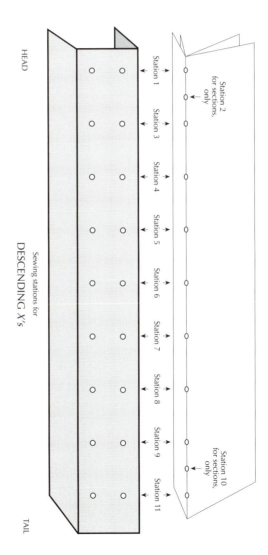

SEWING PROCEDURE

1. Start on the outside of the sections. A needle enters each section from the mountain peak into the valley side at station 2. Center the thread dangling from each section. Pull the sections tightly together. The needle and thread which, for now, is inside the first section, will be referred to as the x needle. The thread and needle inside the second section will be the y needle. They cannot be called *1st* and *2nd* because each needle will alternate sewing one section, then the other.

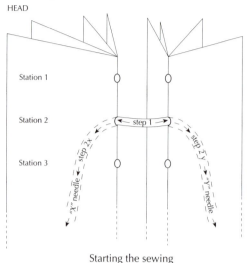

Starting the sewing

Place on the cover.

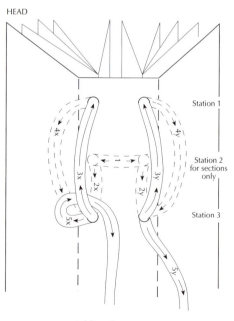

2x. Exit the first section at station 3 to outside of the spine-cover.

2y. Exit the second section through station 3.

3x. Enter station 1.

3y. Enter station 1.

4x. Exit station 3.

4y. Exit station 3.

5x. Slip behind the thread from the outer to the inner side, that is, proceeding from the side-cover towards the spine.

Adding the cover

Step 5x then enters station 4 of the first section, as shown in diagram
below. At each station, the first section will be sewn first, using
whichever needle is in the section. Then the second section is sewn.

5y. Slip behind the thread at station 3 of the second section, from the
outer to the inner side. Enter station 4.

6x. Exit station 5 of the first section.

7x. Angle backward, slip under the thread at station 4 of the second section, from the outer to the inner side. Lap the diagonal thread. Enter
station 6 of the second section.

6y. Exit station 5 of the second section.

7y. Angle backward. Lap the diagonal thread. Slip under the thread at station 4 from the outer to inner side. Lap diagonal thread 7*y*. Slip *under*
7*x* to hold down the long stitch. Enter station 6 of the first section.

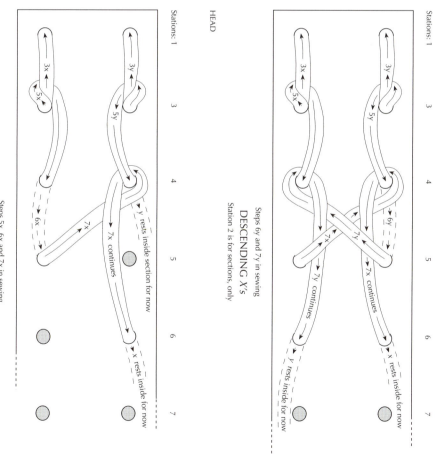

8y. Always sewing the first section first, exit station 7.

9y. Angle backward. Slip under
the thread at station 6 from
the outer to the inner side.
Enter station 8 of the second
section.

8x. Exit station 7 of the second
section.

9x. Angle backward. Lap the
diagonal thread (9y). Slip
under the thread at station 6
from the outer to the inner
side. Lap the diagonal thread
(9x). Slip *under* 9y to hold
down the long stitch. Enter
station 8 of the first section.

10x. Sewing the first section
first, exit station 9.

11x. Angle backward. Slip
under the thread at station 8
from the outer to the inner
side. Enter station 11 of the
second section.

10y. Exit station 9.

11y. Angle backward. Lap the
diagonal thread (11x). Slip
under the thread at station 8
from the outer to the inner
side. Lap the diagonal thread
(11y). Slip *under* 11x to hold
down the long stitch. Enter
station 11 of the first section.

12y. Exit station 10 of the section, only.

12x. Exit station 10 of the section, only. Tie-off in the gap
between the sections.

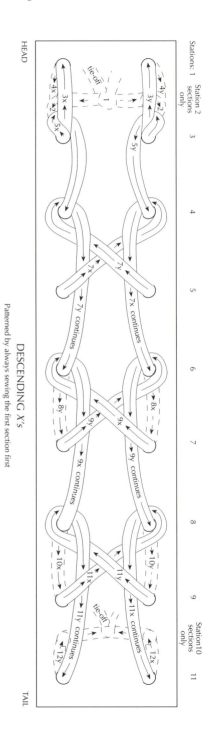

HEAD

DESCENDING X's
Patterned by always sewing the first section first

TAIL

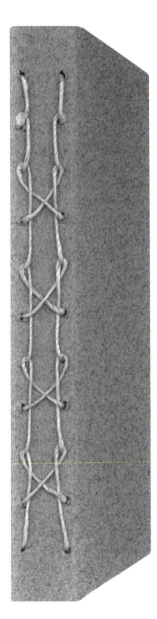

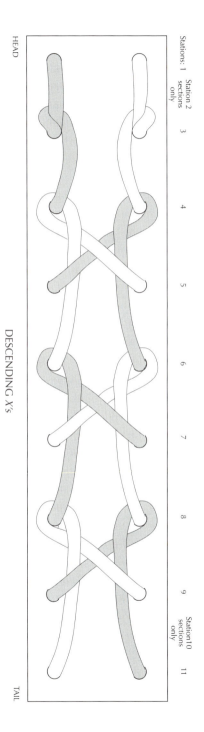

HEAD

Stations: 1

Station 2
sections
only

3

4

5

DESCENDING *X's*

6

7

8

9

Station10
sections
only

11

TAIL

DESCENDING *X's*

Each needle alternately sews the other
section. Two colors of thread could
be tied together to start the sewing.
The sewing path of each needle
would be obvious on the spine.

ALPHA *Alternating Loops*

This is the sign for the Greek letter, and the sometime signature of my godchild, Alpha Gaylord Lillstrom: ∝ It is also the sewing path of this sewing dedicated to her.

Sewing Stations: Station 1 is for the anchor stitch. Each additional station thereafter is for the formation of an alpha loop.

Since each link enters the spine-cover on the opposite side from which it exited, the pattern of the loops will alternate:

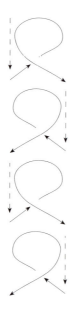
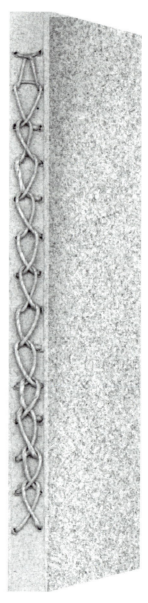

In addition, the threads on the inside of the sections alternate from one section to the other.

Right : An example of the sewing referred to as ALPHA *Alternating Loops.*

SEWING PROCEDURE

1. Start on the inside. Exit the first section at station 1.
2. Span and enter the second section at station 1.
3. Exit station 2.
4. Retreat towards the head. Pass over, then under the anchor stitch (step 2). Angle and enter the first section at station number 2. Tie-off.
5. Exit station 3.
6a. Angle to the outer side of station 2 of the second section. Link under the thread marked step 4a at station 2.
6b. Drop, link under the thread marked step 4b at station 2 of the first section.
6c. Angle forward, pass over the thread 6a and enter the second section at station 3.
7. Exit station 4.
8. Angle to the outer side of station 3 of the first section. Climb, link under threads 6a and 6c. Angle forward, pass over the thread 8a. Enter the first section at station 4.

Remaining Stations:

Continue sewing the remaining stations in the same manner. Odd-numbered steps drop and exit. Even-numbered steps (a) angle, (b) link both feet of the previous *X* stitch, then (c) angle to form an *X*, then enter the other section. Since step *c* always passes over, rather than slipping under step *a,* the pattern of the *X* stitches alternate.

After entering the final station, climb and tie-off.

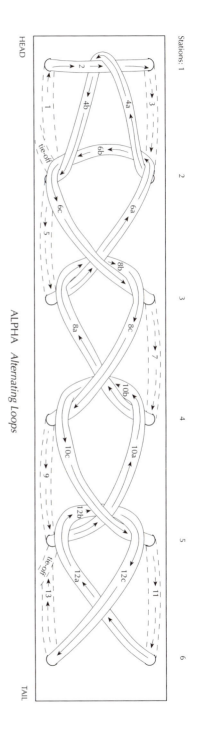

THE WATERFALL

The Waterfall creates a thick repetition of threads on the spine in a 2–section sewing. This twin link stitch is related to the single link stitch sewing, Sewn Chains, for a 1–section sewing, which is described on page 42.

PREPARATION

This sewing requires two needles, one on each end of a single thread. Although there are two sections, the spine-cover has only one row of stations, which is shared by both sections. Pierce each section with however many stations. Pierce the cover.

SEWING PROCEDURE

CHANGE-OVER: To keep track of which needle is sewing which section, the change-over from one needle to the other will be inside the sections, rather than on the spine.

1. Set the cover aside. With one needle, exit station 2 of the second section to be sewn. Leave half the length of thread on the inside. With the needle which is on the outside of the section, enter the first section at the second station from the mountain peak to valley. Pull the thread taut, pulling the sections tightly together. Divide the thread evenly (see illustration at the top of the facing page).

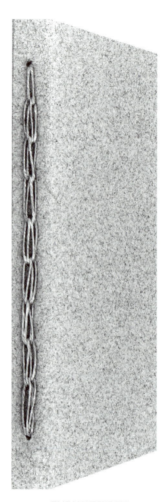

THE WATERFALL
a twin link stitch sewing

Both sections share one set of sewing stations on the cover.

2L. With the needle that is inside the first section, exit station 1 of the first section to be sewn. Add the cover, and exit station 1 of the cover. Remember, both sections will share the singular set of stations on the cover.

2R. With the needle that is inside the second section, exit station 1 of the section and cover.

3R. Enter station 2 of the cover into the *first* section.

3L. Enter station 2 of the cover into station 2 of the *second* section. (The *L* thread will change-over to the second section, the *R* thread to the first. Alternating strengthens the sewing).

4L. Exit the second section and cover through station 3.

5L. Move backward and link under the thread at station 2 (marked 3R), from the outer to the inner side. Enter station 3 into the *first* section.

4R. Exit the first section and cover at station 3.

5R. Move backward and link under the thread (marked step 3L) at station 2 from the outer to the inner side. Enter station 3 into the second section.

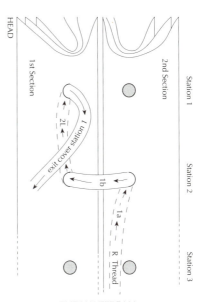

THE WATERFALL

Step 1: Starting the sewing
Step 2: Attaching the cover

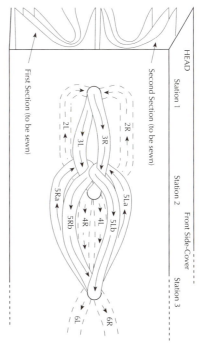

THE WATERFALL

Steps 2L and 2R: Attaching the cover to each section
Steps 3L and 3R: Forming the anchor stitch
Steps 4 through 5: Making the first twin link of the chain

6L. Exit the first section and cover through the next station towards the tail (station 4).

7L a-b. Move backward, link under the threads (steps 5R a-b) at the previous station from the outer to the inner side. Proceed towards the tail one station (4). Enter the second section.

6R. Exit the second section through the next station towards the tail (4). 7R a-b. Move backward and link under the threads at the previous station from the outer to the inner side. Proceed towards the tail one station. Enter the first section.

Remaining Stations:

Repeat steps 6L, 7L, 6R and 7R to form each twin link until you have linked at the next to last station. Proceed to the final station, but enter the cover only. Do the same with the second needle. Tie-off in the gap between the sections on the inside of the spine-cover.

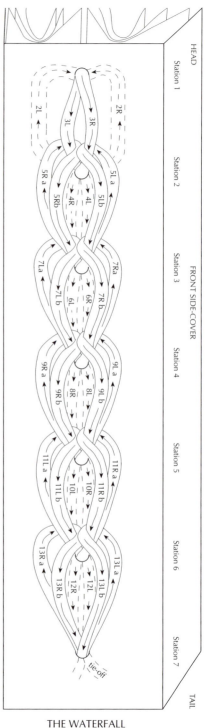

Sewing pattern of the twin link stitch sewing, which I refer to as THE WATERFALL.

THE WATERFALL

Entering alternate sections ties the sewing together

CROSSED SNOWSHOES

PREPARATION

Determine the number and placement of the sewing stations. Pierce the sections. The cover requires two rows of stations, to register with the stations of each section. Place a needle on each end of the thread. This sewing is unusual in that the sewing begins on the outside of the cover. By taking each needle to the inside at station 1, an anchor stitch is formed.

The change-over will always be on the inside of the sections, making it easy to determine which needle is to be used next.

SEWING PROCEDURE

1L. With one needle, enter station 1 of the spine-cover, from the outside, into the inside of the first section. Pull half the thread to the inside of this section.

1R. The other needle enters station 1 of the cover into the second section. This forms the anchor stitch on the spine-cover.

2L. Exit station 2 of the first section.

3L a. Angle backward, over the anchor stitch. Link under close to station 1.

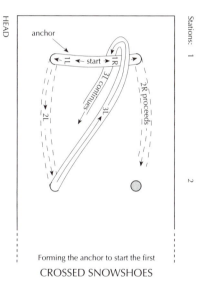

Forming the anchor to start the first
CROSSED SNOWSHOES

2L b. Enter station 2 of the first section. Do not pull tightly, being careful to keep the link close to the end of the anchor.

2R. Exit station 2 of the second section.

3R a. Angle over the previous link, pass over the anchor stitch, and link under, close to station 1.

3R b. Enter station 2 into the second section. Form the chain at an angle, keeping the loop close to the end of the anchor.

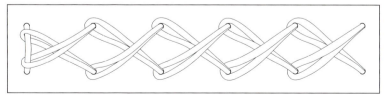

CROSSED SNOWSHOES
A link stitch sewing that gives a chain pattern

HEAD

Stations: 1

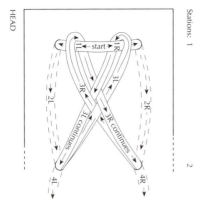

Optional weaving the links

4L. Exit the first section at the next station towards the tail (3).

5L a. Angle to the outer side to the previous station. Link under both threads.

5L b. Angle and re-enter the first section (3).

4R. Exit the second section at the next station towards the tail (3).

5R a. Angle to the outer side to the previous station. Link under both threads.

5R b. Angle and re-enter the second section (3).

Remaining Stations: Repeat steps 4L, 5L, 4R and 5R to form each additional intersecting link of the chain. After forming the final link for the first section, re-enter the final station of the cover, but do not enter the first section.

Form the final link with the *R* thread. Re-enter the final station of the cover, but do not enter the second section. Remove the two needles and tie-off on the inside of the spine-cover in the gap between the two sections.

HEAD

Stations: 1

CROSSED SNOWSHOES

TAIL

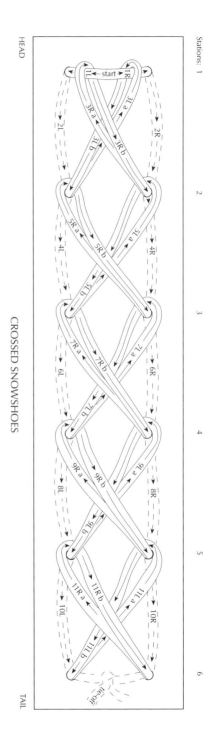

Prototype for the intersecting link stitch sewing, CROSSED SNOWSHOES.

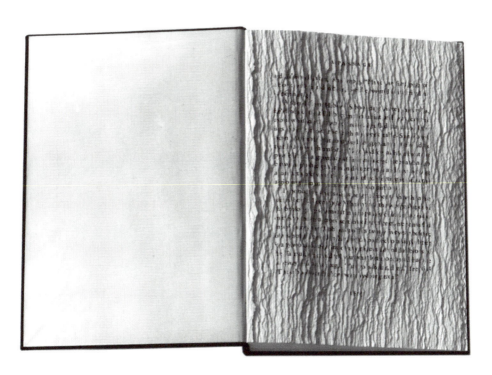

Buzz Spector, *A Passage,* Granary Books, 1994. Edition of 50. Typography by
Philip Gallo, offset printing by Bradley Freeman. Bound by Jill Jevne.
21.5 x 16 cm.

THREAD EYE

The Thread Eye is a spartan, but elegant interlocking of linked threads upon the spine-cover. It requires two needles, and can be done with two colors of thread. I prefer only one for a subtle result. However, if the threads vary only slightly in hue, the result is quite rewarding.

Sewing Stations: To avoid a tie-off at the head and tail inside each section, an extra station is added at the head and tail for the sections, only. These begin, and end the sewing in the gap on the inside of the cover between the sections. There is no corresponding stations for the cover.

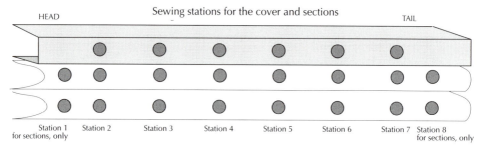

Sewing stations for the cover and sections

HEAD ... TAIL

Station 1 for sections, only — Station 2 — Station 3 — Station 4 — Station 5 — Station 6 — Station 7 — Station 8 for sections, only

The sewing starts without the cover. If two colors are used, tie the two ends of the threads together and clip close to the knot. Thread each color with a needle.

SEWING PROCEDURE

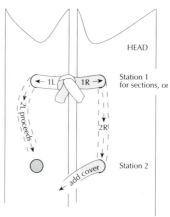

Starting the sewing
prior to adding the cover

1L. Lay aside the cover. With one needle, enter the first section at station 1 from the mountain peak to the valley.

1R. With the other needle, enter the second section at station 1 from the mountain peak to the valley.

Pull on both threads to snug the sections closely together. Divide the thread evenly inside both sections.

2R. Set on the cover. Exit the second section through station 2 of the section and the cover.

3R. Place the needle directly back into station 2 and re-enter the second section.

Pull almost all the thread to the inside, leaving a small loop on the spine.

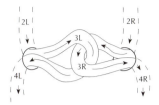

The loop should not extend more than halfway across the spine. Be careful not to lose the loop.

2L. Exit station 2 of the first section and cover.

3L. Link through the loop formed at the second section. Re-enter station 2 into the first section.

4L. Proceed towards the tail one station (3). Exit the first section.

4R. Proceed towards the tail one station (3)Exit the second section.

5R. Place the needle directly back into this station (3). Re-enter the second section. Pull most of the thread to the inside, leaving a small loop on the spine.

5L. Take the needle dangling from the first section and link through the loop formed at the second section. Re-enter the station into the first section.

Remaining Stations: Repeat steps 4L, 4R, 5R and 5L to form each link at the remaining paired stations on the spine-cover. Upon re-entering the final cover station for each section, proceed on the inside to the final station (8). Exit the section, only. Tie-off in the gap between the sections on the inside of the spine-cover.

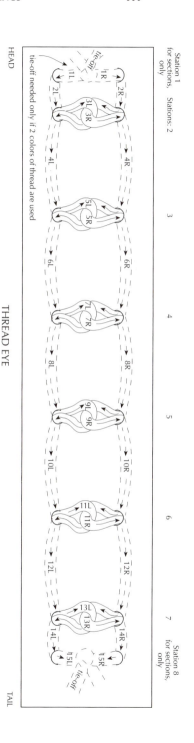

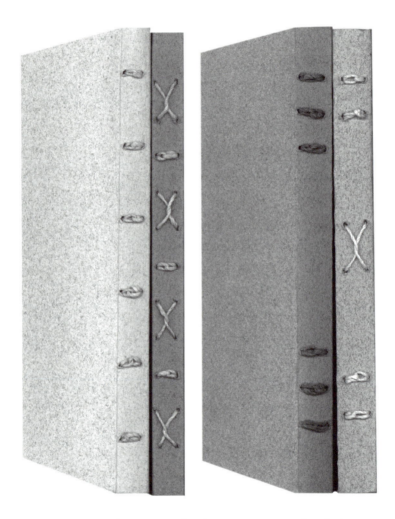

Left: An example of the sewing referred to as THREAD EYE, described on page 110. Next, is the sewing the THREAD EYE WITH *X's*, described on page 113.

Third from the left: Another sewing of THREAD EYE, varying the pattern. On the right is a variation of THREAD EYE WITH *X's*.

THREAD EYE WITH *X's*

The previous sewing, Thread Eye, is modified here. Every other link forms an *X*. Instead of linking and re-entering the same station, two stations are used to create the *X*.

Sewing Stations: Additional stations could be added to the sections, only, at the head and the tail. These would be to start and end the sewing. However, it is just as easy to make double use the of second and the next to last stations to start and end on the inside of the cover in the gap between the sections. That is how the sewing will be described.

STARTING and ENDING PROCEDURE
On page 51 is a description for starting and ending 2–section sewings. It requires an additional sewing station at the head, and another at the tail for the sections, only. These stations are not part of the sewing pattern on the cover. The use of these extra stations avoids double stitches on the inside of the sections.

However, sometimes the pattern of the stitches is so dense that it does not allow room for additional stations whose sole purpose is to start or end the sewing. Often it is simply less complicated to start the sewing through the mountain peak of the sections using station 2 of each of the sections:

After the sewing is started, as illustrated to the right, add the cover, taking each needle through station 1 for each section. Set on the cover and continue the sewing.

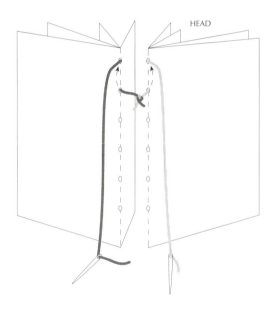

Starting the Sewing

Station 2 doubles its usage. First, without the cover, as a point to begin the sewing. After the cover is added, station 2 is used as part of the sewing pattern.

SEWING PROCEDURE

Two needles are used. Steps are numbered and lettered for left and right needles. The sewing starts without the cover. If two colors are desired, tie the two ends of the threads together and clip close to the knot. Thread each color with a needle.

1. Set aside the cover. With one needle, enter the first section at station 2 from the mountain peak to the valley. With the other needle, enter the second section at station 2 from the mountain peak to the valley. Pull on both threads to snug the sections closely together. Divide the thread evenly inside both sections.

2L. Add the cover. Exit station 1 of the first section, and through station 1 of the cover.

3L. Enter station 2 of the first section. Pull most of the thread to the inside, leaving the stitch on the spine-cover slightly limp.

2R. Exit the second section through station 1.

3R. Link under the stitch (step 3L), and enter station 2b of the cover into the second section. Pull on both needles to tighten and shape the X stitch on the spine.

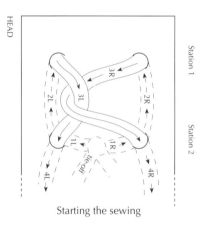

Starting the sewing

4L. Exit station 3 of the first section through 3 of the cover.

5L. Place the needle directly back into station 3 and re-enter the first section. Pull almost all the thread to the inside, leaving a small loop on the spine. The loop should not extend more than halfway across the spine. Be careful not to lose the loop.

4R. Exit the second section at station 3.

5R. Slip under the looped thread and link through the loop. Re-enter station 3 into the second section. Pull on both threads to tighten and shape the link.

6L. In the first section, proceed towards the tail one station (4) and exit.

7L. Enter the next station (5). Pull most of the thread to the inside of the first section, leaving the stitch on the spine-cover slightly limp.

6R. In the second section, exit the next station (4).

7R. Link under the stitch (step 7L), and enter the next station (5).

8L. In the first section, proceed towards the tail one station (6) and exit.

9L. Place the needle directly back into this same station and re-enter the first section. Pull almost all the thread to the inside, leaving a small loop on the spine. Be careful not to lose the loop.

8R. In the second section, exit the next station (6).

9R. Link under the loop. Place the needle directly back into the station (6) and re-enter the second section. Pull on both threads to tighten and shape the link.

Remaining Stations:

Repeat steps 6L through 9R to form each pair of the following extended and simple links.

Form the final *X* stitch (extended link).

Inside the first section, retreat to the previous station. (10). Exit the section, only. Inside the second section, retreat to the previous station. (10). Exit the section, only. Tie-off in the gap between the sections on the inside of the cover.

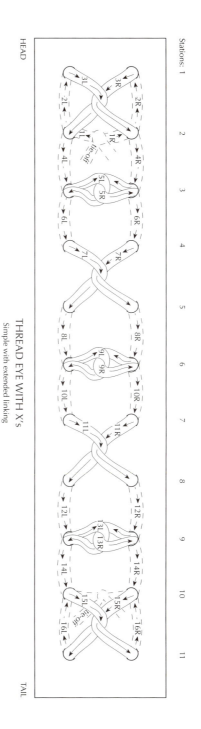

HEAD

Stations: 1   2   3   4   5   6   7   8   9   10   11

THREAD EYE WITH X's
Simple with extended linking

TAIL

2–SECTION RUNNING STITCH SEWING

In Volume I, page 66, two approaches to sewing a 2–section pamphlet were described. The following *figure 8 sewing* is more elegant.

NOTE: Although this sewing is known as the *Double Section Pamphlet Sewing*, it is a misnomer: Betsy Eldridge points out that a pamphlet sewing is a *B* sewing—the path creates the letter *B* (see page 16 in this volume).

What is described *here,* is a *Figure 8* (see page 22). Therefore I will refer to this as a *2–Section Running Stitch Sewing.*

After seeing the omission of this sewing in Volume I, the description of this 2–Section Running Stitch Sewing was sent to me by Albert Borch of Calgary, Alberta. He learned it from Betty Lou Chaika.

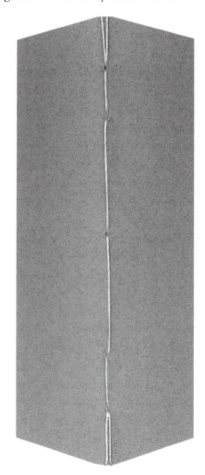

In the sample Bert sent to me, the first tie-off is inside the second section, and the final tie-off within the first. I have taken the liberty to alter the sewing path, so that both tie-offs are in between the sections. Clipping the thread close to the knot, it almost disappears in this new location, since the sewing is tightly fitting, with no gap between the sections.

SEWING PATTERN: The completed sewing will result in a single thread from station to station on the cover, as well as inside each section. There will be two threads on the spine which wrap around the head. One thread continues inside the first section from the head to station 5. The other wraps around the head into the second section to station 5.

There will be two threads on the spine which wrap around the tail. One continues inside the first section to station 1. The other wraps around the tail into the second section to station 1.

2–SECTION
RUNNING STITCH SEWING

PREPARATION

Fold two sections. Make a hard crease on the first section, but only a soft crease on the second.

Prepare a paper cover with a single hinge-fold. It is important that the cover be the same height as the sections, since the thread wraps around the head and tail. The cover would crimp or break if not supported by the sections the full length of the spine (hinge-fold).

Set the first section inside the second, for purposes of piercing. Place on the cover and pierce five sewing stations through the sections and the hinge-fold of the cover.

Sewing Stations: For this sewing, station 1 is at the tail; station 5 is at the head. The first section of the book will be the first to be sewn.

The sewing steps that will take you through a single, continuous sewing are in three parts, each a running stitch. First, the two sections are sewn together. The sewing continues as a second running stitch, connecting the first section to the cover. The third running stitch sews the second section to the cover.

SEWING PROCEDURE
First Run:
SEWING THE SECTIONS

1. Set the cover and second section aside. Enter the first section at station 1, from the mountain peak to the inside. Pull all the thread inside the section, except enough to be able to tie-off later on.

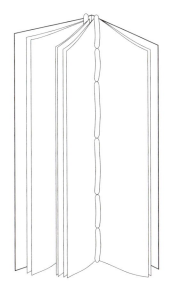

Inside view of the stitches

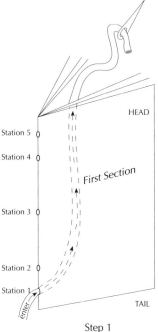

Step 1
2–SECTION RUNNING
STITCH SEWING

2. The approach to Step 2 depends upon whether you are sewing a blank binding or imaged sections. I will describe both methods. I prefer the former, as it is less complicated, but cannot be used if the pages have already been numbered, as it would result in an incorrect imposition of text

STEP 2a, b, c, for a BLANK BINDING: Open the second section. Set the valley of the second section onto the mountain peak of the first. Allow the dangling thread (step 1) of the first section to protrude from the tail:

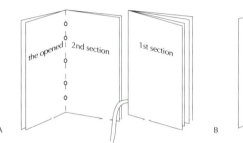

Step 2 for a blank binding
A. Open the second section.
B. Set the second section onto the first.
C. The first section, having been enveloped by the second.

Alternate STEP 2a, b, c, for IMAGED SECTIONS: With both sections closed, side by side, open the second section to the center page. Reverse the fold so that the second section envelops the first:

Alternative step 2 for a imaged sections
A. Set the sections side by side.
B. Reverse the fold of the second section, bringing the second half counter-clockwise around the first.
C. The first section, having been enveloped by the second.

Whether you followed step 2, or alternate step 2, the sewing is the same for the remainder of the thirteen sewing steps.

3. Exit station 2 of the first section, on through station 2 of the second section. Proceed on the mountain peak of the second section. Enter station 3 of the second section, and, continue through the first section, proceeding from the mountain peak to the inside.

Continue this running stitch through both sections to the head, ending at station 5 on the inside of the first section.

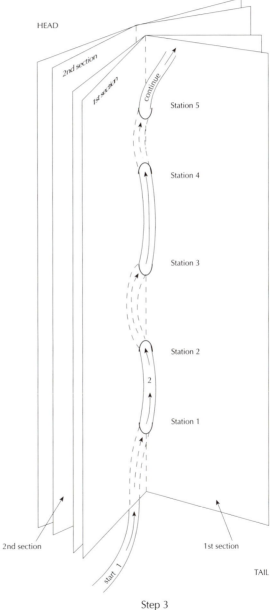

HEAD

2nd section

1st section

continue

Station 5

Station 4

Station 3

Station 2

2

Station 1

2nd section

1st section

start 1

TAIL

Step 3
2–SECTION RUNNING STITCH SEWING

4. Step 4 is the same, whether you followed step 2 for a blank binding, or for imaged sections. Open the second section, keeping the first closed. Grasp the half of the second section whose pages are in front of the first. Reverse the fold of these pages and pull them around to become the final pages of the book block. The two sections are now side by side, with the second section totally behind the first.

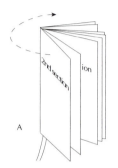

Step 4 for blank or imaged sections
A. Open the front half of the second section.
B. Reverse the fold of these pages.
C. Bring the first half of the second section clockwise around to the back.

Run a bone folder across the spine-edge of the two sections. Tighten the running stitch by holding the thread at the tail and pulling the other end away from the head. Pull parallel to the spine to avoid ripping the paper.

Second Run: *SEWING THE FIRST SECTION TO THE COVER*

5. Set on the cover. Grasp the thread, marked as step 2, and wrap around the head of the first section. Enter the cover at station 5 into the second section. The wrap-around will extend slightly onto the front side-cover.

6. Wrap around the head of the second section. Enter the cover at station 5 into the first section. The wrap-around will extend slightly onto the back side-cover. The two threads on the cover will form a *V* of approximately a 20° angle.

7. Proceed to station 4 on the inside of the first section. Exit. Make a running stitch through the cover and the first section, stopping when you exit the cover at station 2. This will attach the first section to the cover, but will not affect the second section.

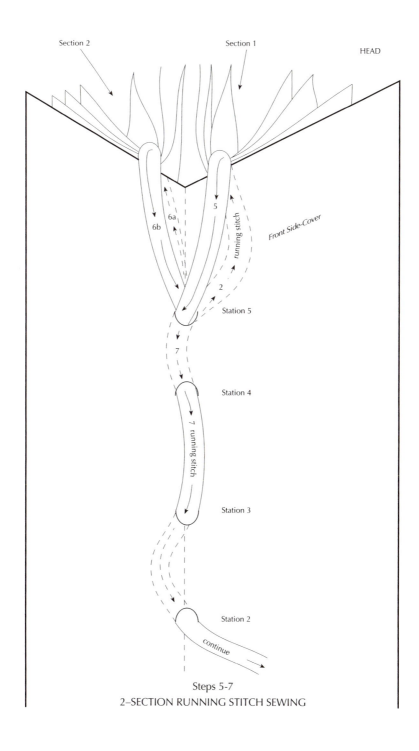

Section 2

Section 1

HEAD

6b 6a

5

running stitch

Front Side-Cover

2

Station 5

7

Station 4

7 running stitch

Station 3

Station 2

continue

Steps 5-7
2–SECTION RUNNING STITCH SEWING

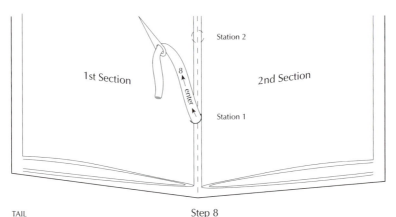

Step 8
2-SECTION RUNNING STITCH SEWING
Inside view of the book

8. Open the book block to the gap between the sections. Section 1 will be against the front side-cover; section 2 will rest against the back. Enter station 1 of the cover only. The needle will proceed in the gap between the two sections. Tie-off at station 1 in the gap between the sections with the dangling thread. Clip only the shorter thread. Pull slightly on the longer thread away from the tail. This will position the knot on the spine, almost out of sight.

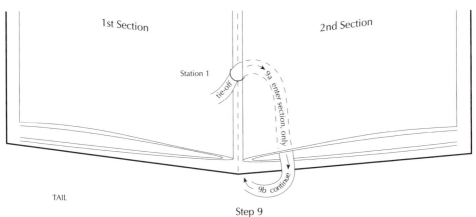

TAIL

Step 9
2-SECTION RUNNING STITCH SEWING
Inside view of the book

9. From the gap between the sections, enter station 1 of the second section, only, from the mountain peak to the valley. Wrap around the tail of the second section.

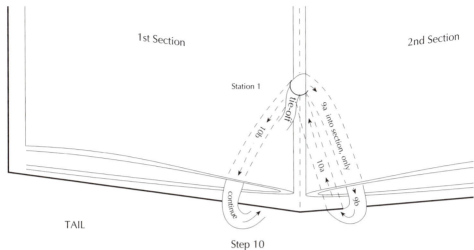

1st Section

2nd Section

Station 1

tie-off

9a into section, only

10b

10a

9b

continue

TAIL

Step 10
2-SECTION RUNNING STITCH SEWING
Inside view of the book

10. On the spine-cover, enter the cover at station 1 into the first section. The wrap-around will extend slightly onto the back side-cover. Wrap around the tail of the first section. Enter the cover at station 1 into the second section. The wrap-around will extend slightly onto the front side-cover. Form the resulting *V* on the cover to be the same angle as that at the head.

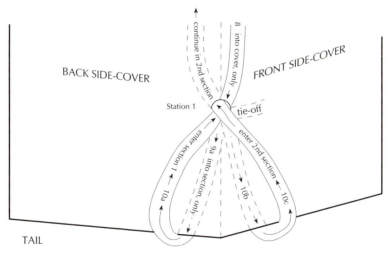

continue in 2nd section

8 into cover, only

BACK SIDE-COVER

FRONT SIDE-COVER

Station 1

tie-off

enter section 1

9a into section, only

enter 2nd section

10a

9b

10b

10c

TAIL

Step 10
2-SECTION RUNNING STITCH SEWING
Outside view of the book

Third Run:
SEWING THE SECOND SECTION TO THE COVER

11. Proceed to station 2 on the inside of the second section. Exit. Make a running stitch through the second section and the cover, stopping when you exit the cover at station 4. This will attach the second section to the cover.

12. Open the book block to the gap between the sections. Section 1 will be against the front side-cover; section 2 will rest against the back. Enter station 5 of the cover only. The needle will proceed in the gap between the two sections.

13. Tie-off with a half hitch in the gap between the two sections at station 5 on the inside of the cover. Clip the thread close to the knot, almost out of sight.

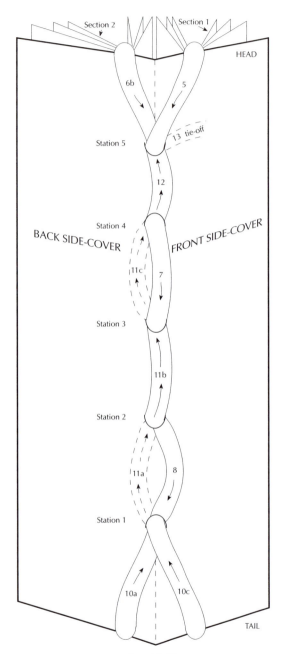

Step 11-13
2-SECTION RUNNING STITCH SEWING
Outside view of the cover

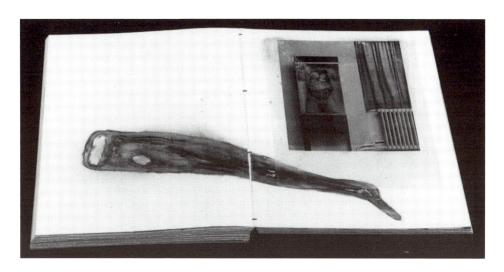

Above: Shelagh Keeley, *A Space for Breathing,* Granary Books, 1992. Color photographic transfers with original drawings in pencil, pigment and gouache 22 copies made. Binding by Daniel Kelm, The Wide Awake Garage. 27.8 x 35.7 cm.

Below: Toni Dove, *Mesmer: Secrets of the Human Frame,* Gramary Books, 1993. 60 copies made. Printed offset by Lori Spencer, Borowsky Center for Publication Arts at the University of the Arts in Philadelphia. Hard metal binding designed by Daniel Kelm, The Wide Awake Garage. 27.8 x 20.4 cm.

Above, Henrik Drescher, *Too Much Bliss,* Granary Books, 1992. The cover is laser cut Davy board, covered in black book cloth. Pattern of the irregular holes is mimicked on the first page, which is latex (see top picture on page 127).

On facing page: Henrik Drescher, *Too Much Bliss,* Granary Books, 1992. Letterpress with extensive hand painting, collage and drawing; embellished by Lauren Drescher. 41 copies made. Letterpress by Philip Gallo, The Hermetic Press. Binding by Daniel Kelm, The Wide Awake Garage. 30.5 x 22.9 cm.

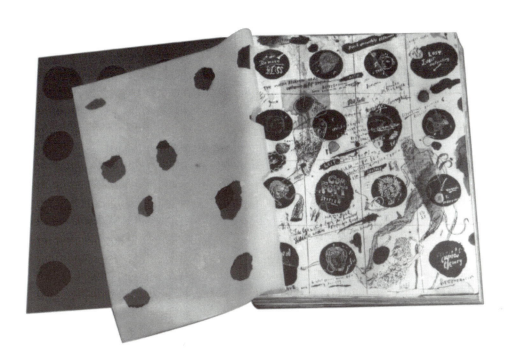

Left: *Nods,* text from five works by John Cage, drawings by Barbara Fahrner. Granary Books, 1991. 45 copies. Typography and letterpress by Philip Gallo, The Hermetic Press; design / binding by Daniel Kelm, The Wide Awake Garage. 33.6 x 17.2 cm.

Below: *The Marriage of Heaven and Hell: A Reading and Study.* Text from William Blake, drawings by Barbara Fahrner. Granary Books, 1993. 41 copies. Typography and letterpress by Philip Gallo, The Hermetic Press; design and binding by Daniel Kelm, The Wide Awake Garage. 31.8 x 30.5 cm.

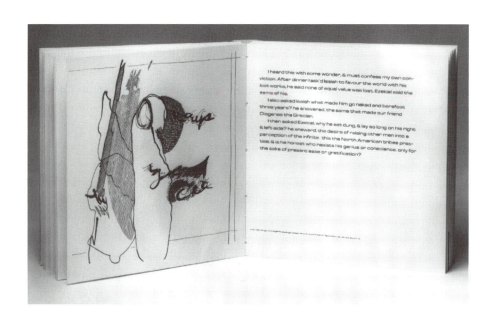

PART 3
3–SECTION SEWINGS

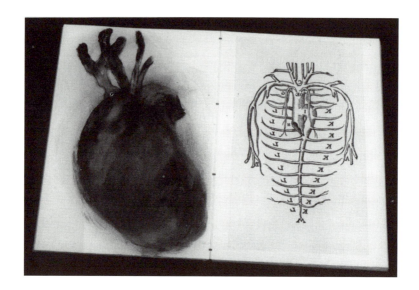

Above: Shelagh Keeley, *Notes on the Body,* Granary Books, 1991. Color photographic transfers with original drawings in pencil, pigment and gouache. 17 copies made. Philip Gallo, typography / letterpress, The Hermetic press; Daniel Kelm, binding, The Wide Awake Garage. 37.5 x 27.9 cm.

Below: Jane Sherry, *Venus Unbound,* Granary Books, 1993. Letterpress with photo-metallic collages, painting and drawing. 41 copies made. Philip Gallo, typography / letterpress, The Hermetic press; Daniel Kelm, binding, The Wide Awake Garage. 30.5 x 22.8 cm.

Each additional section geometrically increases the possibilities of design. All the 1– and 2–section sewings previously described can be used in 3–section patterning. Combinations of earlier stitches can produce new hybrids. The bulk of what can be accomplished lies beyond; it is the additional row of sewing stations. Patterns impossible with the limitations of single or paired pathways give way to this, the first of the multi-numbered sections: three.

I find great excitement in thinking about numbers, and what is meant by a single unit, or a double, as opposed to multiple units. I must contain my investigation to three, and even edit this self-imposed parameter.

On 23 and 24 January, 1994, I sketched out almost a hundred 3–section sewings. The pathways are coded with spartan arrows and numbers, allowing me to "see" the possibility of a thought at a glance, then move on to the next. I work rapidly as one binding suggests another. A polished sketch would kill the creative thought process.

After two twelve hour days of sketching, I started in on the physical act of sewing each of these sketches. My sewing, never at the level of craft of a fine binder, is even more sloppy when I am materializing my sketches as prototypes. Once in a while I find the pathways I have coded are impossible to sew. More often, I discover if I change the path, or resort to sewing with both ends of the thread containing a needle, I can make a much less convoluted pathway. It is discoveries like these that buoy my day and make this book not a task, but the reason for which I jump out of bed each morning so that I might treat myself to the joy of creating.

Now, it is middle February. Some eighty prototypes of 3–section sewings are lined up in my bindery, and, I turn to the computer once again, to describe these in words and drawn illustrations. Later, I will add photo illustrations (digital scans of the spines) of the prototype sewings.

14 February 1994

MULTIPLE SECTION PAMPHLET SEWING

My 3–section sewings should start with the Pamphlet Sewing. The common 1–section Pamphlet Sewing is described in Volume I. It is shown using three, four and five sewing stations. Variation on the 5–Hole has the same sewing path as the 5–Hole Pamphlet Sewing. The difference is that the variation uses three pierced stations and two passive, or *open ended* stations—the head and the tail. Thus, the sewing wraps around the head and the tail to mark the change-over.

The sewing on the following page is based on the 3–Hole Pamphlet Sewing (see page 16 in this book). However, the Multiple Section Pamphlet Sewing could make use of any number of stations. Stitches could be confined to the spine, or as in the case of the 5–Hole Variation, the Multiple Section Pamphlet Sewing would wrap around the head and the tail as many times as there are sections. The sewing would be visually, but not structurally, akin to the Long Stitch through Slotted Wrapper Cover. The following illustration shows six examples. The final one is based on the 5–Hole Variation:

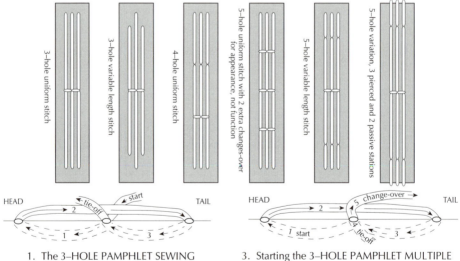

1. The 3–HOLE PAMPHLET SEWING
Tie-off is on the spine. The straight side of the "B" is on the spine.

2. The 3–HOLE PAMPHLET SEWING
Tie-off is on the inside of the section. The straight side of the "B" is on the inside of the section.

3. Starting the 3–HOLE PAMPHLET MULTIPLE SECTION SEWING
Tie-off is on the inside, but the change-over is on the spine. The straight side of the "B" is on the spine.

The Pamphlet Stitch Sewing forms a "B" stitch. The start, tie-off and the straight side of the "B" are on the peak or valley, depending where you start.

The Multiple Section Pamphlet Sewing wants the straight side of the "B" on the spine (peak), *but* the tie-off, and therefore, the start, inside (valley). See diagram directly above, and on page 133.

"B" STITCH: The characteristic of the pamphlet stitch is the pathway of the sewing forms the letter *B*. To avoid the tie-off on the spine, start inside (see diagram to the right, and bottom right on the previous page).

SEWING PROCEDURE

Since Part 3 of this book deals with 3–section sewings, I will describe the sewing using three sections.

1. Start inside of the first section to be sewn. Exit station 1.
2. By-pass station 2, and enter station 3. Tie-off at station 2.
3. Exit station 2. Lap the thread labeled step 2. Set on the second section.
4. Span and enter the cover and second section at station 2. This marks the change-over on the spine.
5. Exit station 1.
6. Enter station 3.
7. Exit station 2. Set on the next section.
8. Span, as change-over, and enter the cover and third section at station 2.
9. Exit station 1.
10. Enter station 3.
11. Exit station 2.
12. Loop thread labeled step 10. Enter station 2, again, so that the tie-off can be inside.
13. Tie-off with a half hitch.

In this manner, any number of sections can be sewn to a continuous support.

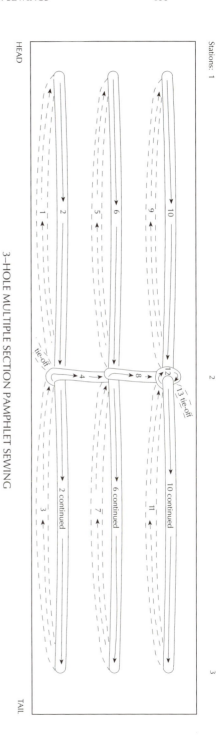

3–HOLE MULTIPLE SECTION PAMPHLET SEWING

The pamphlet stitch is a "B" stitch. In this sewing, the straight side of the "B" is on the spine; the change-over replaces the knot

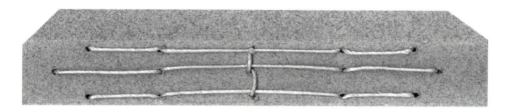

MULTIPLE SECTION PAMPHLET STITCH SEWING, above, is described on the previous page. Compare it to the FIGURE *8* Sewing at the bottom of this page.

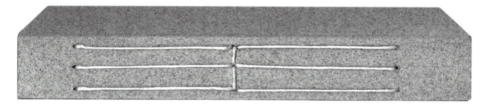

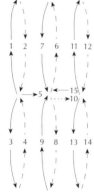

1–Needle sewing

1–needle sewing of the MULTIPLE SECTION FIGURE *8* SEWING is shown as the middle photo on this page, directly above. It is diagrammed to the left, using 3 stations in each section. Although the stitches on the spine superficially appear identical to the photo at the top of the page, the sewings are quite different. The pathway of the Multiple Section Pamphlet Sewing, page 132, necessarily employs the *B* stitch. But the sewing to the left is a Figure *8* Sewing.

In the diagram to the left, the figure *8* pathway is apparent.

Step 5 moves across the spine on the outside, as the change-over. Step 6 enters the cover and the section through the mountain peak. Step 9 enters cover, only. Step 10 changes-over on the inside of the spine-cover and exits the cover, only. Step 14 exits section and cover. Step 15 enters cover and second section to tie-off.

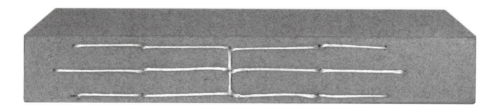

2–needle sewing of the MULTIPLE SECTION FIGURE *8* SEWING is shown directly above. It is described on the following page.

MULTIPLE SECTION FIGURE *8* SEWING

The continuous thread sewing of the Multiple Section Pamphlet Sewing described on page 132 employs the *change-over* on the *outside* of the spine. This offers possibilities of design; it might as well be flaunted. However, in order to alter the location of the change-over on the spine, the pathway of the sewing must necessarily be a Figure *8*. Since the sewing diagrammed on page 136 does not employ the *B* stitch, it is a misnomer to call this sewing a Multiple Pamphlet Stitch Sewing. It is a figure *8* sewing.

1–NEEDLE SEWING: The 1–needle Multiple Section Figure *8* Sewing diagrammed on page 134 uses three sewing stations. The sewing alternately exits to the spine with steps 5, 15, 25. However, after sewing the even-numbered sections, the thread must move on the inside of the spine-cover. This requires backtracking, steps 15, 25, 35, in order to create the horizontal change-over stitch on the cover after each even-numbered section. This requires a convoluted sewing path. The diagram on the previous page is only convenient for a 3–section sewing.

2–NEEDLE SEWING: To resolve this problem, an uncomplicated sewing path is achieved by sewing with two needles, rather than one. It is diagrammed on the following page. The needle in the right hand, designated as *R* for right, enters the cover and the first section at station 3. The length of thread is divided equally, half inside the section, half on the cover. The right needle sews from the center to the tail, then pauses at step 3R.

The other needle, designated as *L*, starts on the outside at station 3 and sews from the center to the head, then pauses at step 3L. Alternate the sewing from right to left needle at the head and the tail.

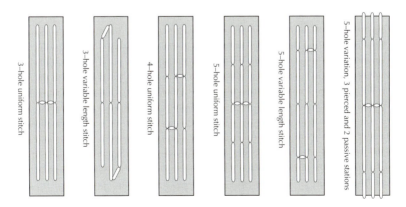

Permutations of the 2–needle sewing of the
MULTIPLE SECTION FIGURE *8* SEWING

SEWING PROCEDURE

To start this 2–needle sewing, take the right needle, enter cover and section to the inside of the first section to be sewn at station 3. Pull enough thread to the inside to evenly divide the thread.

1R. Proceed on the inside. Exit station 4.

2R. Enter station 5.

With the other needle:

1L. Proceed on the spine. Enter station 2.

2L. Exit station 1.

Switch to the right needle:

3R. Exit station 4.

4R. Enter the cover, only, at station 3.

5R. Travel along the inside of the spine-cover. Exit the cover, only, at station 3.

6R. Place on the second section. Enter station 4 through cover and to the inside of the new section.

7R. Exit station 5.

Switch to the left needle:

3L. Enter station 2 of the first section.

4L. Exit station 3.

5L. Proceed horizontally on the spine. Enter station 3 into the second section.

6L. Exit station 2.

7L. Enter station 1.

Switch to the right needle:

8R. Enter station 4.

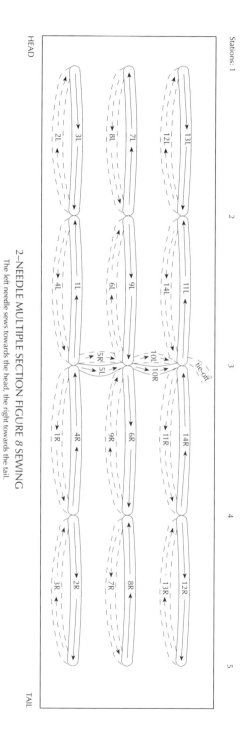

2–NEEDLE MULTIPLE SECTION FIGURE 8 SEWING

The left needle sews towards the head, the right towards the tail.

This 5–hole sewing is *not* a pamphlet stitch sewing.

9R. Exit station 3.

10R. Proceed horizontally on the spine. Set on the third section. Enter station 3 into the third section.

11R. Exit station 4.

12R. Enter station 5.

Switch to the left needle:

8L. Exit station 2 of the second section.

9L. Enter the cover, only, at station 3.

10L. Travel along the inside of the spine-cover. Exit the cover, only, at station 3.

11L. Enter station 2 through cover and to the inside of the third section.

12L. Exit station 1.

Switch to the right needle:

13R. Exit station 4.

14R. Enter station 3.

Switch to the left needle:

13L. Enter station 2.

Remove both needles. Tie-off on the inside at station 3.

MULTIPLE SECTION FIGURE *8* SEWING

Bert Borch, untitled non-adhesive bound blank journal, 1992. 26.5 x 16.5 x 1.3 cm.

MULTIPLE SECTION, MULTIPLE FIGURE *8* SEWINGS

This variation of the previous sewing has two or more figure *8* sewings per section. It is sewn with one needle. Permutation of spine pattern becomes limitless, based on three variables:

- uniform and variable length stitching
- number of stations for the figure 8 stitches,
- whether one or more sections are wrapped at the head and the tail.

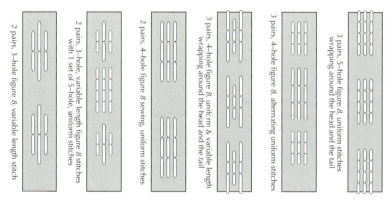

SEWING PROCEDURE

1. Start on the inside of the first section to be sewn. Exit station 3.
2. Enter station 2. Tie-off at station 2.
3-4. Proceed on the inside to station 1. Exit. Enter station 2.
5. Proceed on the inside to station 4. Exit.
6-7. Enter station 5. Exit station 6.
8. Enter the cover, only, at station 5.
9. Travel along the inside of the spine-cover. Enter the new section through the mountain peak to the inside of the section at station 5.
10. Proceed to the tail. Exit station 6 of the section and the cover.

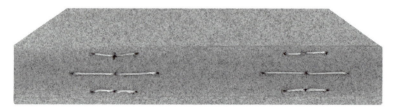

Example of the 1–needle MULTIPLE SECTION, MULTIPLE FIGURE *8* SEWING

11. Enter station 5.
12. Exit station 4.
13. Enter station 5.
14. Exit station 3.
15. Enter station 2.
16. Exit station 1.
17. Enter the cover, only, at station 2.
18. Travel along the inside of the spine-cover. Enter the new section through the mountain peak to the inside of the section at station 2.
19. Proceed to the head. Exit station 1 of the section and the cover.
20. Enter station 2.
21. Exit station 3.
22. Enter station 2
23. Proceed on the inside to station 4. Exit.
24. Enter station 5.
25. Exit station 6.
26. Enter station 5. Tie-off on the inside with a half hitch.

HEAD

Stations: 1   2   3   4   5   6

1–Needle MULTIPLE SECTION and (3-Hole) MULTIPLE FIGURE 8 SEWINGS

Steps 9 and 18 proceed on the inside of the spine-cover to enter the mountain peak of the next section

TAIL

TRIPLE DASH

The Running Stitch can be used for sewing any number of sections. With a 3–section sewing, possibilities of spine patterning expands from the more limited sewings with fewer sections. Here are a few as sketches:

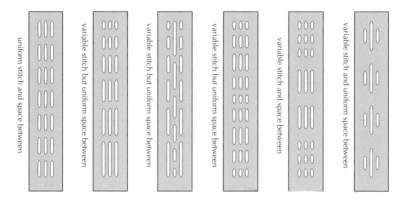

PREPARATION

Fold the sections and gauge the thickness of the book block. Make a paper cover with the spine width precisely, not too narrow and not too wide. If it is too narrow, the sections will not fit. If it is too wide, eventually the cover will get crushed on the book shelf. A tight fit is critical for all paper cover spines.

Draw your design for the stitches on the inside of the spine cover. Use a pencil, as ball point may bleed. Use a light touch, and the design need not be erased; it will not show. Set each section upon the cover design to mark the position of the stations. Pierce the stations for the sections and the cover.

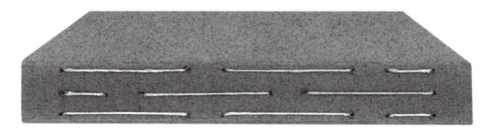

The Brick is an example of the TRIPLE DASH.

SEWING PROCEDURE

1. Start on the inside of the first section to be sewn. Exit station 1.
2. Enter station 2. Tie-off.
3. Exit station 3.
4-7. Proceed sewing a running stitch to the tail, entering station 8 with step 8.
9. Exit the section, only, at station 7.
10. Proceed across the inside of the spine-cover. Enter the new section from the mountain peak to the inside at station 7.
11. Exit the section and the cover at station 8.
12-18.   Make a running stitch to the head.
19. Exit the section, only, at station 2.
20. Proceed across the inside of the spine-cover. Enter the new section from the mountain peak to the inside at station 2.
21. Exit the section and the cover at station 1.
22-28. Make a running stitch to the tail.
29. Proceed on the inside of the section to station 7. Tie-off with a half hitch.

HEAD

Stations: 1 2 3 4 5 6 7 8

Steps 10 and 20 proceed on the inside of the spine-cover to enter the mountain peak of the new section

TRIPLE DASH

TAIL

TRIPLE DASH VARIATION

This triple dash sewing is a running stitch; it is *not* a long stitch. Since it wraps around the head and the tail, it is necessary to measure the cover precisely the same height as the sections, otherwise, the thread wrapping around the head and the tail will crimp the cover paper. I also suggest you reinforce the spine-cover with another ply of paper. This paper may be cut to the dimensions of the spine-cover, and pasted down on the inside. To avoid any adhesives, see: Part 3, *Covers,* in Volume I.

Sewing Stations: There are 6 pierced and 2 *open ended* sewing stations: The head and the tail are designated as "stations". However, they are not pierced stations, but the point at which the thread changes direction by wrapping over the head or tail.

SEWING PROCEDURE

1. Start on the inside of the first section to be sewn. Exit station 2.
2. Proceed over the head, designated as station 1. Tie-off on the inside of the section at station 2.
3. Exit station 3.
4-7. Proceed sewing a running stitch to the tail, exiting station 7 with step 7.
8. Proceed around the tail, designated as station 8.
9. Proceed inside the section. Exit the section, only, at station 7.

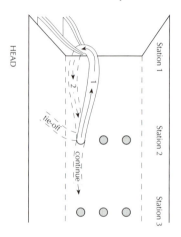

Starting the sewing over the head

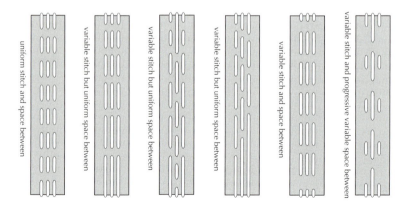

10. Proceed across the inside of the spine-cover. Enter the new section, only, from the mountain peak to the inside at station 7.

11. Wrap around the tail and proceed on the outside of the spine-cover towards the head.

12. Enter station 7.

13-17. Make a running stitch to the head, exiting station 2 with step 17.

18. Proceed around the head to the inside of the section.

19. Exit the section, only, at station 2.

20. Proceed across the inside of the spine-cover. Enter the new section, only, from the mountain peak to the inside at station 2.

21. Proceed inside the section to the head. Wrap around the head.

22-27.   Make a running stitch to the tail, exiting station 7 with step 27.

28. Proceed to the tail. Wrap around to the inside of the section.

29. Proceed on the inside of the section to station 7. Tie-off with a half hitch.

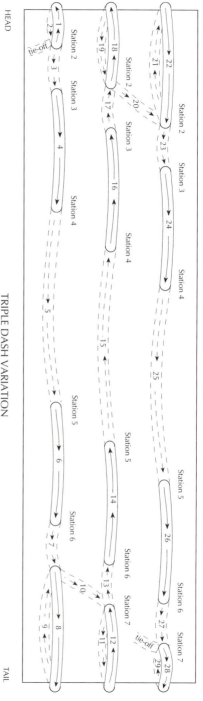

TRIPLE DASH VARIATION

Steps 10 and 20 proceed on the inside of the spine-cover to enter the mountain peak of the new section
Station 1 and 8 are not pierced, but the head and the tail, as open ended sewing stations

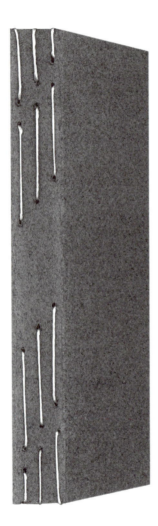 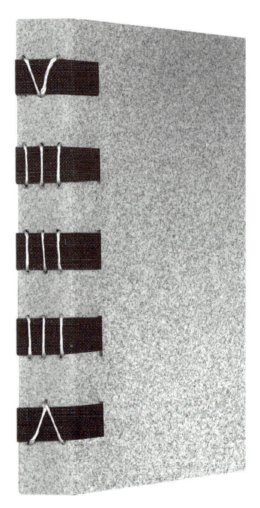

On the left is an example of the TRIPLE DASH VARIATION, described on the previous page.

On the right is an example of the MULTI-SECTION ON TAPES LACED INTO PAPER COVER. Description of this sewing was sent to me by Bert Borch. The sewing is described on page 145. This is the only sewing in Volume II that is sewn onto a raised support. All others are sewn onto continuous support of the paper cover.

MULTI-SECTION ON TAPES LACED INTO PAPER COVER

One description Bert Borch sent to me is a form of the common tape sewing. This variation was learned from Betty Lou Chaika. Changes-over on the spine are a decorative element. This sewing can be used with any number of sections by altering the arrangement of the diagonal stitches.

All sewings in Volume II use continuous support: the sections are sewn through the cover, except this one. Why? It is my oddball sense of aesthetics, and stresses binding, like learning, is an on-going process, *never* complete. Volume I only touched upon raised cords, suggesting to the reader there was *more*. It served as a notation to me to explore raised supports, which I do in Volume III. This page is a note to myself for a future text.

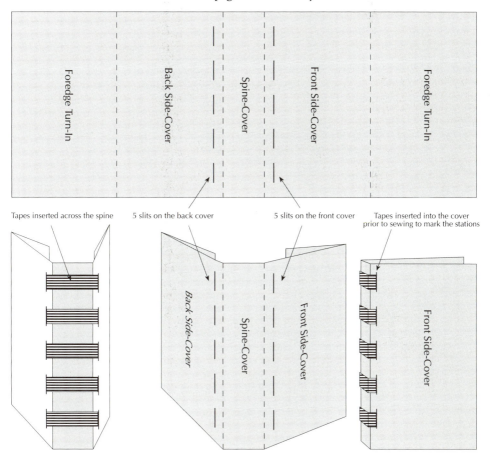

Tapes inserted across the spine   5 slits on the back cover   5 slits on the front cover   Tapes inserted into the cover prior to sewing to mark the stations

PREPARATION

The cover on this sewing should have foredge turn-ins extending all the way back to the hinge-fold, to cover the ends of the tapes. Five tapes will be placed across the outside of the spine and inserted into slits placed on the front and back side-covers. If not vellum, the tapes can be book cloth glued back to back for stiffness, then cut into strips to the size of the tapes. Tapes should be centered, and at least three inches wider than the spine.

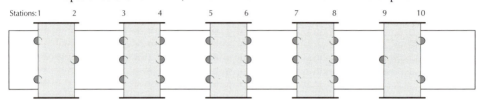

Stations:1   2   3   4   5   6   7   8   9   10

HEAD   Sewing stations for MULTI-SECTION ON TAPES LACED INTO PAPER COVER   TAIL

Sections 1 and 3: Pierce stations 1, 3, 4, 5, 6, 7, 8, and 10. Section 2: Pierce stations 2 through 9.

Sewing Stations: It is important not to pierce all ten stations for each section. Sections 1 and 3 are *not* pierced at sewing stations 2 and 9. Section 2 is not pierced at stations 1 and 10.

To mark the stations, open the cover. Lay the cover on the table with the inside of the cover up. Place the tapes across the spine, but not into the slits. Use them as a guide. Lightly mark the stations on the spine-cover, precisely along the edge of the tapes. Remove tapes and pierce the stations so that half the hole extends above and below the edge of the tape.

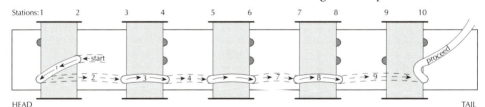

Stations:1   2   3   4   5   6   7   8   9   10

HEAD   TAIL

MULTI-SECTION ON TAPES LACED INTO PAPER COVER
Sewing the first section

Tapes: I sometimes use leather or vellum. If leather, wheat paste a sheet of decorative paper to the back of the pared leather. When it dries, cut it into half or three-quarter inch wide strips to be used as tapes (straps).

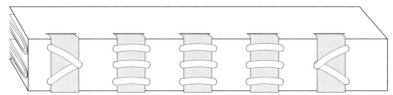

MULTI-SECTION ON TAPES LACED INTO PAPER COVER

Do not cut straps prior to pasting, as alignment would be difficult.

The thinner pared leather with a paper backing is preferred to unpared leather.

- Since it is stiffer, it will not buckle when the thread is wrapped around.
- Since it is thinner than unpared leather, it has a less bulky appearance.

SEWING PROCEDURE

Sewing the First Section:

1. Insert the tapes prior to sewing. Start on the inside of the second section to be sewn. Exit station 2. Pull all but about three inches of the thread to the outside.
2. Enter the first section at station 1.
3. Proceed inside the section. Exit station number 3.
4-9. Proceed sewing a running stitch to the tail, exiting station 10 with step 9. Each exit laps over the tape and enters beyond the other edge of the tape.

Sewing the Second Section:

10. Angle to station 9 of the middle section. Enter.
11. Proceed inside the section. Exit at station 8.
12-17. Make a running stitch towards the head. Exit station 2 with step 17. Tie-off with the beginning thread, but do not cut the longer thread.

Sewing the Third Section:

18. Angle to station 1 of the third section. Enter.
19. Exit station 3.
20-24. Make a running stitch towards the tail. Enter station 8 with step 24.
25. Exit station 10.
26. Angle to station 9 of the middle section. Enter. Tie-off with a half hitch.

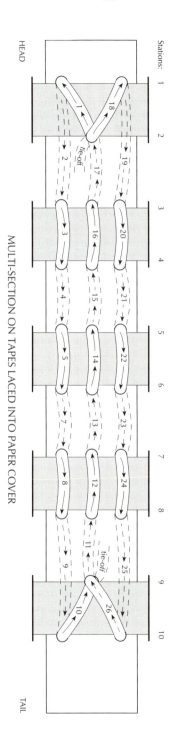

HEAD

MULTI-SECTION ON TAPES LACED INTO PAPER COVER

TAIL

Stations:

Above and below: *A Dog Story,* images by Nicolette Jelen, published by
Vincent Fitzgerald. Binding for this copy is by Daniel Kelm, with painted
leather using acrylic/paste mixture.

The following pages will describe 3–section sewings which span one and/or two sections, always to the same numbered sewing stations. When the book is standing on the tail, these stitches on the spine are horizontal. I refer to them as *bars*.

Examples of 3–section sewings with bars. Left to right:
TANGENT BARS, described on page 150. UNEVEN BARS described on page 154. ALTERNATING BARS described on page 156 and ALTERNATING LOOPED BARS described on page 158.

TANGENT BARS

There are nine stations for each section. In the illustration on the following page, there might appear to be double holes for the middle section. However, the threads share a single set of stations for the middle section.

SEWING PROCEDURE

This is a 2-needle sewing. Thread a needle on each end. One will be referred to as the left, the other the right. Sewing steps are numbered as well as designated *L* for the path of the left needle, and *R* for the other needle. Use stations 1 and 2 of the middle section to start the sewing.

*STARTING THE
SEWING WITHOUT
THE COVER:*

1L. Set aside the
cover. Start on the
outside. Enter the
first section at sta-
tion 2 from the
mountain peak to
the inside. Divide
the thread evenly.

1R. With the right
needle, enter the
third section at
station 2 from the
mountain peak to
the inside.

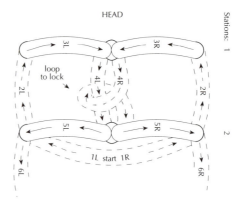

Locking the Stitch in the Middle Section

The right needle loops around the left thread before exiting the middle section, with steps 4R, 8R, 12R and 16R.

Step 1in the diagrams is explained in the written description. Sewing begins without the cover, then it is added.

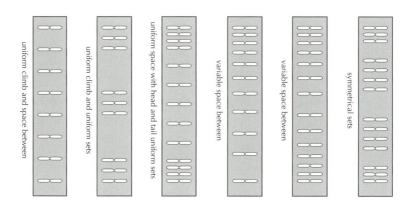

uniform climb and space between

uniform climb and uniform sets

uniform space with head and tail uniform sets

variable space between

variable space between

symmetrical sets

ADDING THE COVER:

2L. Set on the cover. Exit the first section and cover at station 1.

2R. Exit the third section and cover at station 1.

Set on the middle section.

3L. Span, enter the middle section at the same numbered station (1).

4L. Exit the next numbered station (2).

5L. Span and enter the first section at the same numbered station (2).

6L. Exit the next numbered station (3).

3R. Span, enter the middle section at the same numbered station (1).

4R. Exit the next numbered station (2).

5R. Span and enter the third section at the same numbered station (2).

6R. Exit the next numbered station (3).

Remaining Stations:

Repeat steps 3L-6L and 3R-6R until entering station 9 with step 18L in the first section and 18R in the third.

19L. Span and enter the middle section at station 9.

19R. Span and enter the middle section at station 9. Tie-off the two threads with a square knot on the inside of the middle section at station 9.

HEAD

Stations: 1 2 3 4 5 6 7 8 9

Start the sewing without the cover—refer to step 1 in the written instructions

TANGENT BARS
2–Needle Sewing

loop to lock

loop to lock

loop to lock

loop to lock

1L start 1R

tie-off

TAIL

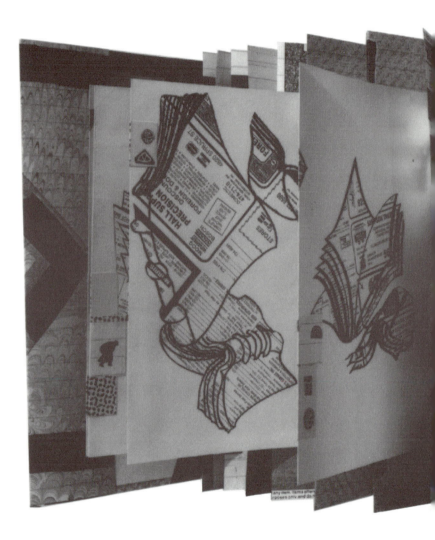

Hedi Kyle, *Con-Cod,* 1993. An imaged one-of-a-kind flag book. Photocopies
from collaged drawings on telephone book pages. This well-used format is one
devised by Hedi Kyle. 18.4 x 14 x 1.3 cm.

UNEVEN BARS

Unlike the previous sewing, Uneven Bars has horizontal stitches that span both one and two sections. This permits a variety of designs for the stitching on the spine-cover:

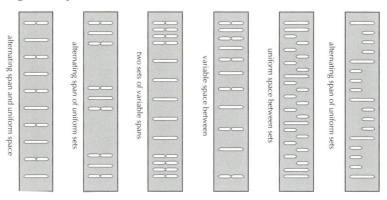

alternating span and uniform space

alternating span of uniform sets

two sets of variable spans

variable space between

uniform space between sets

alternating span of uniform sets

The example described on the facing page is referred to as Beethoven's 5th.

Tennessee Rice Dixon, *Scrutiny in the Great Round,* Granary Books, 1992. Copier, collage, painting, drawing. 22 copies made. Accordion binding by Daniel Kelm, The Wide Awake Garage. 27.8 x 20.3 cm.

SEWING PROCEDURE

1. Exit the first section at station 1.
2. Set on the third section. Span and enter the third section at station 1.
3. Exit station 2 and set on the middle section.
4. Span and enter the middle section at the same numbered station (2).
5. Exit the next station.
6. Span and enter the third section at the same numbered station.
7. Exit the next station.
8. Enter middle section at the same numbered station.
9. Exit the next station.
10. Span and enter the first section at the same numbered station. Tie-off.
11. Exit the next station.
12. Span and enter the middle section at the same numbered station.
13. Exit the next station.
14. Span and enter the first section at the same numbered station.
15. Exit the next station.
16. Span and enter the third section at the same numbered station.
17. Exit the next station.
18-29. Repeat steps 4-15, exiting the first section at station 15 with step 29.
30. Span and enter the third section at station 15.
31. Proceed on the inside to station 11. Tie-off with a half hitch.

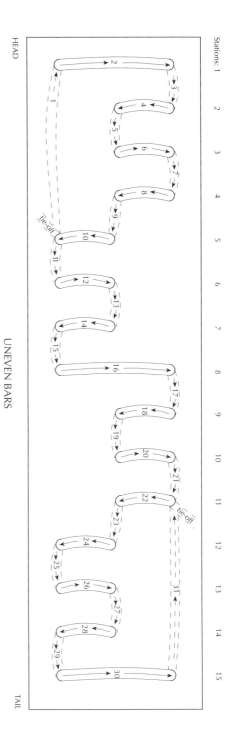

ALTERNATING BARS

A photo of this sewing is on page 149. The following are some patterns for parallel stitches spanning one section with an alternating pattern:

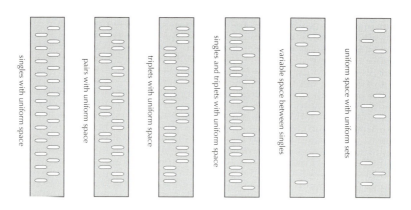

Kathryn Leonard, *Windows Out of Walls,* 1990. Letterpress, edition of 3. Non-adhesive tunnel book cut and slotted Arches cover.
Closes to 12.7 x 20.3 x 5.1 cm.

SEWING PROCEDURE

1. Exit the middle section at station 1.
2. Set on the third section. Span and enter the third section at station 1.
3. Exit station 2.
4. Span and enter the middle section at station 2. Tie-off.
5. Exit the second section at the next station.
6. Span and enter the first section at the same numbered station.
7. Exit the next station.
8. Span and enter the middle section at the same numbered station.
9. Exit the next station.
10. Span and enter the third section at the same numbered station.
11. Exit the next station.
12. Span and enter the middle section at the same numbered station.
13-20. Repeat steps 5-12, entering the middle section at station 10 with step 20.
21-28. Repeat steps 5-12, entering the middle section at station 14 with step 28.
29. Proceed on the inside to station 13. Tie-off with a half hitch.

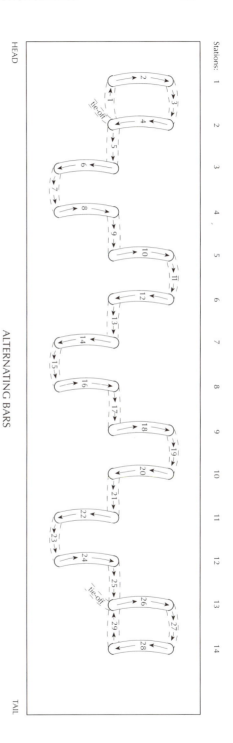

ALTERNATING LOOPED BARS

This sewing is first sewn identical to the previous. Separate sewings in the first and third sections form links on the spine.

SEWING PROCEDURE

First Sewing: Sew precisely as the sewing titled Alternating Bars described on the previous page. A photo is on page 149.

Second Sewing:

1. To sew the links on the first section, start on the inside of the first section. Exit station 3.
2a. Drop to the outside, link under.
2b. Climb and re-enter the same station.
3. Tie-off. Exit station 7.
4a. Drop to the outside, link under.
4b. Climb and re-enter.
5. Exit station 11.
6a. Drop to the outside, link under.
6b. Climb and re-enter.
7. Tie-off with a half hitch.

Third Sewing:

1. Start on the inside of the third section. Exit station 1.
2. Drop to the outside, link under, climb and re-enter the same station.
3. Tie-off. Exit station 5.

Continue to form the links at stations 5, 9 and 13. After re-entering station 13, tie-off with a half hitch.

HEAD

Stations: 1 2 3 4 5 6 7 8 9 10 11 12 13 14

ALTERNATING LOOPED BARS
Sewing the links with two separate sewings

start 1, 2b, 2a, 3 tie-off, the proceed
start 1, 2b, 2a, tie-off, proceed
4b, 4a
4b, 4a, 5
6b, 6a, 5
7 tie-off, 6b, 6a, 7
9 tie-off, 8b, 8a

TAIL

THE ROPE

This dramatic sewing is a favorite, with a thick, rope-like looping on the spine. I was probably influenced by the Caterpillar Sewing, describe in Volume III. The difference is, the Caterpillar wraps several threads as a core to form a raised support from the threads, themselves. The Rope wraps a single thread, forming no structural support; it is merely a decorative sewing.

Pierce as many even-numbered stations as desired. The same number of stations are pierced in each of the three sections.

SEWING PROCEDURE

First Sewing: Sew the middle section in a running stitch from head to tail. Tie-off (see page 20).

Starting the second Sewing: Place a needle on both ends of a new thread.
1. Start on the inside of the first section to be sewn. Exit station 2 of the section, only.
2. Slip under the second section, between the section and the inside of the spine-cover. Enter the third section, only, from the mountain peak to the inside of the section. Pull the thread until equal amounts are within the first and third sections.
3. With the needle that is inside the third section, exit station 1 of the section and cover.
4. With the needle that is inside the first section, exit station 1 of the section and cover.

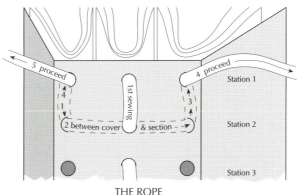

THE ROPE
Starting the second sewing

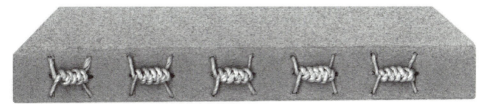

THE ROPE is a 3–section decorative sewing.

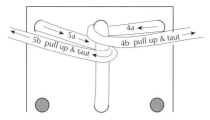

1. Starting to form the Rope

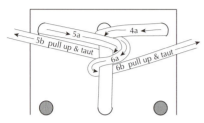

2. Forming the Rope

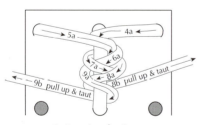

3. Forming the Rope

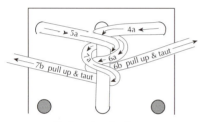

4. Forming the Rope

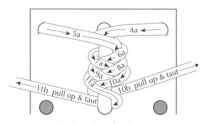

5. Forming the Rope

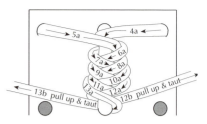

6. Forming the Rope

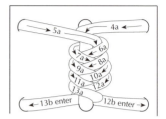

7. Completing 1 unit of the Rope

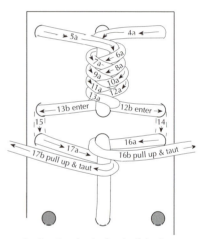

8. Starting the 2nd unit of the Rope

To complete the second sewing of THE ROPE, page 159, follow the diagrams. It is simply a matter of alternately looping the thread of the first sewing with the right thread, then the left:

Slip under with the right thread, then lap the vertical thread of the first sewing. Pull back towards the right and upwards to insure the loop is taut. Repeat the procedure with the left thread. Continue alternately slipping under and lapping to form loops until the vertical thread of the first sewing is solidly packed. Enter the third section with the right needle at station 2. Enter the first section with the left needle at station 2. Continue forming units of the rope. Tie-off on the inside.

SPAN

The following pages will describe 3–section sewings which span one and/or two sections, as well as patterned stitches on the spine. When the book is standing on the tail, these stitches on the spine are both horizontal and vertical. I refer to them as *bars* and *dashes*.

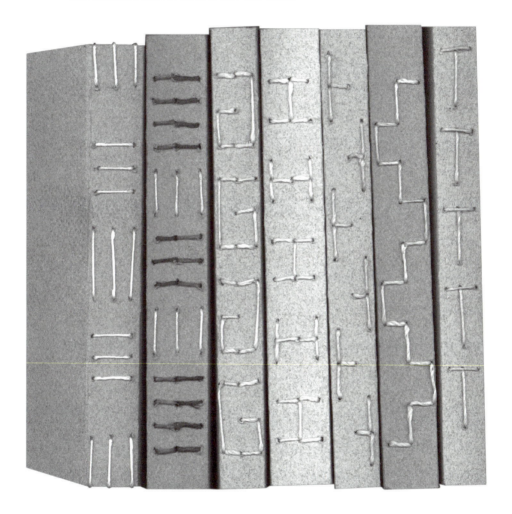

Prototypes of 3–section sewings with bars and dashes. Left to right: TRIPLE PARQUET, described on page 162; PARQUETRY, described on page 164; *G's*, described on page 165; *H's*, described on page 168; BROKEN *H's*, described on page 170; DOVE TAIL, described on page 172; and VERTICAL *T's*, described on page 174.

TRIPLE PARQUET

This might represent sticks of the homonymous margarine.

The alternating direction of this 3-line motif suggests parquetry. It is created by a single sewing with a single needle.

There are ten pierced stations. The head and tail are designated as stations 1 and 12, respectively.

SEWING PROCEDURE
1. Start on the inside of the first section to be sewn. Exit station 2.
2. Proceed over the head to the inside. Tie-off at station 2.
3. Exit station 6.
4. Enter station 7.
5. Exit station 11.
6. Proceed to the tail. Wrap around the tail.
7. Proceed to station 11. Exit the section, only.
8. Proceed along the inside of the spine-cover. Set on the second section. Enter the mountain peak of the second section at station 11.
9. Wrap around the tail.
10. Proceed on the outside of the cover. Enter at station 11.
11. Exit station 7.
12. Enter station 6.
13. Exit station 2.
14. Wrap around the head to the inside.
15. Proceed to station 2. Exit the section, only.
16. Proceed along the inside of the spine-cover. Set on the third section. Enter the mountain peak of the third section at station 2.
17. Wrap around the head.
18. Proceed on the outside of the cover. Enter at station 2.
19. Exit station 6.
20. Enter station 7.
21. Exit station 11.
22. Wrap around the tail.
23. Proceed on the inside. Exit station 10.
24. Span and enter the first section at station 10.

HEAD   TAIL

TRIPLE PARQUET

25. Exit station 9.
26. Span and enter the third section at station 9.
27. Exit station 8.
28. Span and enter the first section at station 8.
29. Exit station 5.
30. Span and enter the third section at station 5.
31. Exit station 4.
32. Span and enter the first section at station 4.
33. Exit station 3.
34. Span and enter the third section at station 3.
35. Proceed on the inside to station 4. Tie-off with a half hitch.

A photo of this book is on page 161.

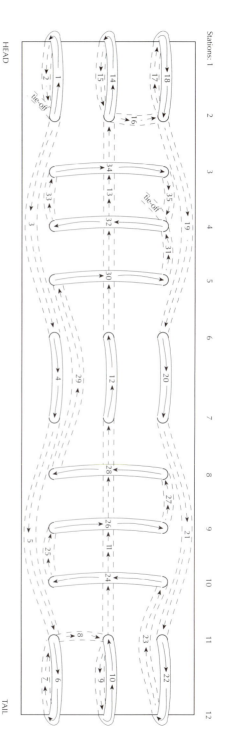

TRIPLE PARQUET

Steps 7 & 15 exit section, only

PARQUETRY

The parquet in this design is created by two separate sewings, perhaps with two colors. There are 13 stations for each section. All stations for both sewings are pre-pierced.

SEWING PROCEDURE

First Sewing: The first sewing is identical as that for Tangent Bars, described on page 150.

Second Sewing: The second sewing is a running stitch, similar to the Triple Dash, page 140.

CHANGES-OVER: In the diagram to the right, step 6 exits the section, only, at station 9. It then passes across the inside of the spine-cover and enters the middle section at station 9 from the mountain peak to the inside.

Step 11 is the cross-over from the middle to the third section at station 4.

A photo of this book is on page 161.

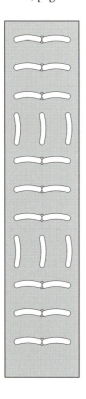

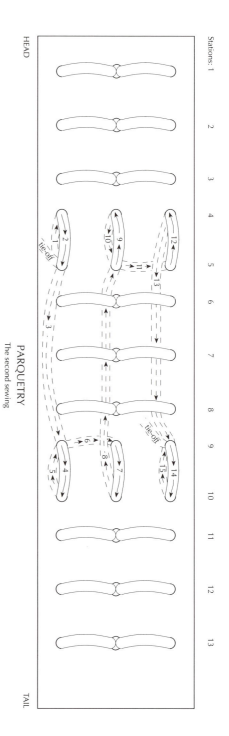

PARQUETRY
The second sewing

Stations: 1 2 3 4 5 6 7 8 9 10 11 12 13

HEAD

TAIL

G's

I refer to this 1-needle sewing as *G's* or Greek Key.

SEWING PROCEDURE

1. Start on the inside of the first section to be sewn. Exit station 1. Set on the middle section.
2. Span and enter the second section at station 1.
3. Exit station 2.
4. Span, enter the first section at station 2. Tie-off.
5. Exit station 3.
6. Span, enter station 2.
7. Exit station 3.
8. Span, enter the second section at station 3.
9. Exit station 4.

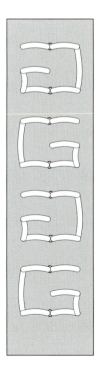

HEAD

Stations:

G's
Beginning the sewing

TAIL

1 2 3 4 5 6 7 8 9 10 11 12

10. Span and enter the first sec-
    tion at station 4.
11. Exit station 6.
12. Enter station 4.
13. Exit station 6.
14. Span and enter the second
    section at station 6.
15. Exit station 7.
16. Span and enter the first sec-
    tion at station 7.
17. Exit station 8.
18. Span and enter the second
    section at station 8.
19. Exit station 9.
20. Span and enter the first sec-
    tion at station 9.
21. Exit station 8.
22. Enter station 9.
23. Exit station 10 of the first
    section.
24. Span, enter the second sec-
    tion at station 10.
25. Proceed inside the section.
    Exit station 12.
26. Span and enter the first sec-
    tion at station 12.
27. Exit station 10.
28. Enter station 12.
29. Exit the section, only, at sta-
    tion 10.
30. Proceed on the inside of the
    spine-cover to the second
    section. Enter the second
    section, only, from the
    mountain peak to the inside.
31. Exit station 12 of the sec-
    ond section and cover.
32. Set on the third section.
    Enter the third section at
    station 12.

HEAD

Continuing the sewing. Step 29 exits the section, only. Step 30 proceeds on the inside of the cover.

G's

Stations:

1
2
3
4
5
6
7
8
9
10
11
12

TAIL

33. Exit the third section at station 11.
34. Enter station 12.
35. Exit station 11.
36. Span, enter the second section at station 11.
37. Exit the second section at station 10.
38. Span and enter the third section at station 10.
39. Exit station 9.
40. Span and enter the second section at station 9.
41. Exit the second section at station 7.
42. Span and enter the third section at station 7.
43. Exit the third section at station 9.
44. Enter station 7.
45. Exit station 6.
46. Span and enter the second section at station 6.
47. Exit the second section at station 5.
48. Span and enter the third section at station 5.
49. Exit station 6.
50. Enter station 5.
51. Exit station 4.
52. Span and enter the second section at station 4.
53. Exit station 3.
54. Span and enter the third section at station 3.
55. Exit station 1.
56. Enter station 2.
57. Exit station 1.
58. Span and enter the second section at station 1. Tie-off on the inside with a half hitch.

HEAD

Continuing the sewing. Step 29 exits the section, only. Step 30 proceeds on the inside of the cover.

G's

TAIL

Stations:

1

2

3

4

5

6

7

8

9

10

11

12

H's

An *H* standing and another on its side seems to say, "hello." The sewing could be thought out as a 2-needle sewing. However, I have plotted it as a single needle sewing. A photo of this book is on page 161.

Sewing Stations: The first and the third sections use all 12 stations. Pierce only stations 1, 2, 4, 6, 7, 9, 11 and 12 for the middle section.

SEWING PROCEDURE

1. Start on the inside the first section. Exit station 1.
2. Set on the second section. Span, enter the second section at station 1.
3. Exit station 2.
4. Enter station 1.
5. Exit station 2.
6. Span and enter the first section at station 2. Tie-off.
7. Exit station 4.
8. Enter station 5.
9. Exit station 4.
10. Enter station 3.
11. Exit station 4.
12. Span, enter the second section at station 4.
13. Exit station 6.
14. Span and enter the first section at station 6.
15. Exit station 7.
16. Span, enter the second section at station 7.
17. Exit station 6.
18. Enter station 7.
19. Exit station 9.
20. Span and enter the first section at station 9.
21. Exit station 10.
22. Enter station 9.
23. Exit station 8.
24. Enter station 9.
25. Exit station 11.
26. Span, enter the second section at station 11.
27. Exit station 12.
28. Span and enter the first section at station 12.
29. Exit station 11, of the section, only.
30. Proceed across the inside of the spine-cover. Enter the second section at station 11 from the mountain peak to the inside.

HEAD

Sewing referred to as *H's*

31. Exit station 12 of the second section.
32. Set on the third section. Span, enter the third section at station 12.
33. Exit station 11.
34. Span, enter the second section at station 11.
35. Exit station 12.
36. Enter station 11.
37. Exit station 9.
38. Span and enter the third section at station 9.
39. Exit station 10.
40. Enter station 9.
41. Exit station 8.
42. Enter station 9.
43. Exit station 7.
44. Span and enter the second section at station 7.
45. Exit station 6.
46. Span and enter the third section at station 6.
47. Exit station 4.
48. Enter station 3.
49. Exit station 4.
50. Enter station 5.
51. Exit station 4.
52. Span and enter the second section at station 4.
53. Exit station 2.
54. Span and enter the third section at station 2.
55. Exit station 1.
56. Span and enter the second section at station 1. Tie-off with a half hitch.

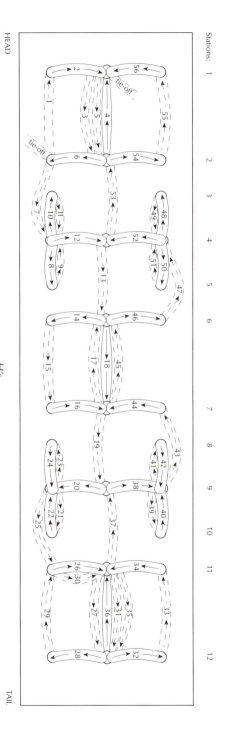

BROKEN *H's*

This is a pleasingly lyrical sewing. A photo of this book is on page 161.

Sewing Stations: For the first section pierce stations 1, 2, 3, 5, 6, 7, 9, 10, 11, 13, 14 and 15. For the middle section pierce stations 2, 3, 6, 7, 10, 11, 14 and 15. For the third section pierce stations 2, 3, 4, 6, 7, 8, 10, 11, 12, 14, 15 and 16.

SEWING PROCEDURE

1. Start on the inside the first section. Exit station 2. Enter station 1.
2. Tie-off at station 2. Exit station 2.
3. Enter station 3.
4. Exit station 2.
5. Set on the second section. Span, enter the second section at station 2.
6. Exit station 6.
7. Span and enter the first section at station 6.
8. Exit station 5.
9. Enter station 6.
10. Exit station 7.
11. Enter station 6.
12. Exit station 10.
13. Enter station 11.
14. Exit station 10.
15. Enter station 9.
16. Exit station 10.
17. Span, enter the second section at station 10.
18. Exit station 14.
19. Span and enter the first section at station 14.
20. Exit station 13.
21. Enter station 14.
22. Exit station 15.
23. Enter the cover, only, at station 14.
24. Proceed across the inside of the spine-cover. Enter the second section, only, at station 14 from the mountain peak to the inside.
25. Link under the thread on the inside of the second section marked as step 18. This will lock the thread. Then, proceed to station 15. Exit.
26. Set on the third section. Span, enter the third section at station 15.
27. Exit station 14.
28. Enter station 15.

HEAD

BROKEN *H's*

29. Exit station 16.
30. Enter station 15.
31. Exit station 11.
32. Enter station 10.
33. Exit station 11.
34. Enter station 12.
35. Exit station 11.
36. Span, enter the second section at station 11.
37. Exit station 7.
38. Span and enter the third section at station 7.
39. Exit station 6.
40. Enter station 7.
41. Exit station 8.
42. Enter station 7.
43. Exit station 3.
44. Enter station 2.
45. Exit station 3.
46. Enter station 4.
47. Exit station 3.
48. Span and enter the second section at station 3.
49. Tie-off at station 7.

BROKEN *H's or* ALTERNATING *T'S*

DOVE TAIL

This stair-stepping design pleases me. I could see adding macramé in other colors of thread to the spine in a separate, non-structural sewing. A photo of this sewing is on page 161.

Sewing Stations: The first section has the following stations pierced: 1, 4, 5, 8 and 9. The middle section uses all ten stations. The third section pierces stations 2, 3, 6, 7 and 10.

SEWING PROCEDURE

1. Start on the inside of the first section to be sewn. Exit station 1.
2. Span and enter station 1 of the middle section.
3. Exit station 2.
4. Enter station 1.
5. Exit station 2.
6. Span, enter station 2 of the third section.
7. Exit station 3.
8. Enter station 2.
9. Exit station 3.
10. Span and enter station 3 of the middle section.
11. Exit station 4.
12. Enter station 3.
13. Exit station 4.
14. Span, enter station 4 of the first section.
15. Exit station 5.
16. Enter station 4.
17. Exit station 5.
18. Span and enter station 5 of the middle section.
19. Exit station 6.
20. Enter station 5.
21. Exit station 6.
22. Span, enter station 6 of the third section.
23. Exit station 7.
24. Enter station 6.
25. Exit station 7.
26. Span and enter station 7 of the middle section.
27. Exit station 8.
28. Enter station 7.
29. Exit station 8.
30. Span, enter station 8 of the first section.
31. Exit station 9.
32. Enter station 8.

HEAD

DOVE TAIL

33. Exit station 9.
34. Span, enter station 9 of the middle section.
35. Exit station 10.
36. Enter station 9.
37. Exit station 10.
38. Span, enter station 10 of the third section.
39. Proceed on the inside to station 7. Tie-off with a half hitch.

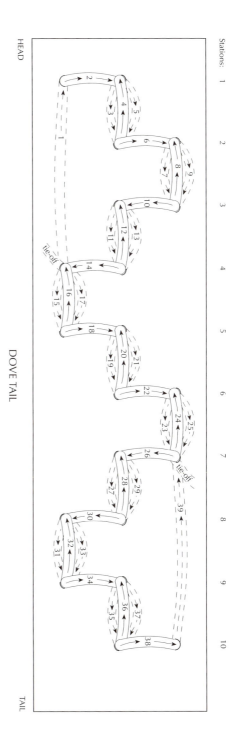

VERTICAL *T's*

Sewing Stations: The first and third sections use only the odd-numbered stations. The middle section uses all ten stations. A photo of this book is on page 161.

SEWING PROCEDURE

1. Start on the inside of the first section to be sewn. Exit station 1.
2. Set on the third section. Span and enter at station 1.
3. Exit at station 3.
4. Span and enter the first section at station 3. Tie-off.
5. Exit station 5.
6. Span and enter the third section at station 5.
7. Exit station 7.
8. Span and enter the first section at station 7.
9. Exit station 9.
10. Span and enter the third section at station 9.
11. Exit the section, only, at station 7.
12. Proceed along the inside of the spine-cover. Set on the middle section. Enter the middle section at station 7 from the mountain peak to the inside.
13. Exit station 10.
14. Enter station 9.
15-22. Make a running stitch to the head, entering station 1 with step 22.
23. Proceed on the inside to station 2. Tie-off.

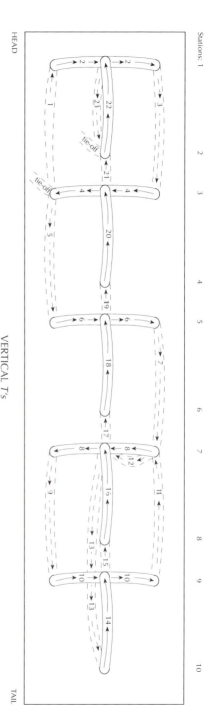

VERTICAL *T's*

HEAD

TAIL

Stations: 1   2   3   4   5   6   7   8   9   10

Pati Scobey, *The Back of Time,* Granary Books, 1992. Relief etchings, watercolor, pen and ink drawing and collage. 25 copies. Etchings were editioned by Scobey and Katherine Kuehn .The book is a French Door format; the binding is by Daniel Kelm, The Wide Awake Garage. 38.1 x 22.8 cm.

Innerzones, Marilyn
Goodrich, 1991.
Hand-made paper
under plexiglass.
Wooden binding
designed by Daniel
Kelm. One-of-a-kind,
collection of the artist.
15.3 X 61 X 91.5 cm.

ANGLE SEWINGS

The following pages will describe about three dozen 3–section sewings which angle, spanning one and/or two sections, as well as contain straight stitches. The diagonal stitches are parallel and/or in opposition to each other. Here is a digital scan of the first half dozen:

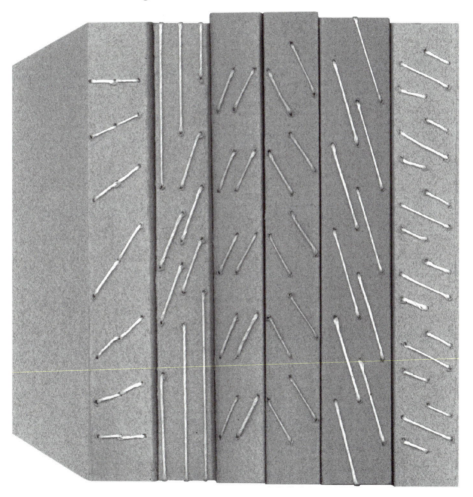

Prototypes of 3–section sewings with diagonal stitches. Left to right:
FALLING DIAGONALS, on the far left is not described. Its sewing pattern is identical to TANGENT BARS, described on page 150.

The remainder of the bindings, from the left, are DASHES & DIAGONALS, described on page 178; PAIRED DIAGONALS, page 180; STAGGERED DIAGONALS, page 182; STAGGERED DIAGONALS VARIATION, page 184; and TRIDENT, described on page 186.

DASHES & DIAGONALS

This design has a feeling of art deco. A photo of this book is on page 177.

This is a straight stitch sewing with diagonals. Like all sewings that wrap around the head and the tail, precautions must be taken to not crimp the paper cover. One solution is to have the sections precisely the same height as the cover. If the cover is taller than the sections, the spine-cover will have to be reinforced. One solution is to glue a stiff paper the same size as the spine-cover on the inside of the cover to make a two ply spine.

Sewing Stations: Diagonal stitches are like diagonal streets—it is easy to get lost straying from a grid. Each section of this sewing has a different number of stations. The sewing path switches between sections. But if you follow the diagram, I think you will be able to chart your course.

OPEN ENDED STATIONS: The head and the tail are designated as stations, but not pierced stations. Rather, they mark the point where the sewing changes direction by wrapping around from the outside to the inside, or vise versa.

The same numbered sewing stations for each section are not the same distance from the head. You must keep track of the location of each station for each section. On the inside of the spine-cover, draw three vertical lines for the sections. Then, draw your diagonal stitches. Pierce the stations for the cover, and appropriately registered stations on each of the sections.

SEWING PROCEDURE

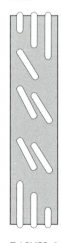

HEAD

1. Start on the inside the first section. Exit station 2. Proceed beyond the head.
2. Wrap over the head, and proceed on the inside of the section. Tie-off at station 2. For a diagram of how to start the sewing, see the illustration on page 142 of the *Triple Dash Variation.*
3. Exit station 3.
4. Set on the second section. Angle, enter the second section at station 3.
5. Exit station 5.
6. Angle to the first section. Enter the first section at station 4.
7. Exit station 6.
8. Proceed along the spine-cover to the tail. Wrap around the tail to the inside of the section.
9. Exit station 5.
10. Angle to the second section. Enter the second section at station 7.

DASHES &
DIAGONALS

11. Exit station 8.
12. Proceed along the spine-cover to the tail. Wrap around the tail to the inside of the section.
13. Exit station 6.
14. Set on the third section. Angle and enter the third section at station 4.
15. Exit station 5.
16. Proceed along the spine-cover to the tail. Wrap around the tail to the inside of the section.
17. Exit station 2.
18. Proceed along the spine-cover to the head. Wrap around the head to the inside of the section.
19. Exit station 3.
20. Angle towards the second section. Enter the second section at station 4.
21. Exit station 2.
22. Proceed along the spine-cover to the head. Wrap around the head to the inside of the section.
23. Proceed on the inside of the second section to station 2. Tie-off with a half hitch.

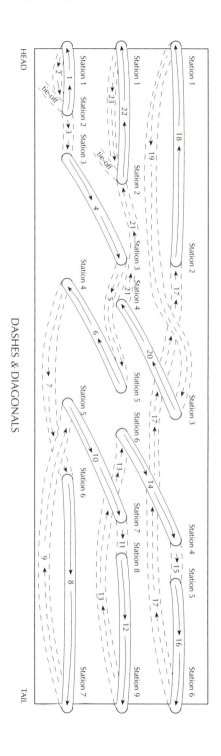

DASHES & DIAGONALS

PAIRED DIAGONALS

This is a 2–needle sewing. A photo of this sewing is on page 177.

Sewing Stations: For the first section pierce the even-numbered stations. For the middle section pierce all ten stations. For the third section pierce only the odd-numbered stations.

SEWING PROCEDURE

Thread a needle on each end of a long piece of thread. One needle will be referred to as the left, the other the right. The sewing steps will be numbered, as well as designated *L* for the path of the left needle, and *R* when the other needle is to be used.

1L. Start on the inside of the middle section. With the left needle, exit station 1 of the section and the cover. Pull the thread to divide the length in half.

2L. Set on the first section. Angle and enter the first section at station 2.

1R. Exit station 2 of the second section and the cover.

2R. Set on the third section. Angle and enter the third section at station 1.

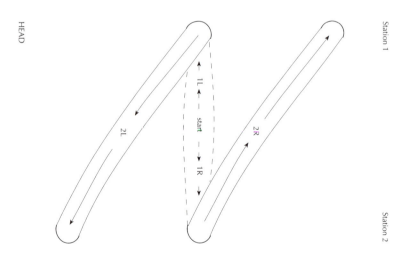

Starting the 2–needle sewing of PAIRED DIAGONALS

1L. The left needle exits station 1 of the middle section and the cover. Pull the thread to divide evenly.

1R. The right needle exits the middle section and the cover at station 2.

3L. Exit station 4.

4L. Angle and enter the second section at station 3.

5L. Exit station 5.

6L. Angle and enter the first section at station 6.

3R. Exit the third section at station 3.

4R. Angle and enter the second section at station 4.

5R. Exit station 6.

6R. Angle and enter the third section at station 5.

7L. Exit the first section at station 8.

8L. Angle and enter the second section at station 7.

9L. Exit station 9.

10L.   Angle and enter the first section at station 10.

11L.   Proceed on the inside. Tie-off at station 8.

7R. Exit the third section at station 7.

8R. Angle and enter the second section at station 8.

9R. Exit at station 10.

10R.   Angle and enter the third section at station 9.

11R.   Proceed on the inside of the third section. Tie-off at station 7.

NOTE: The diagram shows five paired stitches. If your sewing has an even number of paired stitches, there will be only one tie-off, instead of two. It will be inside the second section between the last two stations.

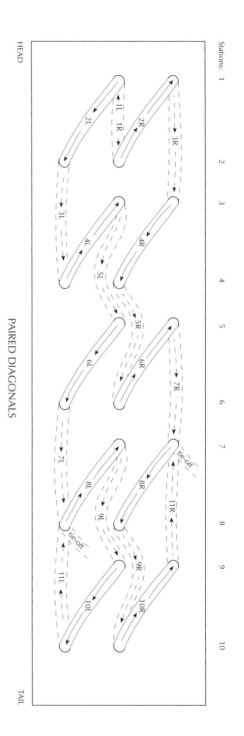

STAGGERED DIAGONALS

This binding could be sewn with two needles with a similar pattern of the previous binding, Paired Diagonals. I will describe it as sewn with a single needle.

Sewing Stations: Stations are based on a grid. For the first section pierce stations 3, 7, 11, 15 and 19. For the middle section pierce stations 1, 4, 5, 8, 9, 12, 13, 16, 17 and 20. For the third section pierce stations 2, 6, 10, 14 and 18.

SEWING PROCEDURE

1. Start on the inside the first section. Exit station 3.
2. Set on second section. Angle and enter the second section at station 1.
3. Exit station 4.
4. Set on the third section. Angle and enter the third section at station 2.
5. Exit station 6.
6. Angle and enter the middle section at station 8.
7. Exit station 5.
8. Angle and enter the first section at station 7. Tie-off.
9. Exit station 11.
10. Angle and enter the middle section at station 9.
11. Exit station 12.
12. Angle and enter the third section at station 10.
13. Exit station 14.
14. Angle and enter the middle section at station 16.
15. Exit station 13.

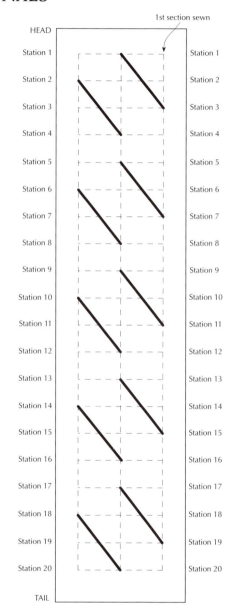

Sewing stations for STAGGERED DIAGONALS
View from INSIDE the spine-cover
A grid is drawn with pencil on the inside of the spine-cover. Note that the design is the reverse of the sewn pattern on the spine.

16. Angle and enter the first
    section at station 15.
17. Exit station 19.
18. Angle and enter the second
    section at station 17.
19. Exit station 20.
20. Angle and enter the third
    section at station 18.
21. Proceed on the inside of the
    third section. Tie-off at
    station 14.

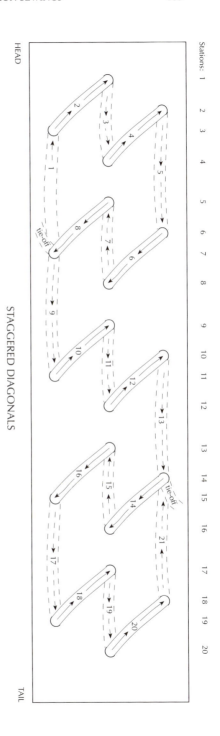

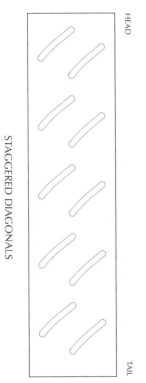

The sewing above, and on
the right, is achieved from
the sewing station diagram
on the previous page. The
stitches on the spine will
be flipped from the draw-
ing on the inside of the
spine-cover.

STAGGERED DIAGONALS VARIATION

Sewing Stations: Stations are based on a grid, similar to the previous binding. With this sewing, the stitches overlap one square of the grid, resulting in a more acute angle to the stitches. See page 177.

The shorter stitches in the upper right and lower left are decidedly a different angle than the other stitches. These were added to give more support for the sections at the head and the tail. If you prefer, omit these two stitches and adjust your sewing path. (Or, maintain the same angle by wrapping over the head and the tail, as in the diagram on the facing page, in steps 2 and 19 marked with an asterisk.)

For the first section pierce stations 1, 3, 5, 7 and 9. The middle section pierces all 10 stations. The third section pierces all the even-numbered stations.

SEWING PROCEDURE

1. Start on the inside the first section. Exit station 2
2. Set on second section. Angle, proceed to the head. Wrap around the head into the second section, as shown on page 185).
3. Exit station 3.
4. Set on third section. Angle and enter the third section at station 1.
5. Exit station 3.
6. Angle and enter the middle section at station 5.
7. Exit station 2.
8. Angle and enter the first section at station 4. Tie-off.

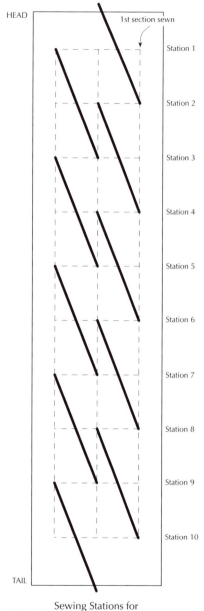

Sewing Stations for
STAGGERED DIAGONALS VARIATION
View from *INSIDE* the Spine-Cover
A grid is drawn with pencil on the inside of the spine-cover.
The design is the reverse of the outside of the spine.

9. Exit station 6.
10. Angle and enter the middle section at station 4.
11. Exit station 7.
12. Angle and enter the third section at station 5.
13. Exit station 7.
14. Angle and enter the middle section at station 9.
15. Exit station 6.
16. Angle and enter the first section at station 8.
17. Exit station 10.
18. Angle and enter the second section at station 8.
19. Exit station 10. (Or, Proceed to the tail. Wrap around to the outside, as shown in this diagram).
20. Angle and enter the third section at station 9.
21. Proceed on the inside of the third section. Tie-off at station 7.

OPEN ENDED STATIONS: The cover can be notched at the head and the tail so that the wrap-around thread is recessed to prevent wear:

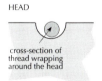

HEAD

cross-section of thread wrapping around the head

The sewing on the right is symmetrical to the sewing station diagram on the previous page. The stitches on the spine will be the reverse of the drawing on the inside of the spine-cover.

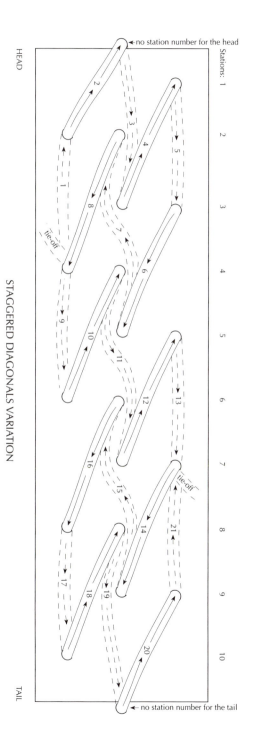

TRIDENT

Sewing Stations: The first section pierces stations 1, 2, 4, 5, 7, 8, 10, 11, 13 and 14. The middle section uses stations 1, 3, 4, 6, 7, 9, 10, 12, 13 and 15. The third section pierces stations 2, 3, 5, 6, 8, 9, 11, 12, 14 and 15.

SEWING PROCEDURE

1. Start inside the middle section. Exit station 1.
2. Set on the third section; angle and enter at station 2.
3. Exit station 3.
4. Set on the first section. Angle and enter at station 1.
5. Exit station 2.
6. Angle, enter the middle section at station 3. Tie-off.
7. Exit the next station (4).
8. Angle and enter the third section at the next numbered station (5).
9. Exit the next numbered station (6).
10. Angle and enter the first section two stations towards the head.
11. Exit the next station towards the tail.
12. Angle and enter the middle section at the next numbered station.

Remaining Stations: Repeat steps 7 through 12 for each additional set of trident stitches. After forming the third stitch of the final trident, proceed on the inside of the middle section two stations towards the head. Tie-off. See page 177.

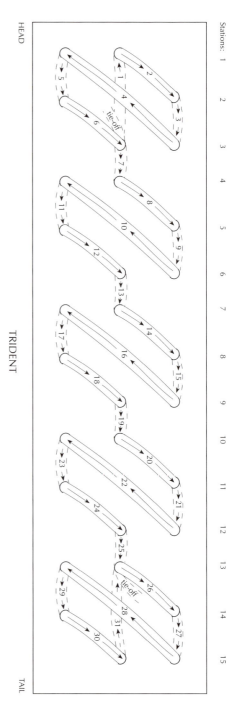

HEAD

TRIDENT

TAIL

Stations: 1 2 3 4 5 6 7 8 9 10 11 12 13 14 15

ANGLE SEWINGS continued
The following pages will describe additional 3–section sewings which
angle, spanning one and/or two sections, as well as contain straight stitches. Here is a digital scan of the second half dozen:

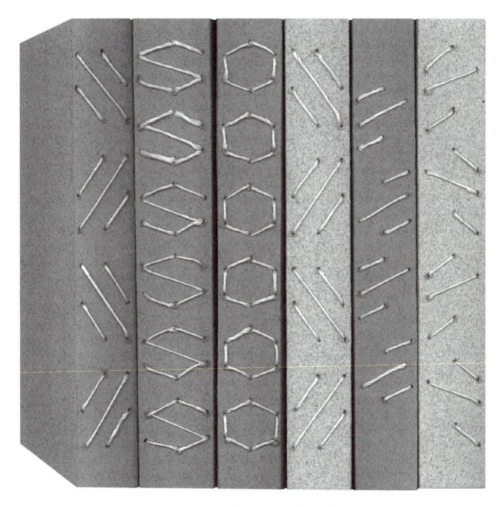

Prototypes of 3–section sewings with diagonal stitches. Left to right:
ALTERNATING TRIDENTS I, described on page 188; S's, page 190; HEXAGO-
NALS, page 192; The three sewings to the left all use identically positioned
sewing stations.

The other three sewings to the right are ALTERNATING TRIDENTS II, described
on page 189; ROCKET, described on page 193; and LEAVES, on page 194.

ALTERNATING TRIDENTS I

Sewing Stations: First and third sections pierce stations 2, 3, 6, 7, 10, 11, 14 and 15. Middle section uses 1, 4, 5, 8, 9, 12, 13 and 16.

SEWING PROCEDURE

Start inside middle section.

1. Exit station (1).
2. Angle, enter third section at next numbered station (2).
3. Exit next station (3).
4. Enter the first section at previous numbered station (2).
5. Exit next station (3).
6. Enter the middle section at next station (4). Tie-off.
7. Exit the next station (5).
8. Angle and enter the first section at the next numbered station (6).
9. Exit the next numbered station (7).
10. Angle and enter the third section at the previous numbered station (6).
11. Exit the next station towards the tail (7).
12. Angle and enter the middle section at the next numbered station.

Remaining Stations: Repeat steps 1 through 12 for each additional paired sets of trident stitches. After forming the final stitch, proceed on the inside of the middle section three stations towards the head. Tie-off.

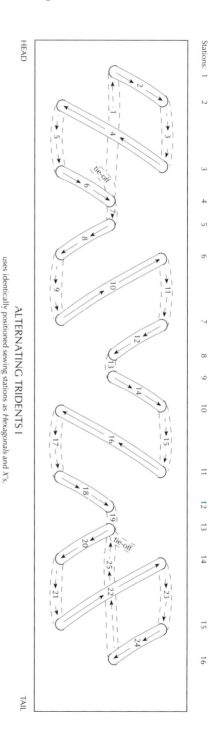

HEAD

TAIL

ALTERNATING TRIDENTS I uses identically positioned sewing stations as *Hexagonals* and *X's*, but a different sewing path

Stations: 1 2 3 4 5 6 7 8 9 10 11 12 13 14 15 16

ALTERNATING TRIDENTS II

Sewing Stations: First section pierces stations 1, 2, 5, 6, 7, 8, 11 and 12. Middle section uses 1, 3, 4, 6, 7, 9, 10 and 12. The third pierces 2, 3, 4, 5, 8, 9, 10 and 11.

SEWING PROCEDURE

Start inside the middle section.
1. Exit station (1).
2. Angle, enter third section at next numbered station (2).
3. Exit next station (3).
4. Angle and enter first section at two stations previously (1).
5. Exit next station (2).
6. Angle, enter the middle section at next station (3). Tie-off.
7. Exit next station (4).
8. Angle, enter the first section at the next numbered station (5).
9. Exit next numbered station (6).
10. Angle and enter the third section at two stations previously (4).
11. Exit the next station towards the tail (5).
12. Angle, enter the middle section at the next numbered station.

Remaining Stations: Repeat steps 1 through 12 for each additional paired sets of trident stitches. After forming the third stitch of the final trident, proceed on the inside of the middle section two stations towards the head. Tie-off.

I prefer this sewing to the previous. Stitches have more stations in common, reducing their number. This places the stations farther apart to avoid perforation.

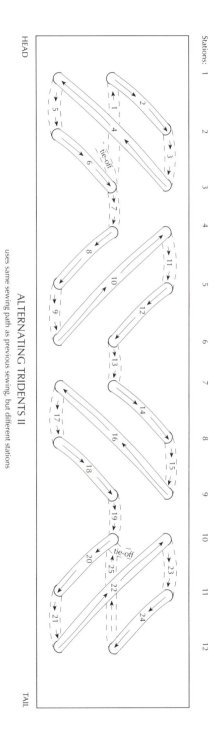

HEAD

TAIL

ALTERNATING TRIDENTS II

uses same sewing path as previous sewing, but different stations

Stations: 1 2 3 4 5 6 7 8 9 10 11 12

S's

A photo of this sewing is on page 187.

Sewing Stations: The first and third sections pierce stations 2, 3, 6, 7, 10, 11, 14 and 15. The middle section pierces stations 1, 4, 5, 8, 9, 12, 13 and 16.

SEWING PROCEDURE

1. Start inside the third section. Exit station 3.
2. Set on the second section. Angle, enter the second section at station 4.
3. Exit station 1.
4. Set on the first section. Angle and enter the first section at station 2.
5. Exit station 3.
6. Angle and enter the second section at station 4.
7. Exit station 1.
8. Angle and enter the third section at station 2. Tie-off.
9. Exit station 3.
10. Angle and enter the first section at station 2.
11. Exit station 6.
12. Angle and enter the third section at station 7.
13. Exit station 6.
14. Angle, enter the second section at station 5.
15. Exit station 8.
16. Angle and enter the first section at station 7.
17. Exit station 6.
18. Angle, enter the second section at station 5.
19. Exit station 8.
20. Angle and enter the third section at station 7.
21. Exit station 11.
22. Angle, enter the second section at station 12.
23. Exit station 9.
24. Angle and enter the first section at station 10.
25. Exit station 11.
26. Angle, enter the second section at station 12.
27. Exit station 9.
28. Angle, enter the third section at station 10.
29. Exit station 11.
30. Angle and enter the first section at station 10.
31. Exit station 14.
32. Angle, enter the third section at station 15.
33. Exit station 14.

HEAD

Sewing titled *S's*

34. Angle, enter the
    second section at
    station 13.
35. Exit station 16.
36. Angle and enter
    the first section at
    station 15.
37. Exit station 14.
38. Angle and enter
    the second section
    at station number
    13.
39. Exit station 16.
40. Angle and enter
    the third section
    at station 15.
41. Proceed in the
    third section to
    station 14. Tie-
    off.

For an additional
binding design, these
identically positioned
sewing stations could
add another stitch to
the *S's* pattern to form
a pattern I would call
Double Diamonds, or a
sort of crude *Figure 8.*

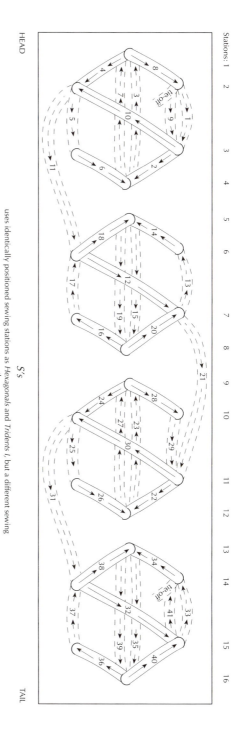

S's

uses identically positioned sewing stations as *Hexagonals* and *Tridents I,* but a different sewing path

HEXAGONALS

This is difficult to sew.

Sewing Stations: The first and third sections pierce stations 2, 3, 6, 7, 10, 11, 14 and 15. The middle section pierces stations 1, 4, 5, 8, 9, 12, 13 and 16.

SEWING PROCEDURE

1. Start inside the middle section. Exit station 1.
2. Set on the first section. Angle and enter the first section at station 2.
3. Exit station 3.
4. Enter station 2.
5. Exit station 3.
6. Angle and enter the second section at station 4. Tie-off.
7. Exit station 1.
8. Set on the third section. Angle and enter the third section at station 2.
9. Exit station 3.
10. Enter station 2.
11. Exit station 3.
12. Angle and enter the second section at station 4.
13. Exit station 5.

Remaining Stations: Repeat steps 2 through 13 to complete each additional hexagon except for the final, which repeats 2 through 12. Then proceed inside three stations towards the head. Tie-off.

A photo of this book, and the following, is on page 187.

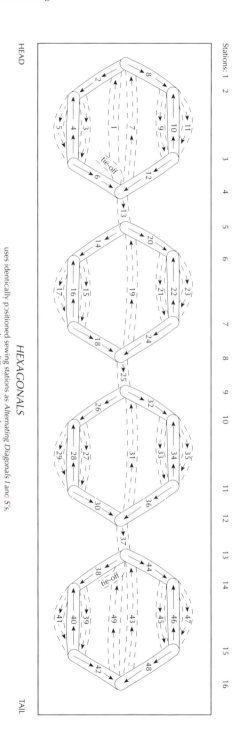

HEAD

Stations: 1 2 3 4 5 6 7 8 9 10 11 12 13 14 15 16

HEXAGONALS uses identically positioned sewing stations as *Alternating Diagonals I* and *S's*, but a different sewing path

TAIL

ROCKET

This design reminds me of the chrome missile on the hood of a 1955 Oldsmobile. The previous binding did not lend itself to sewing; it was a battle. The speed in sewing, and simplicity of the alternating motif makes the Rocket one of my favorites of 3–section spine designs.

Sewing Stations: The first section pierces stations 2, 3, 5, 8, 11, 12, 14 and 17. The middle section pierces stations 1, 4, 6, 9, 10, 13, 15 and 18. The third section pierces 2, 5, 7, 8, 11, 14, 16 and 17.

SEWING PROCEDURE

1. Start on the inside the first section. Exit station 2.
2. Set on the second section. Angle, enter the second section at station 1.
3. Exit station 4.
4. Angle, enter the first section at station 5.
5. Tie-off, then exit station 3.
6. Set on the third section. Angle, enter the third section at station 2.
7. Exit station 5.
8. Angle, enter the second section at station 6.
9. Exit station 9.
10. Angle and enter the third section at station 8.
11. Exit station 7.
12. Angle and enter the first section at station 8.
13. Exit station 11.

Remaining Stations: Repeat the pattern of steps 2 through 12 to form each additional pair of tridents. Tie-off on the inside.

HEAD

ROCKET

TAIL

LEAVES

This is a variation of the sewing titled Rocket. If the sewing stations are based on a grid, the resulting stitches on the spine will *not* be parallel. I find this not objectionable, but as enhancing the design. A photo of this sewing is on page 187.

Sewing Stations: The first section pierces stations 2, 3, 5, 7, 12, 13, 15 and 17. The middle section pierces stations 1, 4, 6, 9, 11, 14, 16 and 19. The third section pierces 2, 7, 8, 10, 12, 17, 18 and 20.

SEWING PROCEDURE

1. Start on the inside the first section. Exit station 2.
2. Set on the second section. Angle and enter the second section at station 1.
3. Exit station 4.
4. Angle, enter the first section at station 5.
5. Tie-off. Exit station 3.
6. Set on the third section. Angle and enter the third section at station 2.
7. Exit station 7.
8. Angle, enter the second section at station 6.
9. Exit station 9.
10. Angle and enter the third section at station 10.
11 Exit station 8.
12. Enter first section at station 7.

Remaining Stations: Repeat the pattern of steps 1 through 12 to form each additional pair of tridents.

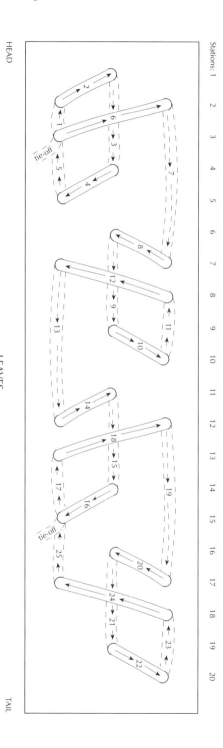

ANGLE SEWINGS continued
The following pages describe additional 3–section sewings which angle,
spanning one and/or two sections, as well as contain straight stitches:

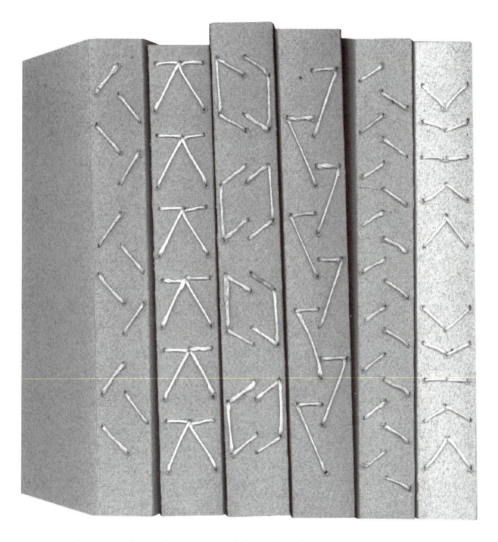

Prototypes of 3–section sewings with diagonal stitches. Left to right:
HOUND'S-TOOTH CHECK, described on page 196; *K's*, described on page
198; BRACKETS, described on page 200; SEVEN *7's*, described on page 202;
BROKEN HERRINGBONE, described on page 204; FOLDING *V's*, described on
page 206.

HOUND'S-TOOTH CHECK

This is a 2–needle sewing. A photo of this book can be seen on page 195.

Sewing Stations: The first section pierces stations 2, 3, 7, 8 and 12. The middle section pierces stations 1, 2, 4, 5, 6, 7, 9, 10, 11 and 12. The third section pierces 3, 4, 8, 9 and 13.

SEWING PROCEDURE
Thread a needle on each end of a long piece of thread. One needle will be referred to as the left, the other the right. The sewing steps will be numbered, as well as designated *L* for the path of the left needle, and *R* when the other needle is used.

1L. Start on the inside the middle section. With the left needle, exit station 1 of the section and cover. Pull the thread to divide the length in half.
2L. Set on the first section. Angle and enter at station 2.

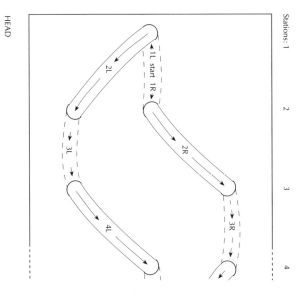
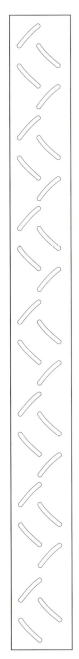

Starting this 2–needle sewing

1L. The left needle starts inside the middle section, exits station 1 on the section and the cover. Divide the thread equally.
2L. Set on the first section. Angle, enter the first section at station 2.
1R. The right needle exits the middle section and cover at station 2.
2R. Set on the third section. Angle and enter the third section at station 3.

1R. Exit station 2 of the middle section and the cover.

2R. Set on the third section. Angle and enter at station 3.

3L. Exit station 3.

4L. Angle and enter the second section at station 4.

5L. Exit station 6.

6L. Angle and enter the first section at station 7.

3R. Exit the third section at station 4.

4R. Angle and enter the second section at station 5.

5R. Exit station 7.

6R. Angle and enter the third section at station 8.

7L. Exit the first section at station 8.

8L. Angle and enter the second section at station 9.

9L. Exit station 11.

10L. Angle and enter the first section at station 12.

11L. Proceed on the inside. Tie-off at station 8.

7R. Exit the third section at station 9.

8R. Angle, enter the second section at station 10.

9R. Exit at station 12.

10R. Angle and enter the third section at station 13.

11R. Proceed on the inside of the third section. Tie-off at station 9.

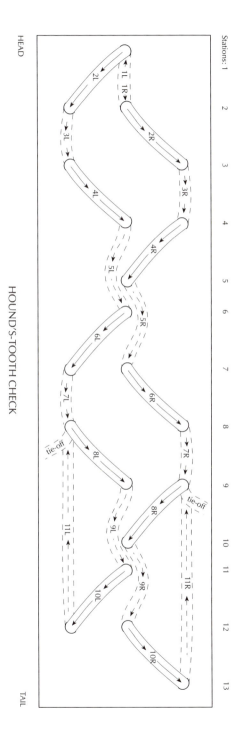

K's

Sewing Stations: Pierce all stations for the first and third sections. The middle section pierces only the odd-numbered stations.

SEWING PROCEDURE

Thread a needle on each end. One will be referred to as the left, the other the right. Sewing steps are numbered as well as designated *L* for the path of the left needle, and *R* for the other needle. Starting the sewing is different than for the previous 2–needle sewing.

1L. Set on the cover and the first section to be sewn. Start on the *outside* of the cover. Enter the cover, and enter the first section from the mountain peak to the valley at station number 1. Divide length of thread.

1R. From the outside of the cover, enter station 1 of the cover, as well as the third section, from the mountain peak to the inside.

2L. Exit station 2.

3L. Set on the middle section. Angle and pass over the thread marked as step 1. Enter the second section at station 1.

4L. Exit station 3.

5L. Span, enter the first section at station 3.

2R. Exit station 2.

Sewing titled *K's*

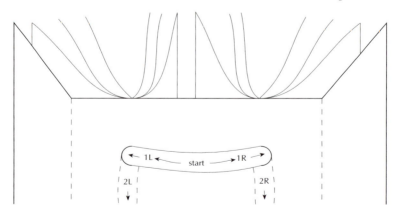

Start on the outside. Enter the cover at station 1 with the left needle into the section from the peak to the valley. The right needle enters the cover into the other section from the peak to the valley at station 1. Divide the thread evenly.

3R. Angle, pass over the thread marked as step 1. Enter the second section at station 1.

4R. Exit station 3.

5R. Span and enter the third section at station 3

6L. Exit station 4.

7L. Angle and enter the second section at station 3.

6R. Exit station 4.

7R. Angle and enter the second section at station 3.

8L. Exit the next station (5).

9L. Span and enter the first section at the same numbered station (5).

10L. Exit the next station towards the tail. (6).

11L. Angle and enter the second section at the previous numbered station (5).

8R. Exit the next station (5).

9R. Span and enter the third section at the same numbered station (5).

10R. Exit the next station towards the tail. (6).

11R. Angle and enter the second section at the previous numbered station (5).

Remaining Stations: Repeat steps 8L through 11L and 8R through 11R to form each additional letter *K*. After completing the last *K*, tie-off the ends of the two threads inside of the middle section.

See photo on page 195.

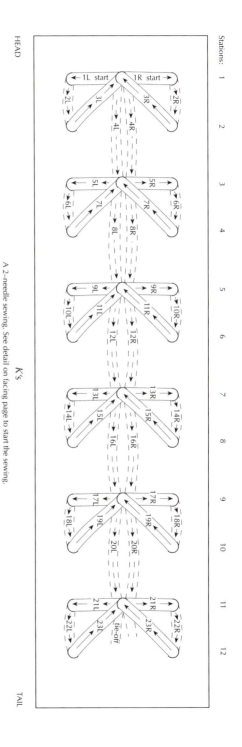

HEAD

A 2-needle sewing. See detail on facing page to start the sewing.

K's

TAIL

Stations: 1 2 3 4 5 6 7 8 9 10 11 12

BRACKETS

Sewing Stations: The first section pierces stations 1, 3, 6, 8, 9, 11, 14 and 16. The middle section pierces all sixteen stations. The third section pierces 2, 4, 5, 7, 10, 12, 13 and 15.

SEWING PROCEDURE

This is a 2–needle sewing. Thread a needle on each end. One will be referred to as the left, the other the right. Sewing steps are numbered as well as designated *L* for the path of the left needle, and *R* for the other needle. Use stations 1 and 2 of the middle section to start the sewing.

1L. Start on the inside the middle section. The left needle exits station 2 of the section and the cover. Divide the length of the thread.

2L. Set on the first section. Angle and enter the first section at station 1.

3L. Exit station 3.

4L. Enter station 1.

1R.Exit the section and cover at station 1. Set on the third section.

2R.Angle and enter the third section at station 2.

3R.Exit station 4.

4R.Enter station 2.

5L. Exit station 3.

6L. Angle and enter the middle section at station 4.

7L. Exit station 5.

8L. Angle and enter the first section at station 6.

9L. Exit station 8.

10L. Enter station 6.

5R.Exit station 4.

6R.Angle and enter the middle section at station 3.

7R.Exit station 6.

8R.Angle and enter the third section at station 5.

9R.Exit station 7.

10R. Enter station 5.

11L. Exit station 8.

12L. Angle and enter the middle section at station 7.

13L. Exit station 10.

14L. Angle and enter the first section at station 9.

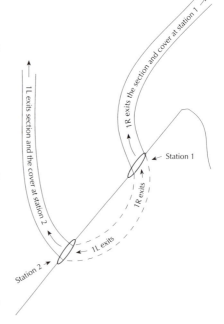

To start the sewing set on the cover. Exit the middle section and cover with the right needle at station 1. Divide the thread evenly. Exit the section and cover with the left needle at station 2.

15L. Exit station 11.
16L. Enter station 9.
11R. Exit station 7.
12R. Angle and enter the
      middle section at station
      number 8.
13R. Exit station 9.
14R. Angle and enter the
      third section at station
      10.
15R. Exit station 12.
16R. Enter station 10.
17L. Exit station 11.
18L. Angle and enter the
      second section at station
      number 12.
19L. Exit station 13.
20L. Angle and enter the
      first section at station
      14.
21L. Exit station 16.
22L. Enter station 14.
17R. Exit station 12.
18R. Angle and enter the
      second section at station
      number 11.
19R. Exit station 14.
20R. Angle and enter the
      third section at station
      13.
21R. Exit station 15.
22R. Enter station 13.
23L. Exit station 16.
24L. Angle and enter the
      second section at station
      number 15.
23R. Exit station 15.
24R. Angle and enter the
      second section at station
      number 16.
25R. Proceed on the inside
      to station 15. Tie-off
      with the other thread.

HEAD

BRACKETS

TAIL

2–needle sewing. To start the sewing see diagram on the facing page.

For steps 1L & 1R
See diagram on the facing page

Stations: 1 2 3 4 5 6 7 8 9 10 11 12 13 14 15 16

SEVEN 7's

This sewing could be sewn with two needles, but the pathways overlap more. I prefer my original procedure which is listed below, and diagrammed on the following page. See photo of this sewing on page 195.

Sewing Stations: The first section pierces stations 2, 6, 10 and 14 for the section and the cover. Station 16 is pierced for the section, only. The middle section pierces all sixteen stations. The third section pierces stations 1, 5, 9 and 13.

SEWING PROCEDURE

1. Start on the inside the first section. Exit station 2.
2. Set on the second section. Angle, enter the second section at station 4. It is important to watch the tension on the diagonal stitches.
3. Exit station 2.
4. Span and enter the first section at station 2. Tie-off.
5. Exit station 6.
6. Span and enter the second section at station 6.
7. Exit station 8.
8. Angle, enter the first section at station 6.
9. Exit station 10.
10. Span and enter the second section at station 10.
11. Exit station 12.
12. Angle, enter the first section at station 10.
13. Exit station 14.
14. Span and enter the second section at station 14.
15. Exit station 16.
16. Angle, enter the first section at station 14.
17. Exit the section, only, at station 16.
18. Proceed along the inside of the spine-cover. Enter the second section, but not the cover, at station 16 from the mountain peak to the inside.
19. Exit the section and the cover at station 15.
20. Angle, enter the third section at station 13.
21. Exit station 9.
22. Angle and enter the second section at station 11.
23. Exit station 13.
24. Span and enter the third section at station 13.
25. Exit station 9.
26. Span and enter the second section at station 9.
27. Exit station 7.
28. Angle and enter the third section at station 5.
29. Exit station 1.

30. Angle and enter the second section at station 3.
31. Exit station 5.
32. Span and enter the third section at station 5.
33. Exit station 1.
34. Span and enter the second section at station 1.
35. Proceed on the inside to station 2. Tie-off with a half hitch.

LOCKING STITCH: At the convergence of the two threads which make up each "7", a locking stitch can be added on the inside of the section, for example, where step 6 and 8 converge:

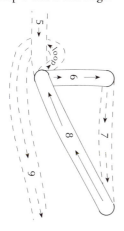

After step 8 enters the first section at station 6, loop around the thread (step 5). Then, continue to station 10 with step 9. This will strengthen the sewing, and help prevent the cover tearing at station 6.

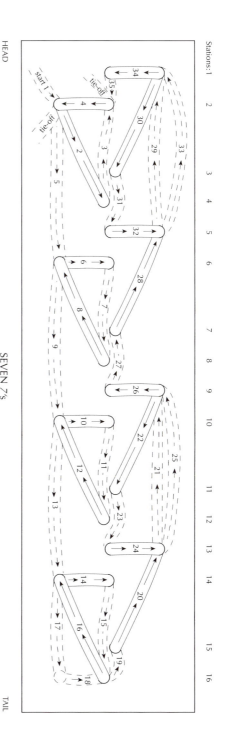

HEAD

SEVEN 7's

Station 16 in the first section is for the section, only. Step 17 exits the section, only.

TAIL

BROKEN HERRINGBONE

A photo of this sewing can be seen on page 195.

Sewing Stations: This is a 2–needle sewing. Number of sewing stations and which stations are pierced in each section depends upon which of the three layouts you chose (see diagram below).

SEWING PROCEDURE

Thread a needle on each end. One will be referred to as the left, the other the right. Sewing steps are numbered as well as designated *L* for the path of the left needle, and *R* for the other needle.

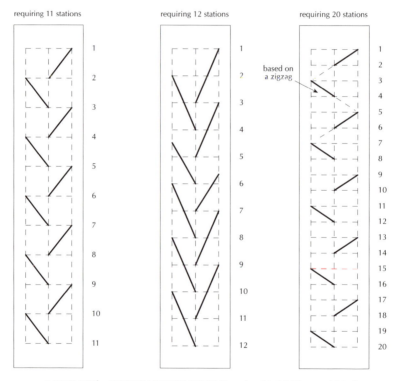

LAYOUTS for BROKEN HERRINGBONE each with 10 Diagonal Stitches

LEFT: Ending and beginning diagonals share the same numbered stations.
MIDDLE: The left diagonals begin and end halfway between stations of the right diagonals. This requires 12 stations for 10 diagonal stitches.
RIGHT: No diagonals share the same numbered stations. This requires 20 stations for 10 diagonals. Each new stitch starts the same distance from the previous. Sewing pattern for each layout is identical.

1L. Start on the inside the middle section. The left needle exits station 4 of the section and the cover. Divide length of thread.

2L. Set on the first section. Angle and enter the first section at station 2.

1R. Exit station 3 of the section and cover. Set on the third section.

2R. Angle and enter the third section at station 1.

3L. Exit station 4.

4L. Angle and enter the second section at station 6.

5L. Exit station 8.

6L. Angle and enter the first section at station 6.

3R. Exit station 3.

4R. Angle and enter the second section at station 5.

5R. Exit station 7.

6R. Angle and enter the third section at station 5.

7L. Exit station 8.

8L. Angle, enter the second section at station 10.

9L. Exit station 12.

10L. Angle and enter the first section at station 10.

11L. Tie-off at station 8.

7R. Exit station 7.

8R. Angle and enter the second section at station 9.

9R. Exit station 11.

10R. Angle and enter the third section at station 9.

11R. Tie-off at station 7.

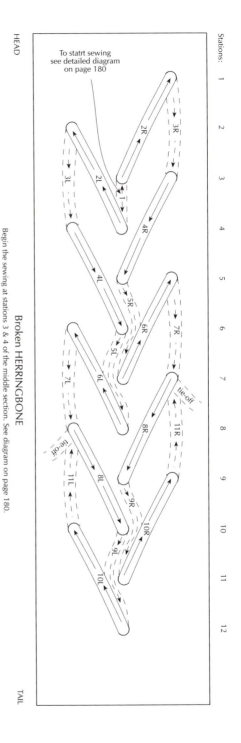

HEAD

Stations:

To statrt sewing see detailed diagram on page 180

Begin the sewing at stations 3 & 4 of the middle section. See diagram on page 180.

Broken HERRINGBONE

TAIL

FOLDING *V's*

A photo of this sewing can be seen on page 195.

Sewing Stations: The first and third sections pierce stations 1, 3, 5, 7, 9, 10, 12, 14, 16 and 18. The middle section pierces stations 2, 4, 5, 6, 8, 11, 13, 14, 15 and 17.

SEWING PROCEDURE

This is a 2–needle sewing. Steps are numbered as well as designated *L* for the path of the left needle, and *R* for the other needle. This sewing starts differently than the previous sewings which began vertically on the out-side fold of the middle section. This 2–needle sewing has a horizontal thread from the first to the third sections on the inside of the spine-cover.

1L. Set aside the cover. Enter the first section from the mountain peak at station 3 of the section, only.

1R. Enter the third section from the mountain peak at station 3 of the sec-tion, only. Place sections almost tangent. Divide length of thread.

2L. Set on the cover. Exit station 1 of the section and the cover.

2R. Exit station 1 of the section and the cover.

3L. Angle and enter the second section at station 2.

4L. Exit station 4.

5L. Angle and enter the first section at station 3.

3R. Angle and enter the second section at station 2.

4R. Exit station 4.

5R. Angle and enter the third section at station 3.

6L. Exit station 5.

7L. Span and enter the second section at station 5.

8L. Exit station 6.

9L. Angle and enter the first section at station 7.

6R. Exit station 5.

7R. Span and enter the second section at station 5.

8R. Exit station 6.

9R. Angle and enter the third section at station 7.

10L. Exit station 9.

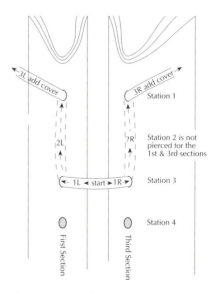

Starting a 2–needle sewing with a horizontal thread entering from the mountain peak of the sections, only.

11L. Angle and enter the second section at station 8.
12L. Exit station 11.13L.
   Angle and enter the first
   section at station 10.
10R. Exit station 9.
11R. Angle and enter the second section at station 8.
12R. Exit station 11.
13R. Angle and enter the
   third section at station 10.
14L. Exit station 12.
15L. Angle, enter the second
   section at station 13.
16L. Exit station 14.
17L. Span and enter the first
   section at station 14.
14R. Exit station 12.
15R. Angle, enter the second
   section at station 13.
16R. Exit station 14.
17R. Span and enter the
   third section at station 14.
18L. Exit station 16.
19L. Angle, enter the second
   section at station 15.
20L. Exit station 17.
21L. Angle and enter the first
   section at station 18.
18R. Exit station 16.
19R. Angle, enter the second
   section at station 15.
20R. Exit station 17.
21R. Angle and enter the
   third section at station 18.
22L. Tie-off on the inside at
   station 16.
22R. Tie-off at station 16.

HEAD

Stations: 1 2 3 4 5 6 7 8 9 10 11 12 13 14 15 16 17 18

Sewing begins on peak of 1st and 3rd sections. See diagram on page 206.

FOLDING V's

TAIL

3L 3R 2L 2R
1L 1R 4L 4R 5L 5R 6L 6R
7L 7R 8L 8R 9L 9R
10L 10R 11L 11R 12L 12R
13L 13R 14L 14R 15L 15R 16L 16R
17L 17R 18L 18R 19L 19R 20L 20R
tie-off tie-off 21L 21R 22L 22R

V's

Sewing Stations: The first and third sections pierce the odd-numbered stations. The middle section pierces the even-numbered stations.

SEWING PROCEDURE

This sewing starts the same as the previous sewing (see diagram on page 206).

The concept of the sewing is the same as that for Folding *V's*. The stations are numbered slightly differently because the previous sewing had diagonal as well as horizontal stitches. Spans in the previous sewing entered the same numbered stations as they exited.

V's II

This sewing is really no different than the one above, but looks completely different. See the illustration of both on the next page.

The difference is that *V's II* shares the same stations for the base of each *V* with the beginning of the next.

A photo is on the following page.

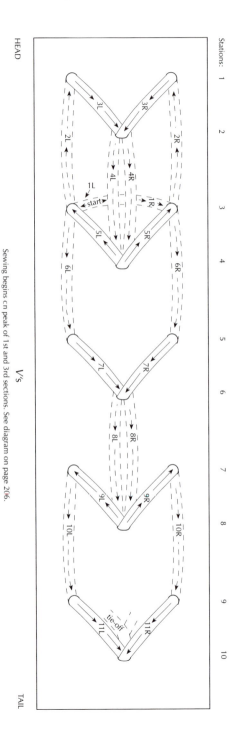

HEAD

Sewing begins on peak of 1st and 3rd sections. See diagram on page 206.

V's

Stations: 1   2   3   4   5   6   7   8   9   10

TAIL

ANGLE SEWINGS continued
The following pages will describe additional 3–section sewings which
angle, spanning one and/or two sections. In addition, they may contain
straight stitches. This is a digital scan of the next sewings:

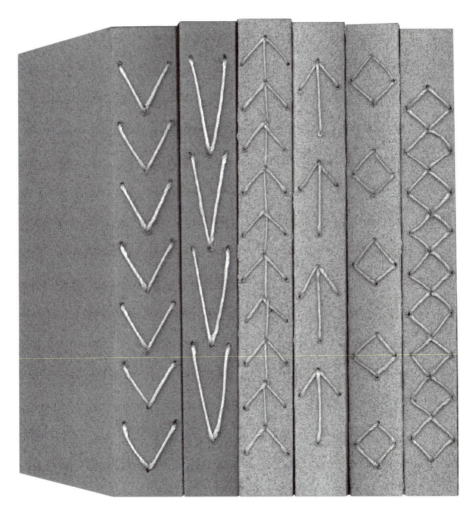

Prototypes of 3–section sewings with diagonal stitches. Left to right:
V's, described on page 208; *V's II*, described on page 208; TOUCHING
ARROWS, on page 210; AEROS *Arrows,* on page 212; ISOLATED DIAMONDS,
described on page 214; and TOUCHING DIAMONDS, described on page 216.

TOUCHING ARROWS

A photo of this sewing can be seen on page 209.

Sewing Stations: For the first and third sections, pierce the even-numbered stations. For the middle section, pierce the odd-numbered stations.

SEWING PROCEDURE

This is one continuous sewing using a single needle.

STEPS 1-10, LACING FIGURE 8:

1. Start on the inside of the middle section. Exit station 1 and enter the next station for the middle section, which is 3.
2.-10. Continue to sew a Lacing Figure *8* to the tail and back to the head (see diagram on the following page, or page 22). Tie-off, but do not clip the thread with the needle; the sewing continues:

STEPS 11-33 SEWING the FIRST and THIRD SECTIONS:

11. Exit the middle section at station 1. Set on the first section. Angle and enter the first section at station 2.
12. Exit station 4.
13. Angle and enter the middle section at station 3.
14. Exit station 1.
15. Set on the third section. Angle and enter the third section at station 2.
16. Exit station 4.
17. Angle and enter the middle section at station 3.
18. Exit station 5.
19. Angle and enter the first section at station 6.
20. Exit station 8.
21. Angle and enter the middle section at station 7.
22. Exit station 5.
23. Angle and enter the third section at station 6.
24. Exit station 8.
25. Angle and enter the middle section at station 7.
26. Exit station 9.
27. Angle and enter the first section at station 10.
28. Exit station 12.

HEAD   TAIL

TOUCHING ARROWS

29. Angle and enter the middle section at station 11.
30. Exit station 9.
31. Angle and enter the third section at station number 10.
32. Exit station 12.
33. Angle and enter the middle section at station 11. Tie-off on the inside at station number 11.

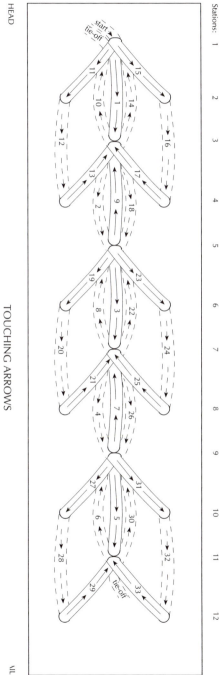

AEROS *Arrows*

This sewing is dedicated to my godchild, Aeros Keith Lillstrom. A photo of this sewing can be seen on page 209.

Sewing Stations: First and third sections pierce stations 2, 5, 8, 11 and 14. The middle section pierces stations 1, 3, 4, 6, 7, 9, 10, 12, 13 and 15.

SEWING PROCEDURE

This is sewn with a single needle.

1. Exit the first section at station 2.
2. Set on the second section. Angle, enter the middle section at station 1.
3. Exit station 3.
4. Enter the first section at station 1.
5. Exit station 4.

STEPS 6-12 RUNNING STITCH to the TAIL:

6. Enter station 6.
7. Exit station 7.
8. Enter station 9.
9. Exit station 10.
10. Enter station 12.
11. Exit station 13.
12. Enter station 15.

SEWING the DIAGONALS:

13. Exit station 13.
14. Angle and enter the first section at station 14.
15. Exit station 11.
16. Angle and enter the middle section at station 10.
17. Exit station 13.
18. Angle and enter the third section at station 14.
19. Exit station 11.
20. Angle and enter the middle section at station 10.
21. Exit station 7.
22. Angle and enter the first section at station 8.

HEAD   TAIL

AEROS *Arrows*

23. Proceed to station 5. Tie-off, but do not clip the thread with the needle. Exit station 5.
24. Angle and enter the middle section at station 4.
25. Exit station 7.
26. Angle and enter the third section at station 8.
27. Exit station 5.
28. Angle and enter the middle section at station 4.
29. Exit station 1.
30. Angle and enter the third section at station 2.
31. Proceed on the inside to station 5. Tie-off.

ISOLATED DIAMONDS

A photo of this sewing can be seen on page 209.

Sewing Stations: The first and third sections pierce stations 2, 5, 8 and 11. The middle section pierces stations 1, 3, 4, 6, 7, 9, 10 and 12.

SEWING PROCEDURE

This is a 2–needle sewing. Steps are numbered as well as designated L for the path of the left needle, and R for the other needle.

This sewing starts without the cover, the same as the diagram on page 206, except different stations are used. To start this sewing there is a horizontal thread which extends from the first to the third sections, entering each section on the mountain peak to the inside at station 5.

1L. Set aside the cover. Enter the first section from the mountain peak to the valley at station 5 of the section, only.

1R. Enter the third section from the mountain peak at station 5 of the section, only. Place sections almost tangent. Divide the length of thread.

2L. Set on the cover. Exit station 2 of the section and the cover.

2R. Exit station 2 of the section and the cover.

3L. Set on the second section. Angle, enter the second section at station 1.

4L. Exit station 3.

5L. Angle and enter the first section at station 2.

3R. Angle and enter the second section at station 1.

4R. Exit station 3.

5R. Angle and enter the third section at station 2.

6L. Exit station 5.

7L. Angle and enter the second section at station 4.

8L. Exit station 6.

9L. Angle and enter the first section at station 5.

6R. Exit station 5.

7R. Angle and enter the second section at station 4.

8R. Exit station 6.

9R. Angle and enter the third section at station 5.

10L. Exit station 8.

HEAD   TAIL

ISOLATED DIAMONDS

11L. Angle and enter the second section at station 7.

12L. Exit station 9.

13L. Angle and enter the first section at station 8.

10R. Exit station 8.

11R. Angle and enter the second section at station 7.

12R. Exit station 9.

13R. Angle and enter the third section at station 8.

14L. Exit station 11.

15L. Angle, enter the second section at station 10.

16L. Exit station 12.

17L. Angle and enter the first section at station 11. Tie-off on the inside.

14R. Exit station 11.

15R. Angle, enter the second section at station 10.

16R. Exit station 12.

17R. Angle and enter the third section at station 11. Tie-off on the inside.

ISOLATED DIAMONDS

To start the sewing see diagram on page 206

TOUCHING DIAMONDS

A photo of this sewing can be seen on page 209.

Sewing Stations: The first and third sections pierce the even-numbered stations. The middle section pierces the odd-numbered stations.

SEWING PROCEDURE
This is a 2–needle sewing. Steps are numbered as well as designated *L* for the path of the left needle, and *R* for the other needle.

1. To start this 2–needle sewing, there is a horizontal thread from the first to the third sections on the inside of the spine-cover. The threads enter on the mountain peak at station 4 of the first and third sections, as opposed to station 5 in the previous sewing (see the diagram on page 206).

2. Step 2 onward is sewn identically to the previous sewing, that is, the same path, but using differently numbered stations (see steps on pages 214 and 215).

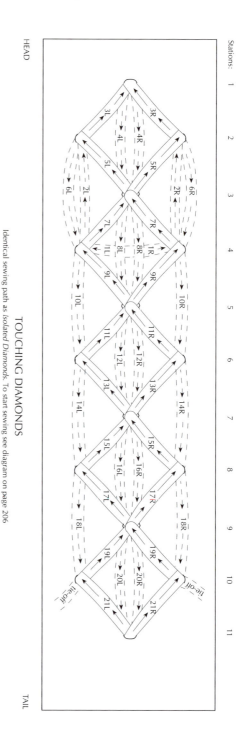

HEAD

Identical sewing path as *Isolated Diamonds*. To start sewing see diagram on page 206

TOUCHING DIAMONDS

Stations:

1

2

3

4

5

6

7

8

9

10

11

TAIL

ANGLE SEWINGS continued
The following pages will describe additional 3–section sewings which
angle, spanning one and/or two sections, as well as containing straight
stitches. This is a digital scan of the next sewings:

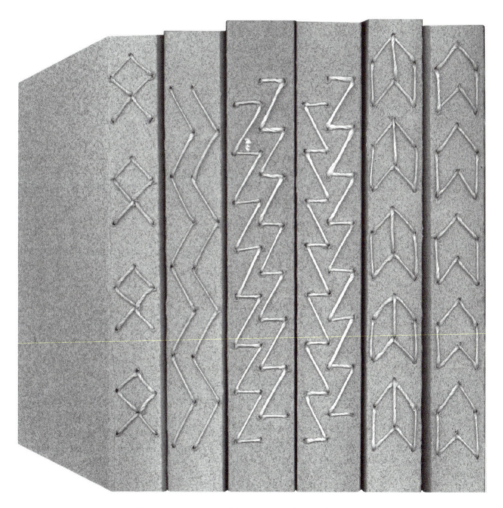

Prototypes of 3–section sewings with diagonal stitches. Left to right:
PISCES, described on page 218; TIRE TRACKS, described on page 220; ASSEM-
BLY LINE Z's, described on page 222; SAW BLADES, described on page 226;
OPEN BOOK, described on page 228 and ARROWHEAD, on page 230.

PISCES

A photo of this sewing can be seen on page 217.

Sewing Stations: The first and third sections pierce the even-numbered stations. The middle section pierces the odd-numbered stations.

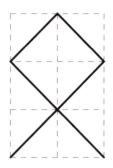

Proportions for the stations is a ratio of 2 to 3

SEWING PROCEDURE

This is a 2–needle sewing. Steps are numbered as well as designated *L* for the path of the left needle, and *R* for the other needle. This 2–needle sewing starts without the cover. A horizontal thread extends from the first to the third sections, entering each on the mountain peak. (see diagram on page 206). For this particular sewing, step 1 is at station 4.

Sewing procedure is closely related to the two previous sewings.

1L. Set aside the cover. Enter the first section from the mountain peak at station 4 of the section, only.

1R. Enter the third section from the mountain peak at station 4 of the section, only. Place sections almost tangent. Divide the length of the thread.

2L. Set on the cover. Exit station 2 of the section and the cover.

2R. Exit station 2 of the section and the cover.

3L. Angle and enter the second section at station 3.

4L. Exit station 1.

5L. Angle and enter the first section at station 2.

3R. Angle and enter the second section at station 3.

4R. Exit station 1.

5R. Angle and enter the third section at station 2.

6L. Exit station 4.

7L. Angle and enter the second section at station 3.

8L. Exit station 7.

9L. Angle and enter the first section at station 6.

6R. Exit station 4.

7R. Angle and enter the second section at station 3.

8R. Exit station 7.

9R. Angle and enter the third section at station 6.

10L. Exit station 8.

11L. Angle and enter the second section at station 7.

12L. Exit station 5.

13L. Angle and enter the first section at station 6.

10R. Exit station 8.

11R. Angle and enter the second section at station 7.

12R. Exit station 5.

13R. Angle and enter the third section at station 6.

14L. Exit station 10.

15L. Angle and enter the second section at station number 11.

16L. Exit station 9.

17L. Angle and enter the first section at station 10.

14R. Exit station 10.

15R. Angle and enter the second section at station 11.

16R. Exit station 9.

17R. Angle and enter the third section at station 10.

18L. Exit station 12.

19L. Angle and enter the second section at station number 11.

18R. Exit station 12.

19R. Angle and enter the second section at station 11.

If you wish to repeat one or more sewn units, sew the next similar to the first, then the second, then the third unit described. Tie-off the two threads on the inside after completing the final sewn unit.

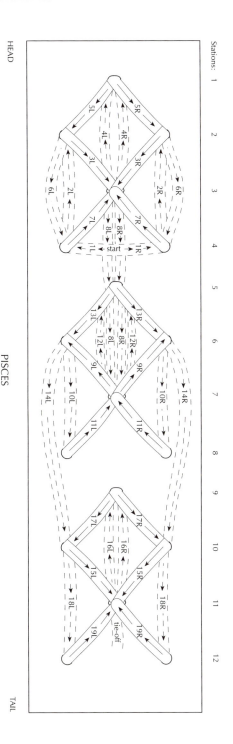

PISCES

To start the sewing, see diagram on page 206

HEAD

TAIL

Stations: 1   2   3   4   5   6   7   8   9   10   11   12

TIRE TRACKS

A photo of this sewing can be seen on page 217.

Sewing Stations: The first section pierces the odd-numbered stations. The middle section pierces all 11 stations. The third sections pierces the even-numbered stations.

SEWING PROCEDURE

This requires two separate sewings, each with a single needle. Steps are numbered as well as designated *a* for the path of the first sewing, and *b* for the second. The *a* sewing stitches the first and second sections to the cover. The *b* sewing is for the second and third sections.

The FIRST SEWING:

1a. Start inside the second section and exit station 2. Set on the first section. Angle and enter the first section at station 1.
2a. Exit station 3.
3a. Angle and enter the second section at station 2. Tie-off.
4a. Exit station 4.
5a. Angle and enter the first section at station 3.
6a. Exit station 5.
7a. Angle and enter the middle section at station 4.
8a. Exit station 6.
9a. Angle and enter the first section at station 5.
10a. Exit station 7.
11a. Angle and enter the second section at station 6.
12a. Exit station 8.
13a. Angle and enter the first section at station 7.
14a. Exit station 9.
15a. Angle and enter the second section at station 8.
16a. Exit station 10.
17a. Angle and enter the first section at station 9.
18a. Exit station 11.

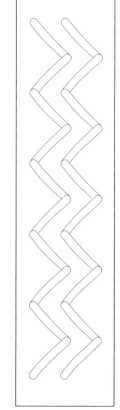

19a. Angle and enter the second section at station 10.
Tie-off.

The SECOND SEWING:

Thread a needle with the same
or a different color thread.

1b. Set on the third section.
Exit the third section at
station 2. Angle and enter
the second section at station 1.

2b. Exit station 3.

3b. Angle and enter the third
section at station 2. Tie-
off.

4b. Exit station 4.

5b. Angle and enter the second
section at station 3.

6b. Exit station 5.

7b. Angle and enter the third
section at station 4.

8b. Exit station 6.

9b. Angle and enter the second
section at station 5.

10b.   Exit station 7.

11b. Angle and enter the
third section at station 6.

12b. Exit station 8.

13b. Angle and enter the second section at station 7.

14b. Exit station 9.

15b. Angle and enter the
third section at station 8.

16b. Exit station 10.

17b. Angle and enter the second section at station 9.

18b. Exit station 11.

19b. Angle and enter the
third section at station 10.
Tie-off.

ASSEMBLY LINE *Z's*

A photo of this sewing can be seen on page 217.

Sewing Stations: The first section pierces the even-numbered stations. The middle section pierces all 18 stations. The third sections pierces the odd-numbered stations.

SEWING PROCEDURE

This requires two separate sewings, each with a single needle. Steps are numbered as well as designated *a* for the path of the first sewing, and *b* for the second. The *a* sewing stitches the first and second sections to the cover. The *b* sewing is for the second and third sections.

The FIRST SEWING:

1a. Start inside the second section and exit station 2. Set on the first section. Angle, enter the first section at station 4.

2a. Exit station 2.

3a. Span and enter the second section at station 2. Tie-off.

4a. Exit station 4.

5a. Angle and enter the first section at station 6.

6a. Exit station 4.

7a. Span and enter the middle section at station 4.

8a. Exit the middle section two stations towards the tail.

9a. Angle and enter the first section two stations towards the tail.

10a. Exit two stations towards the head.

11a. Span and enter the second section at the same numbered station.

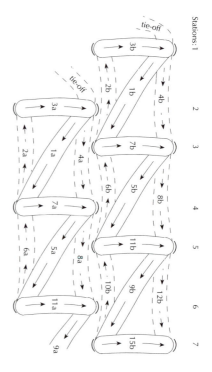

Detail of starting each sewing of
ASSEMBLY LINE *Z's*

***Remaining Stations of the
First Sewing:*** Repeat steps 8-
11 for each successive *Z*. To
complete the final *Z*, span
and enter the first section.
Tie-off with a half hitch.

The SECOND SEWING:
Thread a needle with the
same or a different color
thread.

1b. Start inside the third section and exit station 1.
Angle and enter the sec-
ond section at station 3.

2b. Exit station 1.

3b. Span and enter the third
section at station 1. Tie-
off.

4b. Exit station 3.

5b. Angle and enter the second section at station
number 5.

6b. Exit station 3.

7b. Span and enter the third
section at station 3.

8b. Exit the third section two
stations towards the tail.

9b. Angle and enter the second section two stations
towards the tail.

10b. Exit two stations
towards the head.

11b. Span and enter the
third section at the same
numbered station.

Remaining Stations: Repeat
steps 8-11 for each successive
Z.
To complete the final *Z*, span
and enter the middle section.
Tie-off with a half hitch.

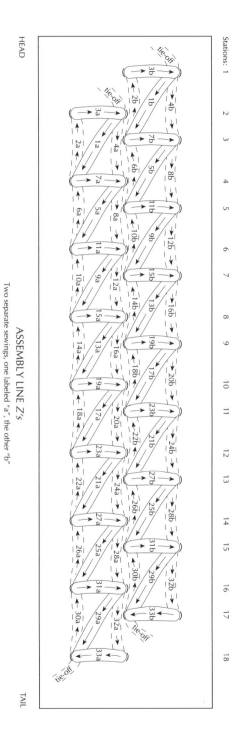

HEAD

Two separate sewings, one labeled "a", the other "b"

ASSEMBLY LINE Z's

TAIL

Stations: 1 2 3 4 5 6 7 8 9 10 11 12 13 14 15 16 17 18

STAIR-STEPS

This sewing was derived from The 2–section Twisted *X* (page 84), and the 3–section Twisted *X* (page 248). I like that it laps and loops two of the spans.

Perhaps the angle, lap and loop could be a continuous thread that zigzags down, then back up the spine, as it laps and loops every span in sight! This would be reminiscent of a great multiple play in checkers.

Sewing Stations: The first section pierces stations 1 through 10. The middle section pierces stations 2 through 11. The third sections pierces stations 3 through 12.

SEWING PROCEDURE

1. Start inside the third section. Exit station 3.
2. Set on the second section. Span, enter station 3 of the second section.
3. Exit station 2.
4. Set on the first section. Span, enter station 2 of the first section.
5. Exit station 1.
6a. Angle, lap and loop thread labeled step 4.
6b. Angle, lap, loop thread 2.
6c. Angle, enter third section at station 4. Tie-off.

Repeat steps 2-6 to form each additional unit of the stair-step. The next tie-off will be upon completion of the final unit.

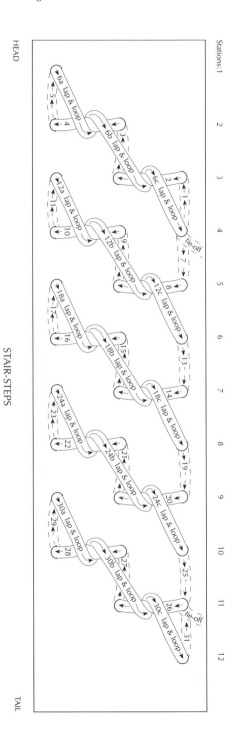

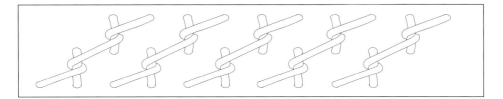

STAIR-STEPS

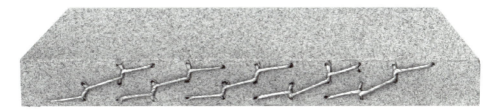

STAIR-STEPS, a 3–section sewing. This sewing is diagrammed as a single
sewing. However, the spans could be sewn first, in one color. A second color
could be used for a second sewing, which angles, laps and loops the spans.

Sewings in Volume II are on continuous paper support. It is critical that the
spine be reinforced. Examples of 2– and 3–ply paper covers are diagrammed in
Volume I. Those examples do not use paste or glue, and are always on the
inside of the spine.

Above, the reinforcement is glued to the outside of the spine, around the head
and tail to the inside. The top example is suède; the middle is leather; the bottom is (non-archival) gummed strapping tape. Tyvec is a strong material, ph-
neutral, and is starting to be used in contemporary bindings.

SAW BLADES

This sewing is dedicated to my dear friend Philip Zimmermann. A photo of this sewing can be seen on page 217.

Sewing Stations: The first section pierces the odd-numbered stations. The middle section pierces all 18 stations. The third section pierces the even-numbered stations.

SEWING PROCEDURE

This requires two separate sewings, each with a single needle. Steps are numbered as well as designated *a* for the path of the first sewing, and *b* for the second. The *a* sewing stitches the first and second sections to the cover. The *b* sewing is for the second and third sections.

The FIRST SEWING:

1a. Start inside the second section and exit station 1. Set on the first sec-
     tion. Angle, enter the first section at station 3.

2a. Exit station 1.

3a. Span and enter the second section at station 1. Tie-off.

4a. Exit station 3.

5a. Angle and enter the first section at station 5.

6a. Exit station 3.

7a. Span and enter the middle section at station 3.

8a. Exit the middle section two stations towards the tail.

9a. Angle and enter the first section two stations towards the tail.

10a. Exit two stations towards the head.

11a. Span and enter the second section at the same numbered station.

Remaining Stations of the First Sewing: Repeat steps 8-11 for the top portion of, and the angle of, each successive *Z*.

To complete the final *Z*, span and enter the first section. Tie-off with a half hitch.

HEAD   TAIL

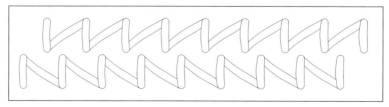

SAW BLADES

The SECOND SEWING:

Thread a needle with the same or a different color thread.

1b. Start inside the second section and exit station 2. Angle and enter the third section at station 4.

2b. Exit station 2.

3b. Span and enter the second section at station 2. Tie-off.

4b. Exit station 4.

5b. Angle and enter the third section at station 6.

6b. Exit station 4.

7b. Span and enter the second section at station 4.

8b. Exit the second section two stations towards the tail.

9b. Angle and enter the third section two stations towards the tail.

10b. Exit two stations towards the head.

11b. Span and enter the second section at the same numbered station.

Remaining Stations: Repeat steps 8-11 to form each successive Σ.

To complete the final Σ, span and enter the third section. Tie-off with a half hitch.

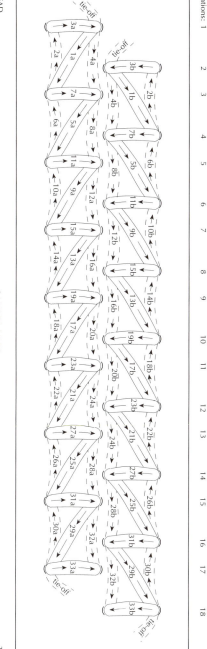

HEAD

Stations: 1 2 3 4 5 6 7 8 9 10 11 12 13 14 15 16 17 18

Two separate sewings, one labeled "a", the other "b"

SAW BLADES

TAIL

OPEN BOOK

This sewing is like my heart, for my partner, Scott. A photo of this sewing can be seen on page 217.

Sewing Stations: The first and third sections pierce the even-numbered stations. The middle section pierces the odd-numbered stations.

SEWING PROCEDURE

This is a 2–needle sewing. Steps are numbered as well as designated L for the path of the left needle, and R for the other needle. The sewing starts without the cover. A horizontal thread enters the mountain peak of the first to the third sections at station 4. A diagram of how to start the sewing is illustrated on page 206.

1L. Set aside the cover. Enter the first section from the mountain peak at station 4 of the section, only.

1R. Enter the third section from the mountain peak at station 4 of the section, only. Place the two sections almost tangent. Divide the length of the thread.

2L. Set on the cover. Exit station 2 of the section and the cover.

2R. Exit station 2 of the section and the cover.

3L. Set on the second section. Angle, enter the second section at station 1.

4L. Exit station 3.

5L. Angle and enter the first section at station 4.

3R. Angle and enter the second section at station 1.

4R. Exit station 3.

5R. Angle and enter the third section at station 4.

6L. Exit station 6.

7L. Angle and enter the second section at station 5.

6R. Exit station 6.

7R. Angle and enter the second section at station 5

8L. Exit station 7.

9L. Angle and enter the first section at station 8.

8R. Exit station 7.

9R. Angle and enter the third section at station 8.

10L. Exit station 10.

11L. Angle and enter the second section at station 9.

12L. Exit station 11.

13L. Angle and enter the first section at station 12.

10R. Exit station 10.

11R. Angle and enter the second section at station 9.

12R. Exit station 11.

13R. Angle and enter the third section at station 12.

14L. Exit station 14.

15L. Angle, enter the second section at station 13.

16L. Exit station 15.

17L. Angle and enter the first section at station 16.

14R. Exit station 14.

15R. Angle, enter the second section at station 13.

16R. Exit station 15.

17R. Angle and enter the third section at station 16.

18L. Exit station 14.

19L. Enter station 16.

20L. Exit station 12.

21L. Enter station 10.

22L. Exit station 8.

23L. Enter station 6.

24L. Exit station 4.

25L. Enter station 2 of the cover, only.

26L. Proceed on the inside of the spine cover. Angle and enter the second section, only, from the peak to the valley at station 3.

27L. Exit station 1 of the section and the cover.

28L-34L. Make a running stitch to the tail. Tie-off on the inside at station 15.

18R. Exit station 14.

19R. Enter station 16.

20R. Exit station 12.

21R. Enter station 10.

22R. Exit station 8.

23R. Enter station 6.

24R. Exit station 4.

25R. Enter station 2. Tie-off.

HEAD

OPEN BOOK

TAIL

Sewing begins on peak of 1st & 3rd sections. See diagram on page 206 to begin

Stations: 1   2   3   4   5   6   7   8   9   10   11   12   13   14   15   16

ARROWHEAD

A photo of this sewing can be seen on page 217.

Sewing Stations: The first and third sections pierce the even-numbered stations. The middle section pierces the odd-numbered stations.

The stations are designed on a grid. The three verticals represent the sections. The distance they are spread apart depends upon the thickness of the sections. Space at the head and tail are considered. The remainder of the height of the spine is divided horizontally among how ever many sewing stations needed.

SEWING PROCEDURE

This 2–needle sewing is almost identical to the previous, the Open Book. The difference is that in this sewing, the running stitch in the middle section is eliminated.

Follow steps 1R-25R and 1L-24L diagrammed on page 228-229. Then, with the left needle, the new step 25L is to enter the first section at 2, and tie-off on the inside with a half hitch.

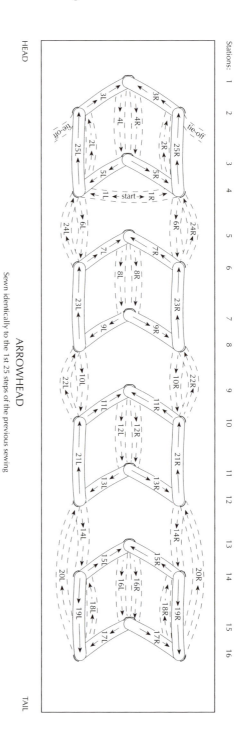

ARROWHEAD

Sewn identically to the 1st 25 steps of the previous sewing

HEAD

TAIL

Stations: 1 2 3 4 5 6 7 8 9 10 11 12 13 14 15 16

ANGLE SEWINGS continued

The following pages will describe additional 3–section sewings which angle, spanning one and/or two sections, as well as containing straight stitches. This is a digital scan of the next sewings:

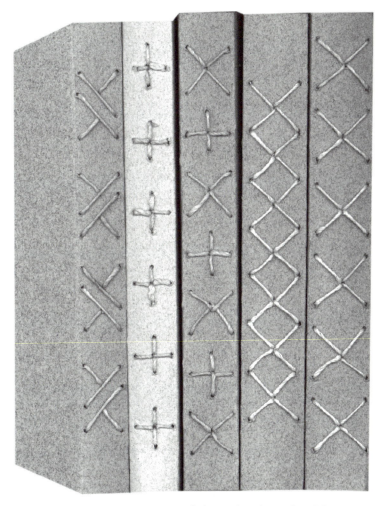

Prototypes of 3–section sewings with diagonal stitches. Left to right: DIAGONAL *T's*, described on page 232; *+'s*, on page 234; *+'s & X's*, on page 236; CONTIGUOUS *X's*, described on page 238 for an even number, and on page 242 for an odd number of *X's*. ISOLATED *X's* is described on page 240.

DIAGONAL *T's*

A photo of this sewing can be seen on page 231.

Sewing Stations: The first section pierces stations 1, 2, 4, 5, 7, 8, 9, 10 and 12. The middle section pierces stations 2, 3, 6, 7, 10 and 11. The third pierces stations 1, 3, 4, 5, 6, 8, 9, 11 and 12.

It is easy to become confused in piercing these stations. It will help to draw a light vertical pencil line on the inside of the spine-cover representing the location of each of the sections. Then mark off the twelve evenly spaced horizontal lines for each numbered station.

Draw the pattern of the stitches lightly with a sharpened pencil. Pierce only those stations needed for each section. Line up each section with the cover to mark the stations on the sections.

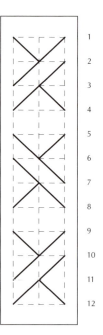

Drawing a grid on the inside of the spine-cover to position the sewing stations

SEWING PROCEDURE

1. Start inside the first section. Exit station 1.
2. Set on the third section. Angle, enter the third section at station 3.
3. Exit station 1.
4. Set on the middle section. Angle and enter at station 2.
5. Exit the second section at station 3.
6. Angle and enter the first section at station 4. Tie-off at station 2.
7. Exit station 2.
8. Angle and enter the third section at station 4.
9. Exit station 5.
10. Angle and enter the first section at station 7.
11. Exit station 5.
12. Angle and enter the middle section at station 6.
13. Exit station 7.
14. Angle and enter the third section at station 8.
15. Exit station 6.
16. Angle and enter the first section at station 8.

DIAGONAL T's

Sewing on the spine is symmetrical to the drawing inside, as shown on the facing page

17. Exit station 9.
18. Angle and enter the third section at station 11.
19. Exit station 9.
20. Angle and enter the middle section at station 10.
21. Exit station 11.
22. Angle and enter the first section at station 12.
23. Exit station 10.
24. Angle and enter the third section at station 12.
25. Proceed on the inside of the third section to station 11. Tie-off with a half hitch.

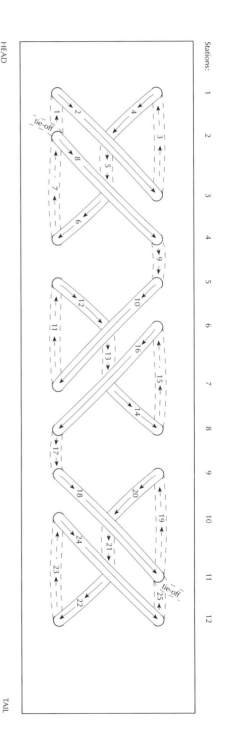

DIAGONAL T's

+'s

A photo of this sewing can be seen on page 231.

Sewing Stations: The first and third sections pierce stations 2, 5, 8, 11 and 14. The middle section pierces all fifteen stations.

SEWING PROCEDURE

This is a 2–needle sewing. Steps are numbered as well as designated L or R to differentiate the needles. The sewing starts without the cover. A horizontal thread enters the peak of the first and third sections, to the inside, at station 5. A diagram of how to start the sewing is illustrated on page 206.

1L. Set aside the cover. Enter the first section from the mountain peak at station 5 of the section, only.

1R. Enter the third section from the mountain peak at station 5 of the section, only. Place the two sections almost tangent. Divide the length of the thread.

2L. Set on the cover. Exit station 2 of the section and the cover.

2R. Exit station 2 of the section and the cover.

3L. Set on the second section. Span, enter the second section at station 2.

4L. Exit station 5.

5L. Span and enter the first section at station 5.

3R. Span and enter the second section at station 2.

4R. Exit station 5.

5R. Span and enter the third section at station 5.

6L. Exit station 8.

7L. Span and enter the second section at station 8.

8L. Exit station 11.

9L. Span and enter the first section at station 11.

6R. Exit station 8.

7R. Span and enter the second section at station 8.

8R. Exit station 11.

HEAD   TAIL

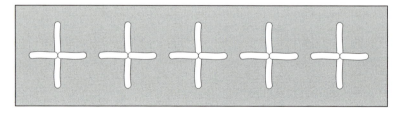

+'s

9R. Span and enter the third
section at station 11.
10L. Exit station 14.
11L. Span and enter the second section at station
number 14.
12L. Exit station 13.
13L. Enter station 14.
10R. Exit station 14.
11R. Span and enter the second section at station
number 14.
12R. Exit station 15.
13R. Enter station 14. Tie-
off with a half hitch.
14L. Exit station 12.
15L. Enter station 11.
16L. Exit station 10.
17L. Enter station 11.
18L. Exit station 9.
19L. Enter station 8.
20L. Exit station 7.
21L. Enter station 8.
22L. Exit station 6.
23L. Enter station 5.
24L. Exit station 4.
25L. Enter station 5.
26L. Exit station 3.
27L. Enter station 2.
28L. Exit station 1.
29L. Enter station 2. Tie-off
with a half hitch.

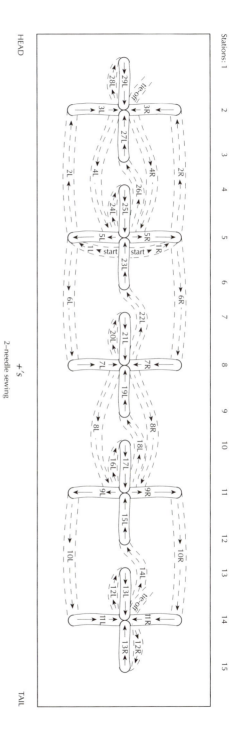

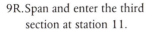

+'s & X's

Sewing Stations: First and third sections pierce the odd-numbered stations. The middle section pierces stations 2, 4, 5, 6, 8, 10, 11, 12 and 14.

SEWING PROCEDURE

This is a 2–needle sewing. Steps are numbered as well as designated *L* or *R* to differentiate the needles. The sewing starts without the cover. A horizontal thread enters the peaks of the first and third sections to the inside at station 5. A diagram to start the sewing is illustrated on page 206.

1L. Set aside the cover. Enter the first section from the mountain peak at station 5 of the section, only.

1R. Enter the third section from the mountain peak at station 5 of the section, only. Place sections almost tangent. Divide the length of the thread.

2L. Set on the cover. Exit station 3 of the section and the cover.

2R. Exit station 3 of the section and the cover.

3L. Set on the second section. Angle, enter the second section at station 2.

4L. Exit station 5.

5L. Span and enter the first section at station 5.

3R. Angle and enter the second section at station 2.

4R. Exit station 5.

5R. Span and enter the third section at station 5.

6L. Exit station 1.

7L. Angle and enter the second section at station 2.

8L. Exit station 4.

9L. Enter station 5.

10L. Exit station 8.

11L. Angle and enter the first section at station 7.

6R. Exit station 1.

7R. Angle and enter the second section at station 2.

8R. Exit station 5.

9R. Enter station 6.

10R. Exit station 8.

HEAD   TAIL

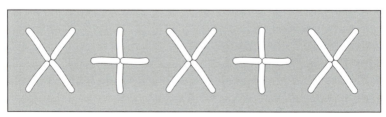

+'s & X's

11R. Angle and enter the
    third section at station 7.
12L. Exit station 9.
13L. Angle and enter the
    second section at station
    number 8.
14L. Exit station 10.
15L. Enter station 11.
16L. Exit station 14.
17L. Angle, enter the first
    section at station 13.
12R. Exit station 9.
13R. Angle and enter the
    second section at station
    number 8.
14R. Exit station 11.
15R. Enter station 12.
16R. Exit station 14.
17R. Angle and enter the
    third section at station
    number 13.
18L. Exit station 15.
19L. Angle and enter the
    second section at station
    number 14.
20L. Exit station 11.
21L. Span and enter the first
    section at station 11.
22L. Proceed on the inside
    to station 13. Tie-off with
    a half hitch.
18R. Exit station 15.
19R. Angle and enter the
    second section at station
    number 14.
20R. Exit station 11.
21R. Span and enter the
    third section at station
    number 11.
22R. Proceed on the inside
    to station 13. Tie-off with
    a half hitch.

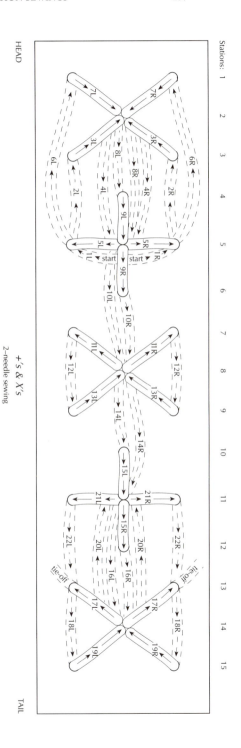

CONTIGUOUS *X's* (for an even number of *X's*)

To sew Contiguous *X's* for an odd number of *X's*, see page 242.

Sewing Stations: First and third sections pierce the odd-numbered stations. The middle section pierces the even-numbered stations. If your design needs an odd number of *X's*, it must be sewn as described on page 242 (see the diagram on page 206 to start this 2–needle sewing).

SEWING PROCEDURE

1L. Set aside the cover. Enter the first section from the mountain peak to the valley at station 3 of the section, only.

1R. Enter the third section from the mountain peak at station 3 of the section, only. Place sections almost tangent. Divide the thread.

2L. Set on the cover. Exit station 1 of the section and the cover.

2R. Exit station 1 of the section and the cover.

3L. Set on the second section. Angle, enter the second section at station 2.

4L. Exit station 4.

5L. Angle and enter the first section at station 3.

3R. Angle and enter the second section at station 2.

4R. Exit station 4.

5R. Angle and enter the third section at station 3.

6L. Exit station 5.

7L. Angle and enter the second section at station 4.

8L. Exit station 2.

9L. Angle and enter the first section at station 3.

6R. Exit station 5.

7R. Angle and enter the second section at station 4.

8R. Exit station 2.

9R. Angle and enter the third section at station 3.

10L. Exit station 5.

11L. Angle and enter the second section at station 6.

12L. Exit station 8.

13L. Angle and enter the first section at station 7.

HEAD   TAIL

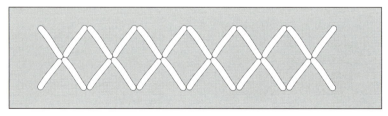

CONTIGUOUS *X's* for an even number of *X's*

10R. Exit station 5.

11R. Angle and enter the second
section at station 6.

12R. Exit station 8.

13R. Angle and enter the third section at station 7.

14L. Exit station 9

15L. Angle and enter the second section at station 8.

16L. Exit station 6.

17L. Angle and enter the first section
at station 7.

14R. Exit station 9.

15R. Angle and enter the second
section at station 8.

16R. Exit station 6.

17R. Angle and enter the third
section at station 7.

18L. Exit station 9.

19L. Angle, enter the second section at station 19.

20L. Exit station 12.

21L. Angle and enter the first
section at station 11.

18R. Exit station 9.

19R. Angle, enter the second
section at station 19.

20R. Exit station 12.

21R. Angle and enter the third
section at station 11.

22L. Exit station 13.

23L. Angle, enter the second section
at station 12.

24L. Exit station 10.

25L. Angle and enter the first section
at station 11. Tie-off with a half
hitch.

22R. Exit station 13.

23R. Angle, enter the second section
at station 12.

24R. Exit station 10.

25R. Angle and enter the third section at station 11. Tie-off with a
half hitch.

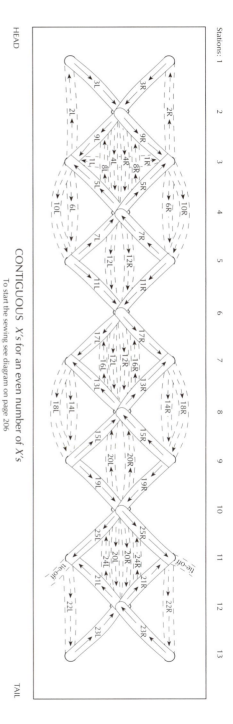

HEAD

CONTIGUOUS *X's* for an even number of *X's*

To start the sewing see diagram on page 206

TAIL

Stations: 1 2 3 4 5 6 7 8 9 10 11 12 13

ISOLATED *X's*

Sewing Stations: The first and third sections pierce stations 1, 3, 4, 6, 7, 9, 10, 12, 13, 15, 16 and 18. The middle section pierces stations 2, 5, 8, 11, 14 and 17.

SEWING PROCEDURE

This sewing *path* is identical to the previous sewing, Contiguous *X's*. However, the *stations* are numbered differently, since the isolated X's share no stations.

Of the 3–section sewings I have devised, the *X* Pattern is the most satisfying. I struggled to create an *X*. Attempts meandered with 56 steps without any sense of logic; a spine with six *X's* had no repeated steps.

The *X* Patterns described here have only eight steps yielding two *X's*. The eight steps are repeated for additional pairs of *X's*.

Previous attempts had stations for all three sections on the same horizontal, with a tendency to perforate. Staggering stations places more space between them. Designing an *X* pattern was resolved by threading both ends of the thread. It is less circuitous and makes the sewing easier to learn. I take pleasure in problem solving.

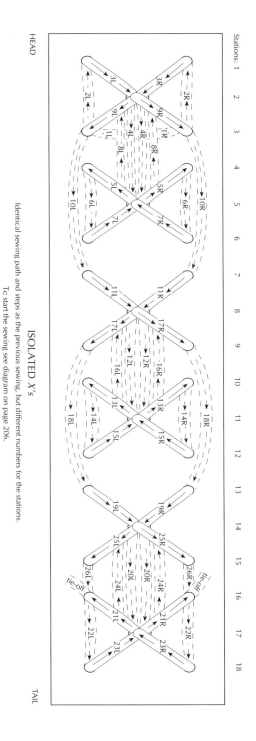

HEAD

Identical sewing path and steps as the previous sewing, but different numbers for the stations.

To start the sewing see diagram on page 206.

ISOLATED *X's*

TAIL

Stations: 1
2
3
4
5
6
7
8
9
10
11
12
13
14
15
16
17
18

ANGLE SEWINGS continued
The following pages will describe additional 3–section sewings which angle, spanning one and/or two sections, as well as containing straight stitches. This is a digital scan of the next X sewings:

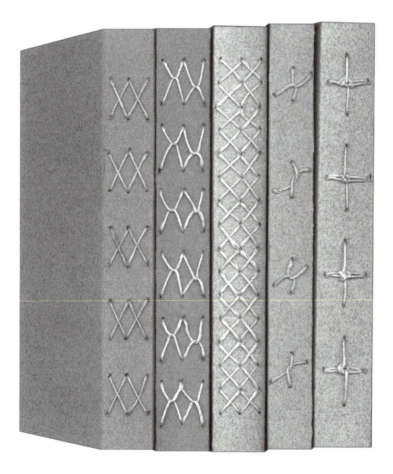

Prototypes of 3–section sewings with diagonal stitches. Left to right: DOS ESQUIS, described on page 244; HURRICANE FENCE, described on page 245; DIAMOND X, page 246; TWISTED X, page 248 and TIED CROSS, on page 250.

CONTIGUOUS X's (for an odd number of X's)

To sew Contiguous X's for an even number of X's, see pages 238. A photo of this sewing can be seen on page 231.

Sewing Stations: First and third sections pierce the odd-numbered stations. The middle section pierces the even-numbered stations.

SEWING PROCEDURE

1R. Set aside the cover. Exit the second section, only, at station 6.

2R. Proceed along the ridge of the mountain peak and enter station 4 of the section, only. Divide the length of thread.

3R. Set on the cover. Exit station 2 of the section and the cover.

4R. Set on the third section. Angle and enter the third section at station 1.

1L. Exit station 2 of the second section and the cover.

2L. Set on the first section. Angle and enter the first section at station 1.

3L. Exit station 3.

4L. Angle and enter the second section at station 2.

5L. Exit station 4.

6L. Angle and enter the first section at station 3.

5R. Exit station 3.

6R. Angle and enter the second section at station 2.

7R. Exit station 4.

8R. Angle and enter the third section at station 3.

7L. Exit station 5.

8L. Angle and enter the second section at station 4.

9L. Exit station 6.

10L. Angle and enter the first section at station 5.

9R. Exit station 5.

10R. Angle and enter the second section at station 4.

11R. Exit station 6.

12R. Angle and enter the third section at station 5.

11L. Exit station 7.

12L. Angle and enter the second section at station 6.

13L. Exit station 8.

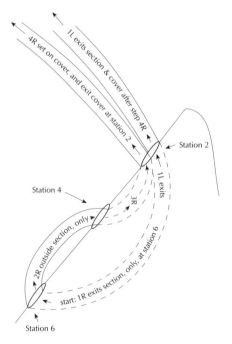

Start the sewing with the 2nd section prior to adding the cover

14L. Angle and enter
the first section at
station 7.

13R. Exit station 7.

14R. Angle and enter
the second section at
station 6.

15R. Exit station 8.

16R. Angle and enter
the third section at
station 7.

15L. Exit station 9.

16L. Angle and enter
the second section at
station 8.

17L. Exit station 10.

18L. Angle and enter
the first section at
station 9.

17R. Exit station 9.

18R. Angle and enter
the second section at
station 8.

19R. Exit station 10.

20R. Angle and enter
the third section at
station 9.

19L. Exit station 11.

20L. Angle and enter
the second section at
station 10.

21R. Exit station 11.

22R. Angle and enter
the second section at
station 10. Tie-off
with the left thread.

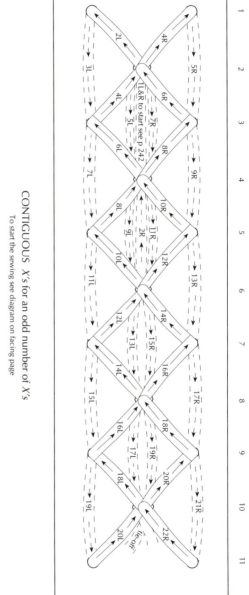

CONTIGUOUS *X's* for an odd number of *X's*

To start the sewing see diagram on facing page

DOS ESQUIS

This is a fine looking sewing which is also quick and easy. A photo of this sewing can be seen on page 241.

Sewing Stations: All three sections pierce all the stations.

SEWING PROCEDURE
This is a single needle sewing.

1. Exit the first section at station 1. Set on the second section.
2. Angle and enter the second section at station 2.
3. Exit station 1.
4. Set on the third section. Angle and enter the third section at station number 2.
5. Exit station 1.
6. Angle and enter the second section at station 2.
7. Exit station 1.
8. Angle and enter the first section at station 2. Tie-off.
9. Exit station 3.

Remaining Stations: Repeat the pattern of steps 2 through 8 to form each additional pair of *X's*. Repeat step 9 to continue to another pair. When the final *X* is sewn, enter the first section and tie-off with a half hitch.

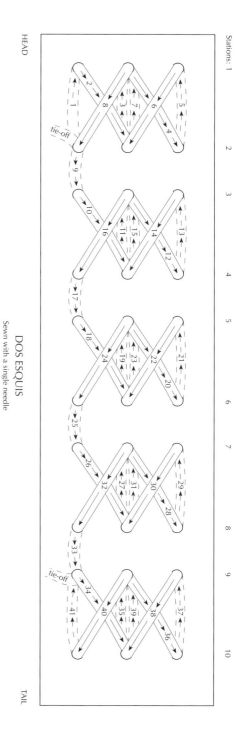

HEAD

DOS ESQUIS
Sewn with a single needle

TAIL

Stations: 1 2 3 4 5 6 7 8 9 10

HURRICANE FENCE

Sewing Stations: All three sections pierce all the stations.

SEWING PROCEDURE

This sewing is identical to the 2–section Linked *X,* described on page 88.

First, sew a column of the linked *X's* using the first and second sections.

Then, make a separate sewing, using the second and third sections.

A photo of this sewing is on page 241.

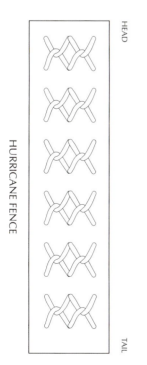

DIAMOND *X*

The Diamond *X* appears to have many more stations than in fact it does. It is an interestingly textured spine. A photo of this sewing is on page 241.

Sewing Stations: All three sections pierce all the stations.

SEWING PROCEDURE

FIRST SET of FOUR X's:

1. Start on the inside of the first section. Exit station 1.
2. Set on the second section. Angle, enter the second section at station 2.
3. Exit station 1.
4. Set on the third section. Angle and enter the third section at station 2.
5. Exit station 1.
6. Angle and enter the second section at station 2.
7. Exit station 1.
8. Angle and enter the first section at station 2. Tie-off.
9. Exit station 3.
10. Angle, enter the second section at station 2.
11. Exit station 3.
12. Angle and enter the third section at station 2.
13. Exit station 3.
14. Angle and enter the second section at station 2.
15. Exit station 3.
16. Angle and enter the first section at station 2.
17. Exit station 3. This ends the pattern. Repeat the pattern:

NEXT SET of FOUR X's:

18. Angle and enter the second section at the next numbered station.
19. Retreat one station and exit.
20. Angle and enter the third section at the next numbered station.
21. Retreat one station and exit.
22. Angle and enter the second section at the next numbered station.
23. Retreat one station and exit.
24. Angle and enter the first section at the next numbered station.
25. Advance one station and exit.
26. Angle and enter the second section at the previous numbered station.
27. Advance one station and exit.
28. Angle and enter the third section at the previous numbered station.
29. Advance one station and exit.
30. Angle and enter the second section at the previous numbered station.
31. Advance one station and exit.
32. Angle and enter the first section at the previous numbered station.
33. Advance one station and exit.

Remaining Stations: Repeat steps 18 through 32 to form each additional set of four *X's.*

Repeat step 33 to proceed to the next set of *X's.* When the final set is completed, tie-off inside the first section with a half hitch.

NOTE: Upon entering with step 10, you can loop around thread 7 before proceeding with step 11. Entering with step 14, loop around thread 3 before proceeding with step 15. Locking at each station will strengthen the sewing.

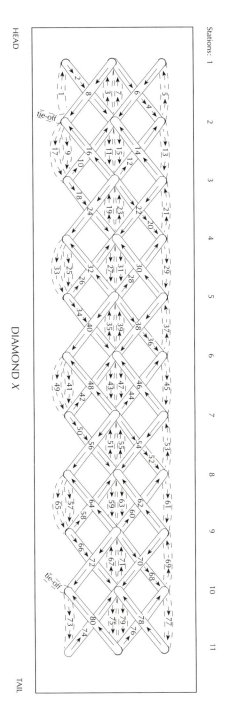

DIAMOND X

DIAMOND X

3–SECTION TWISTED *X*

The 3–section Twisted *X* is similar to the 2–section Twisted *X*, as illustrated on page 84. This version permits a different angle by use of three sections. The pattern is exaggerated by alternating the pattern. A photo of this sewing can be seen on page 241.

Sewing Stations: The second section pierces stations 1, 3, 4, 6, 7, 9, 10 and 12. The first and third sections to pierce stations 2, 5, 8 and 11. This makes the *X* at a right angle. I prefer an oblique *X,* so I pierce the stations in the third section slightly higher than center. The first section is pierced slightly below where they would have been for a right angle.

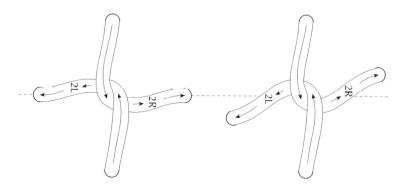

On the left, sewing stations for the first and third sections are horizontally lined up. This makes the stitch approximately at a right angle to the vertical member.
At the right is an oblique *X* by slightly lowering the stations for the first section, and raising for the third. This is more dynamic, and, by alternating (flipping) every other *X,* the result is more lyrical (see drawing on the next page).

SEWING PROCEDURE
NOTE: In this sewing, sometimes the left needle will enter the first section, and at others, it will be used to sew the third. The same is true with the right needle.

The start of this 2–needle sewing is simple.

1L. Exit the second section and the cover at station 3.

1R.Exit the second section and the cover at station 1. Divide the length of thread.

2L. Set on the first section. Enter the first section at station 2. Allow a slight slack in the thread on the spine.

2R.Set on the third section. Link under the (left) thread on the spine.

Enter the third section at station 2. Adjust the tension to form the *X*.

3R. Exit station 5.

4R. Enter the second section at station 6. Allow a slight slack in the thread on the spine.

3L. Exit station 5.

4L. Link under the thread (step 4R), and enter the second section at station 4. Carefully adjust the tension to form the *X*.

5R. Exit station 9.

6R. Enter the *first* section at station 8. Allow a slight slack in the thread on the spine.

5L. Exit station 7.

6L. Link under the thread (step 6R). Enter the *third* section at station 8. Carefully adjust the tension to form the *X*.

7L. Exit the third section at station 11.

8L. Enter the second section at station 12. Allow a slight slack in the thread on the spine.

7R. Exit the first section at station 11.

8R. Link under the thread (step 8L). Enter the second section at station 10. Adjust the tension to form the *X*.

9L. Proceed to station 10. Tie-off with the right thread with a square knot.

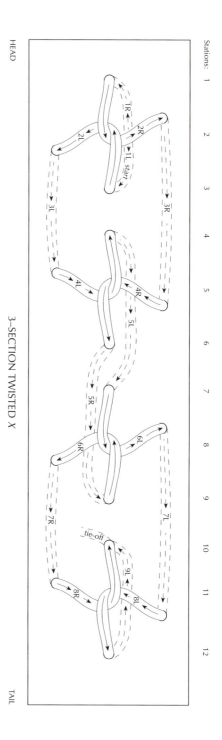

HEAD

3–SECTION TWISTED X

TAIL

Stations: 1 2 3 4 5 6 7 8 9 10 11 12

TIED CROSS

Tied Cross has two separate sewings. First, sew the first and third sections with a 2–needle sewing. This makes the double spans at each of the stations for those sections. Secondly, sew the middle section. This forms and ties the crosses. Variations on the second sewing yield a variety of Tied Crosses (see page 252). A photo of this sewing can be seen on page 241.

Sewing Stations: First and third sections pierce stations 2, 5, 8 and 11. The second section pierces stations 1, 3, 4, 6, 7, 9, 10 and 12.

SEWING PROCEDURE

The FIRST SEWING: To start this 2–needle sewing see the diagram on page 206.

1L. Set aside the cover. Enter the first section at station 5 of the section, only, from the mountain peak to the valley.

1R. Enter the third section at station 5 of the section, only, from the mountain peak to the valley. Divide the length of the thread.

2L. Set on the cover. Exit station 2 of the section and the cover.

3L. Span and enter the third section at station 2.

2R. Exit station 2 of the section and the cover.

3R. Span and enter the first section at station 2.

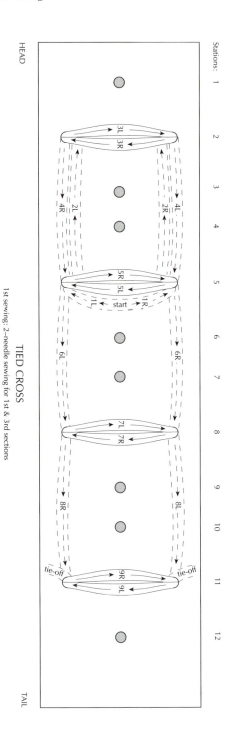

4R. Exit station 5 of the first
    section.
5R. Span and enter the third
    section at station 5.
4L. Exit station 5 of the third
    section.
5L. Span and enter the first
    section at station 5.

Remaining Stations: Continue
in this manner for the remaining stations for the first and
third sections. Tie-off on the
inside.

The SECOND SEWING: Set
on the second section.

1. Exit station 1.
2a. Lap and link under the
    first thread (3L).
2b. Lap both threads.
2c. Link under the second
    thread. Proceed to station
    3 and enter. Tie-off.
    NOTE: Other ties are
    illustrated on page 252.

3. Exit the next station.
4a. Lap and link the next
    thread.
4b. Lap both threads.
4c. Link under the second
    thread. Proceed to next
    station and enter.

Remaining Stations: Repeat
steps 3 and 4 for each additional cross to be tied. After
tying the final cross and
entering the section, tie-off
on the inside at the previous
station towards the head.

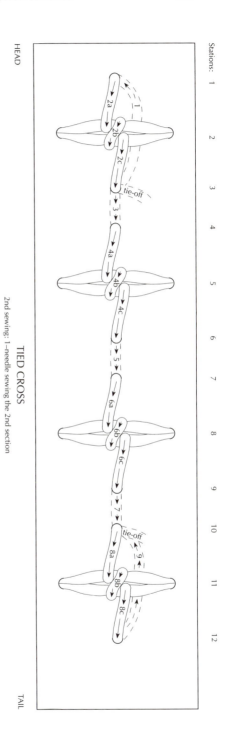

TIED CROSS

2nd sewing: 1–needle sewing the 2nd section

HEAD

TAIL

Stations: 1   2   3   4   5   6   7   8   9   10   11   12

VARIATIONS on the TIED CROSS: Each of the following are patterns you might consider for sewing the second section of the Tied Cross:

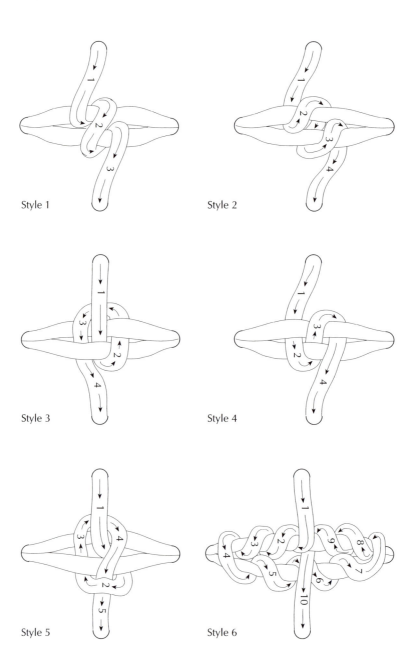

Style 1

Style 2

Style 3

Style 4

Style 5

Style 6

LINK SEWINGS

Link is a stitch, *chain* is a pattern. "Chain Stitch" is a misnomer. It is a *link stitch*. Linking forms a chain.

The following pages will describe additional 3–section sewings which drop, span or angle and link. This is a digital scan of the first six examples of the sewings:

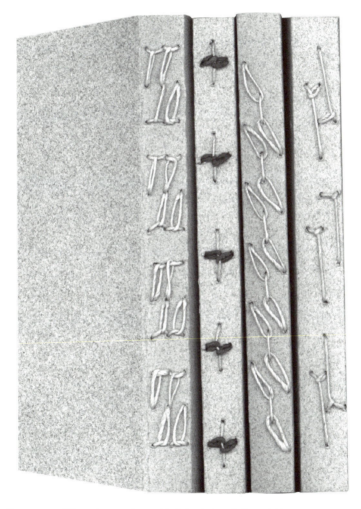

Prototypes of 3–section sewings with link stitches. Left to right:
BOW TIED, described on page 254; HORSESHOES, described on page 258;
LOOP THE LOOP, page 260; PINCHED *P's,* page 262; BOBBIN, on page 264
and SIDE BOW, described on page 268.

BOW TIED

The second section is sewn with a running stitch which provides anchors for the link stitches, which originate from the first and third sections.

Sewing Stations: All sections pierce all stations.

SEWING PROCEDURE

SEWING the FIRST and SECOND SECTIONS, HEAD to TAIL:

1. Exit station 1 of the second section. Set on the first section.
2. Span and enter the first section at station 1.
3. Exit station 2.
4. Angle and link under the thread near the second section. Enter station 2 of the first section.
5. Exit station 3.
6. Span, enter the second section at station 3.
7. Exit station 2.
8. Angle and link under the thread near the first section at station 3. Enter station 2 of the second section.
9. Exit station 4.

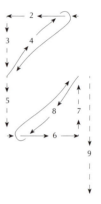

Sewing pattern for a double set of spans and links to the tail

Remaining Stations to the Tail: Form each succeeding double set of spans and links following steps 2-9. After forming the final link (step 24 in the diagram), exit the next station (9).

SEWING the SECOND and THIRD SECTIONS, TAIL to HEAD:

26. Set on the third section. Span and enter the third section at station 9.
27. Exit station 8.
28. Angle and link under the thread near the second section at station 9. Enter station 8 of the third section.
29. Exit station 7.
30. Span, enter the second section at station 7.
31. Exit station 8.
32. Angle and link under the thread near the third section at station 7. Enter station 8 of the second section.
33. Exit station 6.

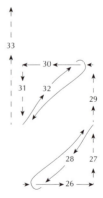

Sewing pattern for a double set of spans and links to the head

Remaining Stations to the Head: Form each succeeding double set of spans and links following steps 26 through 33. After forming the final link (step 48 in the diagram), Enter station 2 and tie-off.

See photo on page 253.

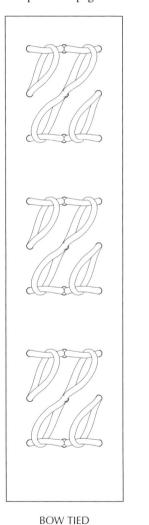

BOW TIED

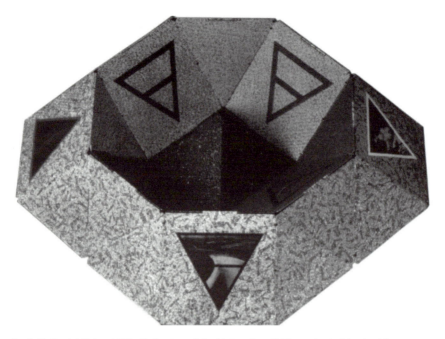

Earth III, Daniel Kelm, 1989. Collection of the University of Wisconsin, Kohler Art Library
9.5 X 48.2 X 48.2 cm.

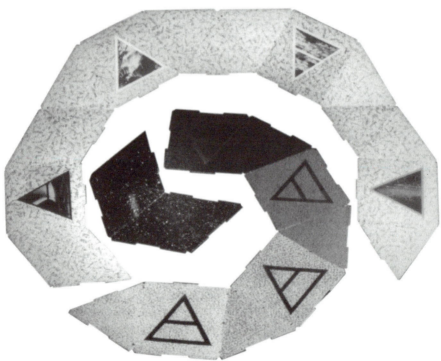

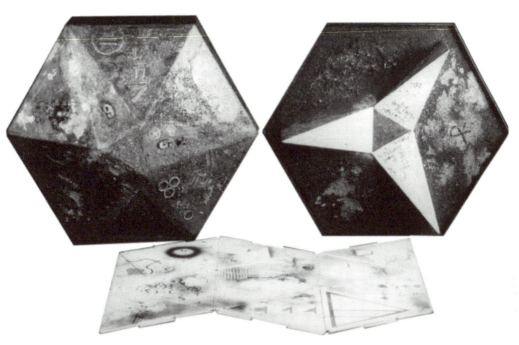

Rubeus, Timothy C. Ely. Binding by Daniel Kelm, 1990. Paper, stainless steel, linen, acrylics, sand and metal leaf. Collection of the artist. Box is 17.8 X 30.5 X 35.6 cm. Book, pinned together, is 14 X 25.4 X 27.9 cm.

HORSESHOES

The second section is sewn with a running stitch which provides the anchors for the links. The first and third sections are sewn separately with a 2–needle sewing. A photo of this sewing can be seen on page 253.

Sewing Stations: The second section pierces stations 1, 3, 4, 6, 7, 9, 10, 12, 13 and 15. The first and third sections pierce 2, 5, 8, 11 and 14.

SEWING PROCEDURE

FIRST SEWING:

1. Start inside the second section. Exit station 1.
2. Enter station 3. Tie-off.

3-11. Continue a running stitch to the tail. Exit station 4, enter 6, exit 7, enter 9, exit 10, enter 12. Proceed inside to station 10. Tie-off with a half hitch.

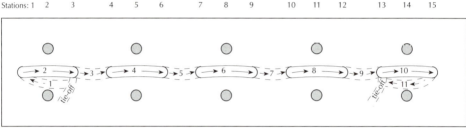

Stations: 1   2   3   4   5   6   7   8   9   10   11   12   13   14   15

HEAD   HORSESHOES   TAIL
1st sewing

SECOND SEWING:

The second sewing might be of a different color. To start this 2–needle sewing see the diagram on page 206:

1L. Enter the first section, only, at station 5 from the mountain peak to the valley. Divide the thread.

1R.Slip the right needle between the inside of the spine-cover and the second section. Enter the third section at station 5 of the section, only, from the mountain peak to the valley. Pull thread to the inside, so that the thread is evenly divided within the first and third sections.

2R.Exit station 3 of the third section and the cover.

2L. Exit station 3 of the first section and the cover.

3L. Link under the running stitch which extends from station 1 to 3 in the middle section. Re-enter the first section at station 2,

3R.Link under the running stitch which extends from station 1 to 3 in the middle section. Re-enter the third section at station 2,

4L. Exit the next station (5).

5L. Link under the running stitch and re-enter the first section.

4R. Exit next station (5).

5R. Link under the running stitch and re-enter the third section.

Remaining Stations: Repeat steps 3L, 4L 3R and 4R to form the links at each successive station.

For both the right and left needles, after completing the last link, upon re-entering the section, proceed one station towards the head. Tie-off with a half hitch.

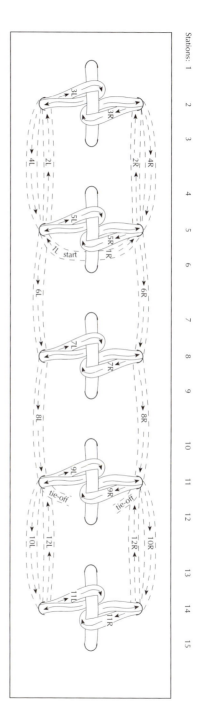

HORSESHOES
2nd sewing

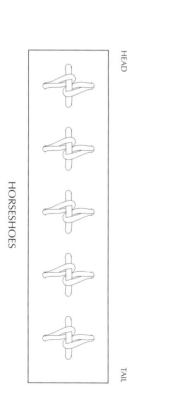

HORSESHOES

LOOP THE LOOP

A photo of this sewing can be seen on page 253.

Sewing Stations: The first section pierces all the odd-numbered stations, except 11. The second section pierces all stations, except station 1. In addition, the second section pierces station 12 for the section, only. This is for the change-over to section 3 on the inside of the spine-cover with step 12. The third section pierces all even-numbered stations, except station 2. In addition, pierce station 1 for the section, only. This is for the change-over to section 1 on the inside of the spine-cover with step 23.

SEWING PROCEDURE

1. Start inside the second section. Exit station 2.
2. Enter station 3. Tie-off.
3-10. Continue a running stitch to station 11. Enter station 11 with step 10.
11-12. Exit station 12 of the section, only. Proceed on the inside of the spine-cover towards the third section. Exit station 12 of the cover, only.
13. Angle and link under the running stitch at station 11. Set on the third section. Re-enter station 12 of the cover, and enter the third section to the inside.

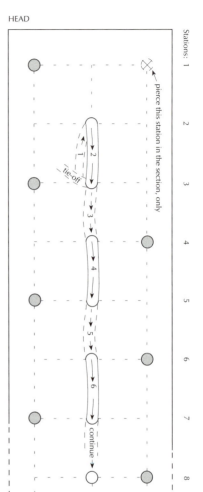

HEAD

LOOP THE LOOP
Starting the sewing and showing the grid for layout of the stations

LOOP THE LOOP

14. Proceed to station 10. Exit the section and cover.

15. Angle and link under the stitch at station 9. Re-enter the third section at station number 10.

16-21. Continue three more times proceeding two stations toward the head. Each time, exit, angle and link under the running stitch. Re-enter the station.

22. Upon re-entering station 4 with step 21, proceed to station 1. Exit the section, only.

23. Proceed on the inside of the spine-cover towards the first section. Exit station 1 of the cover, only.

24. Angle and link under the running stitch at station 2. Set on the first section. Re-enter station 1 of the cover, and enter the first section to the inside.

25. Exit station 3.

26. Angle and link under the stitch at station 4. Re-enter station 3 of the first section.

27- 32. Continue three more times proceeding two stations toward the tail. Each time, exit, angle and link under the running stitch. Re-enter the station.

Upon re-entering station 9 with step 32, tie-off with a half hitch.

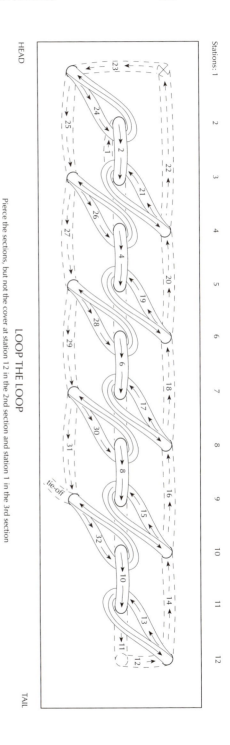

HEAD

Stations: 1 2 3 4 5 6 7 8 9 10 11 12

Pierce the sections, but not the cover at station 12 in the 2nd section and station 1 in the 3rd section

LOOP THE LOOP

tie-off

TAIL

PINCHED *P's*

HEAD

This is one sewing with a single needle. A photo of this sewing can be seen on page 253.

Sewing Stations: First section pierces stations 2, 6 and 10. In addition, the first section pierces station 1 for the section, only. The middle section pierces all stations, except for station 7. The third section pierces stations 3, 5, 7 and 11.

SEWING PROCEDURE

1. Exit the third section at station 3.
2. Set on the middle section. Enter the second section at station 1.
3. Exit station 3.
4. Angle and link under the diagonal thread. Re-enter station 3 in the middle section. Adjust the tension to form the desired angle for the diagonal thread.
5. Exit station 5.
6. Angle and enter the third section at station 7. Tie-off.
7. Exit station 5.
8. Angle and link under the diagonal thread (step 6). Re-enter station 5 in the third section. Adjust the tension.
9. Exit station 11.
10. Angle and enter the middle section at station 9.
11. Exit station 11.
12. Angle and link under the diagonal thread (step 10). Re-enter station 11 in the middle section. Adjust the tension.
13. Exit station 12.
14. Set on the first section. Angle and enter the first section at station 10.

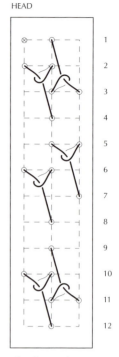

Sewing stations
View of the outside of
the spine-cover

HEAD   TAIL

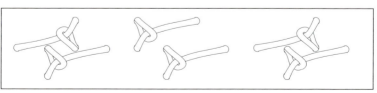

PINCHED *P's*

15. Exit station 6.
16. Angle and enter the middle section at station 8.
17. Exit station 10.
18. Angle and link under the diagonal thread (step 14). Re-enter station 10 in the middle section. Adjust the tension.
19. Exit station 6.
20. Angle and link under the diagonal thread (step 16). Re-enter station 6 in the middle section. Adjust the tension.
21. Exit station 4.
22. Angle and enter the first section at station 2.
23. Exit the section, only, at station 1.
24. Proceed inside the spine-cover. Enter the second section, only, at station 1 from the mountain peak to the inside of the section.
25. Exit the section and the cover at station 2.
26. Angle and link under the diagonal thread (step 22). Re-enter station 2 in the middle section. Adjust the tension. Tie-off on the inside with a half hitch.

NOTE: All the odd-numbered steps are straight line stitches inside the sections. Those inside the middle section appear curved in the diagram, only so that their path can be seen and followed easily.

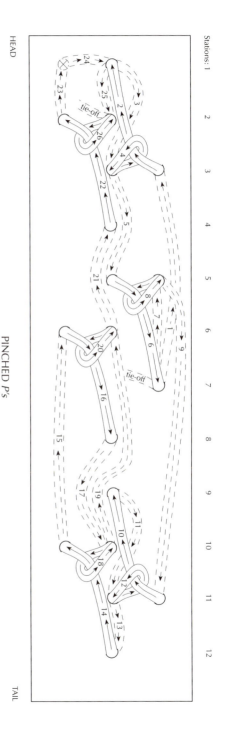

BOBBIN

The name I gave to this sewing sounds like the song of a bird. In attaching photographs and drawings to pages, I often use a sewing machine. I set the stitches to the maximum length so as not to perforate the paper. The bobbin is threaded with a different color of thread, and the tension loosened. This pulls the bobbin to the front surface. The result is a dotting of the color of the bobbin punctuating the stitches. The sewing machine stitches are used not only to attach, but the means of a linear "drawing". The concept of the dotting color on the surface by means of a bobbin inspired this sewing. A photo of this sewing can be seen on page 253.

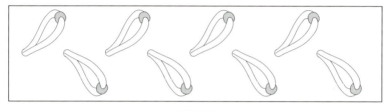

BOBBIN

Sewing Stations: First section pierces stations 3, 5, 7 and 9. The second section pierces the first eight stations. The third section pierces all the even-numbered stations.

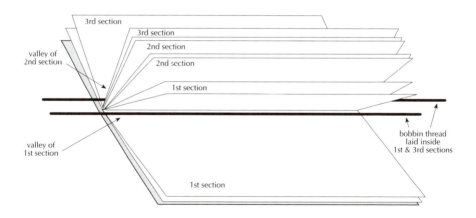

The bobbin thread is laid in the valley of the first and third sections after the stations have been pierced. Upon completing sewing the links on the spine, the ends of the bobbin thread inside each section can be tied to secure the sewing.

SEWING PROCEDURE

Much like a sewing machine, the bobbin thread must be in place prior to sewing with the needle. In this instance, cut a bobbin thread for the first and third sections approximately twice the height of the section. This will allow enough to tie-off later on.

Lay the bobbin thread in the valley of the middle of the first and third sections. Center the thread so there will be excess at each end to later tie-off.

1. Start on the inside of the middle section. Exit station 1.
2. Set on the third section, with the bobbin thread laid inside. Angle and enter station 2 of the third section. Link under the bobbin on the inside of the section. Exit station 2, applying enough tension to sightly pull the bobbin onto the outside of the spine-cover. Angle to the outside and enter the middle section at station 1.
3. Tie-off on the inside with a half hitch, then proceed to station 2. Exit.
4. Set on the first section. Angle and enter station 3 of the first section. Link under the bobbin on the inside of the section. Exit station 3, applying enough tension to sightly pull the bobbin onto the outside of the spine-cover. Angle to the outside and enter the middle section at station 2.
5. Exit station number 3.

Sewing procedure continued on the following page.

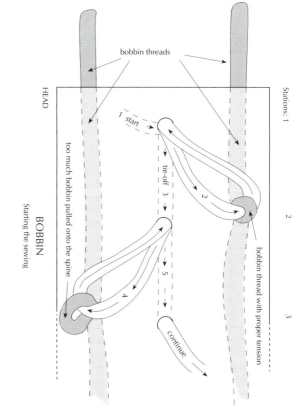

6. Angle, enter station 4 of the third section. Link under the bobbin on the inside of the section. Exit station 4, pulling slightly on the bobbin towards the tail to make sure the bobbin is taut on the inside of the third section between stations 2 and 4. On the outside of the spine, apply sufficient tension to sightly pull the bobbin onto the spine-cover. Angle to the outside and enter the middle section at station 3.

7. Exit station 4.

8. Angle, enter station 5 of the first section. Link under the bobbin on the inside of the section. Exit station 5, pulling slightly on the bobbin towards the tail to make sure the bobbin is taut on the inside of the first section between stations 3 and 5. On the outside of the spine, apply sufficient tension to sightly pull the bobbin onto the spine-cover. Angle to the outside and enter the middle section at station 4.

9. Exit station 5.

10. Angle, enter station 6 of the third section. Link under the bobbin. Exit station 6, pulling slightly on the bobbin towards the tail to make sure the bobbin is taut between stations number 4 and 6.

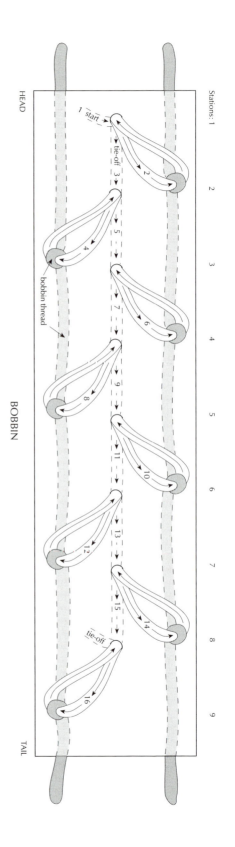

On the outside of the spine, apply sufficient tension to sightly pull the bobbin onto the spine-cover. Angle to the outside and enter the middle section at station 5.

Remaining Stations: Repeat steps 7-10 to form the remaining links. With step 16, upon re-entering the middle section at station 8, tie-off with a half hitch.

The bobbin threads inside the first and third sections will tend to hold in place. However, you can thread the bobbin with a needle in order to tie-off each end with a half hitch.

Gisela Reschke, four examples of the Langstitch und Kettenstitch, 1991.

SIDE BOW

Sewing Stations: All three sections pierce all ten stations. Photo of this sewing is on page 253.

SEWING PROCEDURE

1. Exit the third section at station 1.
2. Enter station 2. Tie-off.
3-10. Do a running stitch to the tail. Enter station 10 with step 10.
11. Exit station 9 of section, only.
12. Set on the middle section. Proceed on the inside of the spine-cover. Enter the second section, only, at station 9 from the mountain peak to the valley.
13. Exit the section and the cover at station 10.
14. Angle to the outside. Lap and link the thread (between stations 9 and 10). Enter the second section at the next station (9). Use just enough tension to slightly bow the running stitch.
15. Exit the next station (8).

Remaining Stations for the Second Section: Repeat steps 14 and 15 until entering station 1 with step 22.

23. Exit the second section, but not the cover, at station 2.
24. Set on the first section. Proceed along the inside of the spine-cover. Enter the first section at station 2 from the mountain peak to the valley.
25. Exit the first section and the cover at station 1.
26a. Angle to the outside and lap both threads marked as steps 2 and 22. Slip under both threads (2 and 22).

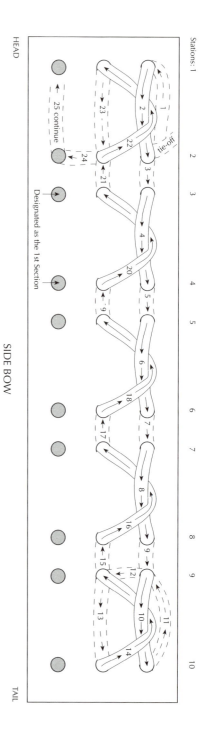

26b. Angle and enter station 2 of the first section. Use just enough tension so that the thread is taut, but not enough to distort the other two threads.

27. Exit station 3.

Remaining Stations for the Final Section: Repeat steps 26a, b, and 27 to form the remaining stitches until entering station 10 with step 34b.

35. Proceed inside the final section to station 9. Tie-off with a half hitch.

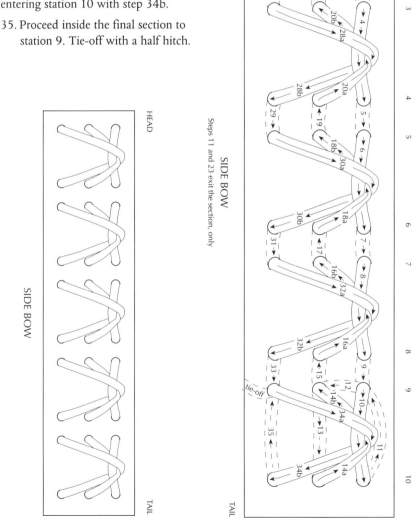

COILED LINE

Sewing Stations: The first section pierces stations 2, 5, 8 and 11. The second section pierces stations 1, 2, 4, 5, 6, 7, 8, 9, 11 and 12. The third section pierces stations 1, 3, 6, 7, 10 and 12.

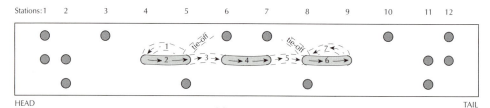

COILED LINE

1st sewing is a running stitch from station 4 to 9 for the 2nd section

SEWING PROCEDURE

FIRST SEWING:

The first sewing is a running stitch in the second section. It uses stations 4 through 9.

1-2. Start inside second section. Exit station 4. Enter station 5. Tie-off.

3.-7. Exit station 6. Enter 7, exit 8, enter 9. Tie-off at station 8.

SECOND SEWING:

The second sewing loops around the first, but not in a solid pack. This permits an equal amount of the first and second color to appear on the looped running stitch. Visually, it reminds me of the sewing Barber Pole, page 94, although the procedure is quite different. In the barber pole, both threads are twisted. Here, the first sewing is static or passive. The second has all the action in creating the pattern. I used a contrasting color thread for the second sewing to emphasize the alternating colors for the middle section.

COIL VARIATION (This version is not diagrammed)

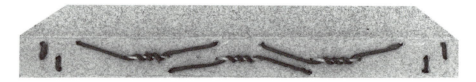

Example of the sewing referred to as COILED LINE

1. Start inside the third section. Exit station 1.
2. Span and enter station 1 of the second section.
3. Exit station 2.
4. Set on the first section. Span and enter station 2 of the first section.
5. Exit station 5.
6. Angle and slip under the thread at station 6 of the second section.
7. Loop, packing loosely clockwise to reveal and equal amount of the coil and the running stitch.
8. Angle and enter the first section at station 8.
9-10. Exit station 11. Span and enter station 11 of the second section.
11-12. Exit station 12. Span and enter the third section at station number 12.
13-14. Exit station 10. Angle and slip under the thread at station 9 of the second section.
15. Loop, counter-clockwise the same number of revolutions as in step 7.
16-17. Angle and enter the third section at station 7. Exit station 6.
18. Angle and slip under the thread at station 5 of the second section.
19. Loop, counter-clockwise the same number of revolutions as before.
20. Angle and enter the third section at station 3. Tie-off.

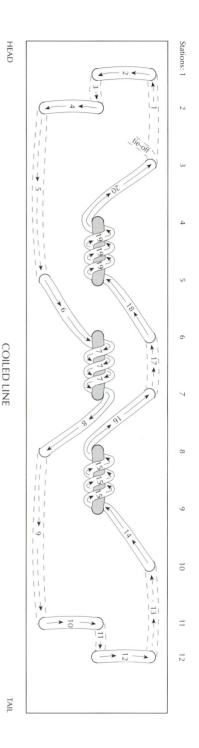

Above and below: *Found Poems,* Philip Gallo, The Hermetic Press, 1994. Letterpress, 23 pages, edition of 70. Distributed by Granary Books.

This "showcases Gallo's virtuoso typography and his quirky found and concrete poetry"—Granary Books flyer. Bound by Daniel Kelm, The Wide Awake Garage. 33.5 x 28 cm.

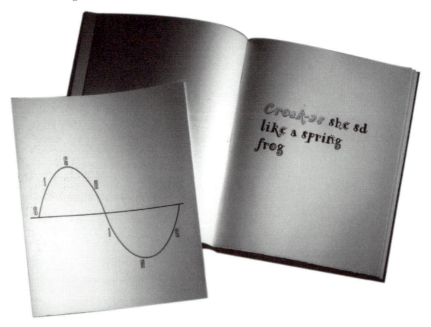

LINK SEWINGS

The following pages will describe additional 3–section sewings which drop, span or angle and link. This is a digital scan of the next three examples of link sewings:

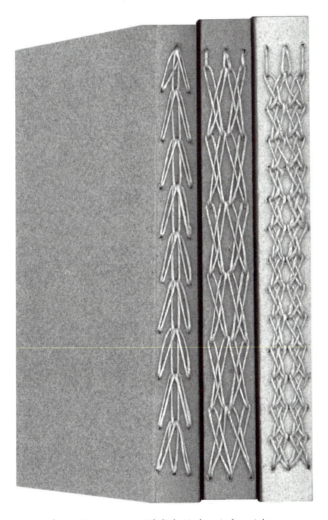

Prototypes of 3-section sewings with link stitches. Left to right:
TRIPLE CHAIN, described on page 274 and WOVEN CHAIN, page 279.

Another WOVEN CHAIN (not described) is shown on the far right. The sewing stations are closer together, giving a nice texture to the spine. This sewing is reproduced as the spine-cover for Volume II of *Non-Adhesive Binding*.

TRIPLE CHAIN

The Triple Chain, like Sewn Chains, page 42, is a *link stitch* sewing. The linking process creates a *chain effect*. There is no "chain stitch," as such.

To begin the Triple Chain, the second section is sewn head to tail, linking, forming a chain with a double anchor, which is to suggest the double thread of a link. The double anchor is shown as steps 2 and 4 in the diagram in the lower right. Also, see page 43. A photo of this sewing can be seen on page 273.

HEAD   TAIL

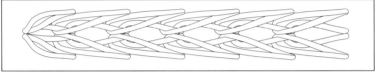

TRIPLE CHAIN

The first sewing continues, linking the first section from tail to head. Link to the closer thread in the chain of the second section (see page 276-7).

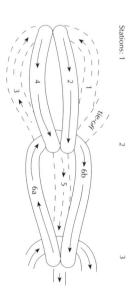

The third section is sewn separately from tail to head. Link to the closer thread of the chain of the middle section (see diagram on page 278). The two separate sewings each use a single needle.

Sewing Stations: The second section pierces all the stations. The first and third sections pierce all stations, except for the first.

SEWING PROCEDURE
FIRST SEWING:
1. Start inside the second section. Exit station 1.
2. Enter station 2. Tie-off.
3. Exit station 1 of second section.
4. Enter station 2 of the second section. This forms the double anchor.
5. Exit station 3 of second section.

Starting the TRIPLE CHAIN
with a single chain
Using a double anchor (steps 1-4)

6a. Reverse direction, link under the two threads at the previous station.

6b. Re-enter the station (3).

Remaining Stations: Repeat steps 5, 6a and 6b to form each additional link, until re-entering station 7 with step 14b.

15. Exit station 6 of the section, only.

16. Set on the first section. Enter the first section, but not the cover, at station 6 from the mountain peak to the valley.

17. Exit the first section and the cover at station number 7.

The written sewing procedure continues on the following page with the next diagram.

Description continues on the following page with a detailed illustration.

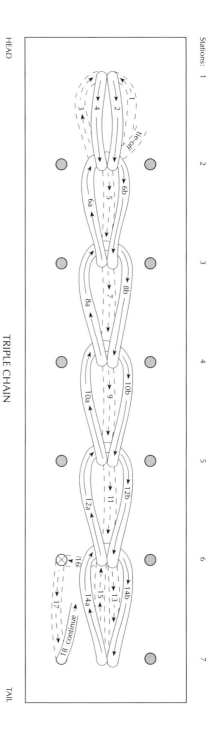

HEAD

Stations: 1   2   3   4   5   6   7

Continuing the sewing, step 15 exits the section, only

TRIPLE CHAIN

TAIL

The first sewing continues by attaching the first section from the tail to the head with link stitches.

18a. Angle towards station 6 of the middle section. Link under only one thread, labeled as step 12a.

18b. Re-enter station 7 of the first section.

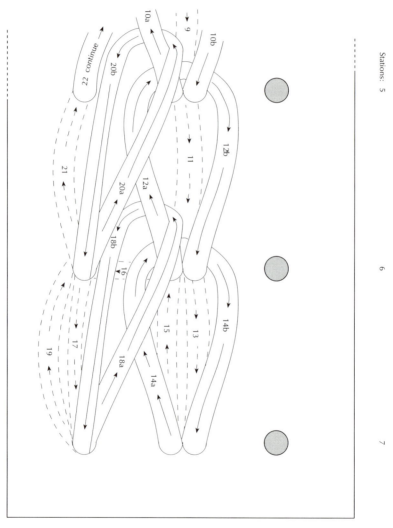

TRIPLE CHAIN
Sewing section 1

19. Exit the first section at
the next station towards
the head (6).

20a. Angle towards the
head to the next station
of the middle section.
Link under only the
thread closer to the first
section.

20b. Re-enter the previous
station of the first sec-
tion.

Remaining Stations:
Repeat steps 19, 20 a and
20b to form the links at
each successive station, until
re-entering station 3 with
step 26b.

27. Exit station 2.

28a. Angle and enter the
cover and second sec-
tion at station 1.

28b. Link under the thread
on the inside of the sec-
tion at station 1. Exit
station 1.

28c. Enter station 2 of the
first section. Tie-off on
the inside of the section
with a half hitch.

The second sewing is
described on the following
page.

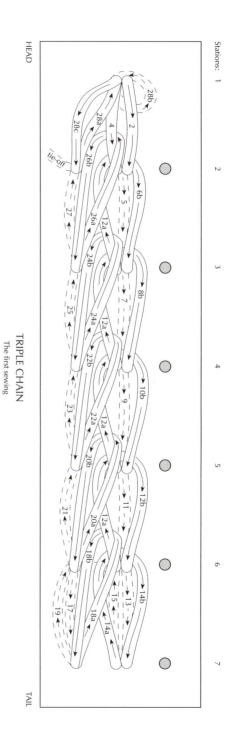

HEAD

TRIPLE CHAIN
The first sewing

TAIL

Stations: 1

2

3

4

5

6

7

SECOND SEWING:

The second sewing attaches the third section from tail to head. Link to the closer thread in the chain of the second section.

1a. Set on the third section. Exit station 7. Angle towards station 6 of the second section. Link under the thread closer to the third section.

1b. Re-enter station 7 of the first section. Tie-off.

2. Exit the next station (6).

3a. Angle towards the second section, to the next station towards the head. Link under the thread closer to the final section.

3b. Re-enter the previous station of the third section.

Remaining Stations: Repeat steps 2, 3a and 3b to form the links at each successive station, until re-entering the third section at station 3 with step 9b.

10. Exit station 2.

11a. Angle and enter the cover and second section at station 1.

11b. Link under the thread on the inside of the section at station 1. Exit station 1.

11c. Angle and enter station 2 of the third section. Tie-off on the inside with a half hitch.

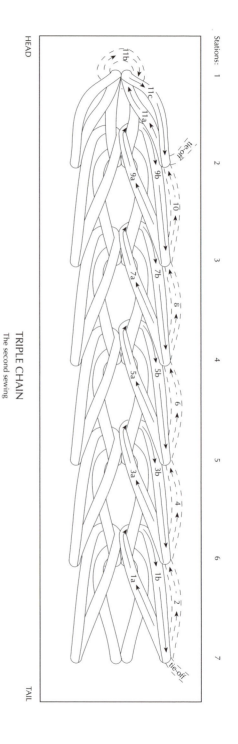

HEAD

TRIPLE CHAIN
The second sewing

TAIL

Stations: 1 2 3 4 5 6 7

WOVEN CHAIN

There are two separate sewings, each a 2–needle sewing. A photo of this sewing can be seen on page 273.

Sewing Stations: All three sections pierce all 8 stations.

SEWING PROCEDURE

FIRST SEWING:

To start this 2–needle sewing see the diagram on page 206:

1L. Enter the first section, only, at station 2 from the mountain peak to the valley. Divide the thread.

1R. Enter the second section at station 2 of the section, only, from the mountain peak to the valley. Pull thread to the inside, so that the thread is evenly divided within the first and third sections.

2L. Exit station 1 of the section and the cover.

2R. Exit station 1 of the section and the cover.

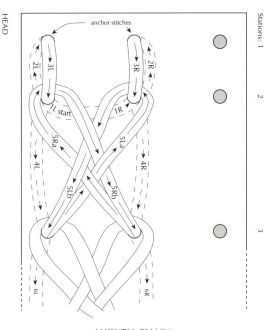

WOVEN CHAIN
Starting the first sewing using the
1st and 2nd sections

HEAD   TAIL

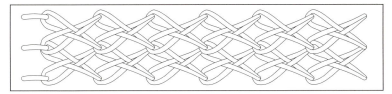

WOVEN CHAIN

3L. Enter station 2.

4L. Exit station 3.

3R.Enter station 2.

4R.Exit station 3.

5La. Angle to the outside. Link under the anchor stitch (3R) at station 2 of the second section.

5Lb. Re-enter station 3 of the first section.

5Ra. Angle to the outside towards station 2 of the first section. Lap thread 5La and slip under the thread marked as step 5Lb. Link anchor stitch, thread 3L at station 2 of the first section.

5Rb. Angle towards station 3 of the second section. Lap 5Lb. Slip under thread 5La. This forms a basket weave. Re-enter station 3 of the second section.

Remaining Stations:

Repeat steps 4L, 5La and b, 4R, 5Ra and b to form the links at each successive station. Starting with step 7, link under *both* threads (7R will link under 5Lb *and* 5La. Thread 7L will link under 5Rb and 5Ra).

Upon re-entering the first section at station 8 with step 15Lb, tie-off with a half hitch. Upon re-entering the second section at station 8 with step 15Rb, tie-off.

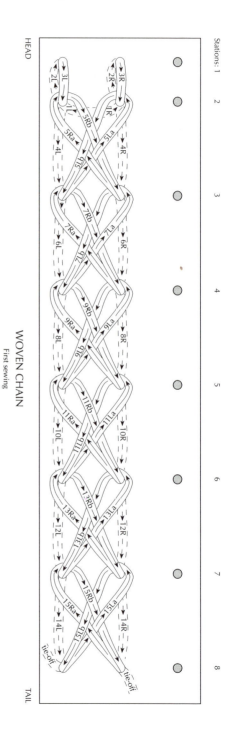

SECOND SEWING:

This time the left needle uses the stations of the second section. The right needle uses the third section (see diagram to the right).

The second sewing is identical to the first, except there is no need for an anchor for the second section—it already has one. Therefore, step 1L exits station 3 of the second section, to begin linking. All the step numbers for the left needle are different from the first sewing, but the linking process is the same.

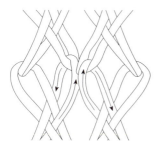

Linking under one thread, only

NOTE: A variation is to link under only one thread with the right needle in the first sewing, and one thread with the left in the second. This results in less bulky links at the second section (see detail above).

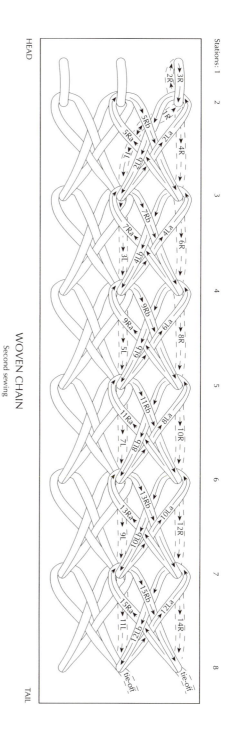

HEAD

WOVEN CHAIN
Second sewing

TAIL

Stations: 1   2   3   4   5   6   7   8

LINK SEWINGS

Link is a *stitch*. *Chain* is the resulting *pattern*, not a stitch. "Chain Stitch" is a misnomer.

The following pages will describe final 3–section sewings which drop, span or angle and link. This is a digital scan of these three examples of link sewings:

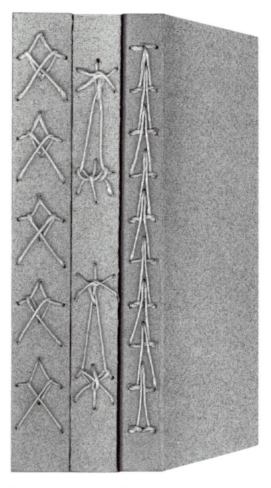

Prototypes of 3–section sewings with link stitches. Left to right:
LINKED STAR, described on page 283; BUTTERFLY STROKE, page 286; and
SHOOTING STAR, described on page 290.

LINKED STAR

Sewing Stations: The first and third sections pierce the even-numbered stations. The middle section pierces the odd-numbered stations. Position of the stations is the same as for Open Book, page 228. A photo of this sewing is on the facing page.

SEWING PROCEDURE

This is a 2–needle sewing. Steps are numbered as well as designated *L* for the path of the left needle, and *R* for the other.

1L. Set aside the cover. Exit the middle section at station 1 of the section, only. Divide the length of the thread.

2L. Proceed along the ridge of the mountain peak. Enter the section, only, at station 3.

3L. Set on the cover. Exit station 1 of the section and the cover.

1R. Link under the thread on the inside of the section, then exit station 1 of the section and the cover. This will lock the thread.

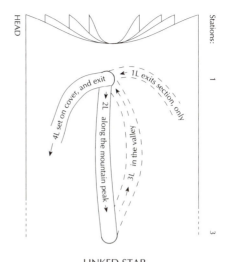

LINKED STAR

Start the sewing with the 2nd section without the cover
2L runs along the ridge of the peak

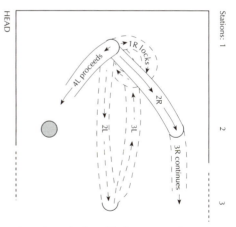

Locking the right thread before exiting the section and cover

HEAD   TAIL

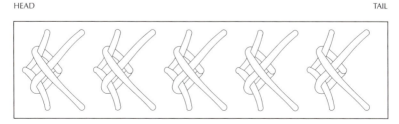

LINKED STAR

4L. Set on the first section. Angle forward. Enter the first section at station 2.

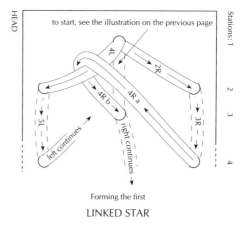

Forming the first
LINKED STAR

5L. Exit station 4.

2R. Set on the third section. Angle and enter the third section at station 2.

3R. Exit station 4.

4R. Angle backwards, lap the thread labeled as step 4L. Link under the thread. Angle forward and enter the second section at station 3.

6L. Angle backwards, lap the thread labeled 4R, as well as the thread 2R. Link under the thread labeled 2R. Angle forward, slip under thread 4R. Enter the second section at station 3.

5R. Exit station 5.

7L. Exit station 5.

8L. Angle forward. Enter the first section at station 6.

9L. Exit station 8.

6R. Angle forward. Enter the third section at station 6.

7R. Exit station 8.

8R. Angle backwards, lap the thread labeled as step 8L. Link under the thread. Angle forward and enter the second section at station 7.

10L. Angle backwards, lap the thread labeled 8R, as well as the thread 6R. Link under 6R. Angle forward, slip under 8R. Enter the second section at station 7.

9R. Exit station 9.

11L. Exit station 9.

12L. Angle forward. Enter the first section at station 10.

13L. Exit station 12.

10R. Angle forward. Enter the third section at station 10.

11R. Exit station 12.

12R. Angle backwards. Lap the thread labeled 12L, then link under the thread. Angle forward and enter the second section at station 11.

14L. Angle backwards, lap the thread labeled 12R, as well as the thread 10R. Link under 10R. Angle forward. Slip under 12R. Enter the second section at station 11.

13R. Exit station 13.

15L. Exit station 13.

16L. Angle forward. Enter the first section at station 14.

17L. Exit station 16.

14R. Angle forward. Enter the third section at station 14.

15R. Exit station 16.

16R. Angle backwards. Lap the thread labeled 16L, then link under the thread. Angle forward and enter the second section at station 15.

18L. Angle backwards. Lap the thread labeled 16R, as well as the thread 14R. Link under 14R. Angle forward. Slip under 16R. Enter the second section at station number 15.

17R. Exit station 17.

19L. Exit station 17.

20L. Angle forward. Enter the first section at station 18.

21L. Exit station 20.

18R. Angle forward. Enter the third section at station 18.

19R. Exit station 20.

20R. Angle backwards. Lap the thread labeled 20L, then link under the thread. Angle forward. Enter the second section at station 19.

22L. Angle backwards, lap the thread labeled 20R, as well as the thread 18R. Link under 18R. Angle forward. Slip under 20R. Enter the second section at station 19. Tie-off on the inside with a square knot with the other thread.

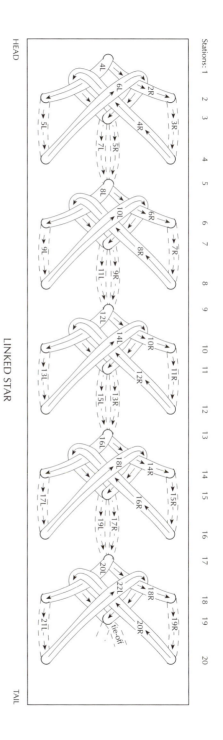

HEAD

LINKED STAR

TAIL

Stations: 1 2 3 4 5 6 7 8 9 10 11 12 13 14 15 16 17 18 19 20

BUTTERFLY STROKE

Butterfly Stroke is dedicated to Philip Lange, who taught me to swim at the age of 44. A photo of this sewing can be seen on page 282.

Originally I designed this sewing from the tail to the head. The thread would exit, link under the span, then angle. In re-formulating a new sewing path from the head to the tail, linking was eliminated.

Sewing Stations: For each star unit, the first and third sections pierce stations 2, 4, 6 8, 10, and 11. The middle section pierces all 11 stations.

SEWING PROCEDURE

This is a 2–needle sewing. Steps are numbered as well as designated *L* for the path of the left needle, and *R* for the other needle.

1L. Set aside the cover. Exit the second section, only, at station 2. Divide the length of the thread.
2L. Proceed along the ridge of the mountain peak. Enter the section from the peak to the valley. Set on the cover.

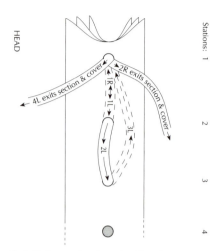

Start with the second section, only, without the cover. 2L runs along the mountain peak.

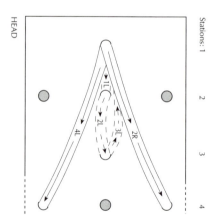

Add the cover. 2R and 4L exit the section and cover.

Beginning the BUTTERFLY STROKE

HEAD   TAIL

BUTTERFLY STROKE

3L. Exit station 1 of the section and the cover.

4L. Set on the first section. Angle, enter the first section at station 4.

1R. Exit station 1 of the section and cover.

2R. Set on the third section. Angle, enter third section at station 4.

5L. Exit station 2.

6L. Span and enter the middle section at station 2.

3R. Exit station 2.

4R. Span and enter the middle section at station 2.

7L. Exit the next station towards the tail (3).

8L. Angle, enter the first section 3 stations towards the tail (6).

9L. Exit two station towards the head (4).

10L. Span, enter middle section at the same-numbered station.

5R. Exit the next station towards the tail (3).

6R. Angle and enter the first section 3 stations towards the tail (station 6).

7R. Exit two station towards the head (4).

8R. Span, enter the middle section at the same-numbered station.

Remaining Stations: Repeat steps 7L through 10L and 5R through 8 R to form each additional unit. Upon spanning and entering the final station with the left and right threads, tie-off on the inside of the middle section with a square knot at station 10, or, add another span at station 11, as diagrammed.

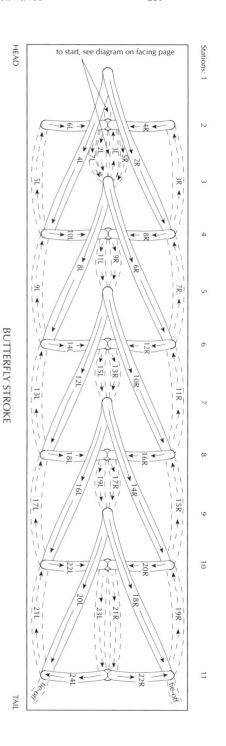

A Maze in Book, Suzanne Moore, 1991. Binding by Daniel Kelm. One-of-a-kind, dyed paper, paste paper, calligraphic drawing.

Private collection in Portland, Maine. Pages are 11.5 x 11.5 cm.

A Maze in Book, Suzanne Moore, 1991. Binding by Daniel Kelm.

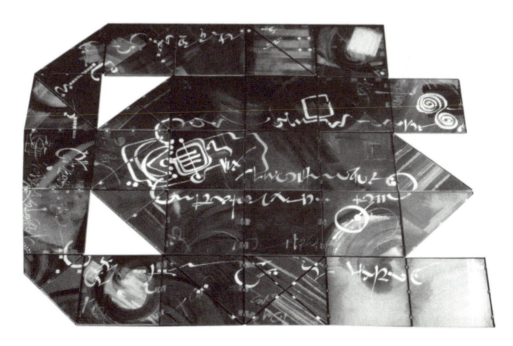

SHOOTING STAR

A photo of this sewing can be seen on page 282.

Sewing Stations: For each star unit, the first and third sections pierce stations 2, 3, 6 and 7. The middle section pierces stations 1, 4, 5 and 8. The first 4 stations form a hexagon, as do the next 4 stations.

SEWING PROCEDURE

This is a 2–needle sewing. Steps are numbered as well as designated *L* for the path of the left needle, and *R* for the other needle.

1R. Exit the middle section and cover at station 1. Divide the length of the thread.

1L. Exit station 4.

2L. Set on the first section. Angle backwards over the thread labeled step 1R. Enter the first section at station 2.

3L. Exit station 3.

2R. Link under thread 2L. Set on the third section. Angle and enter the third section at station 2. Adjust the tension to center the intersecting threads.

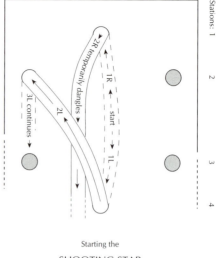

Starting the
SHOOTING STAR

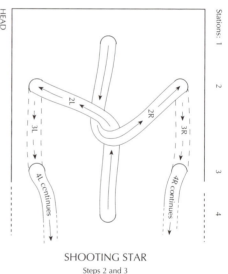

SHOOTING STAR
Steps 2 and 3

HEAD   TAIL

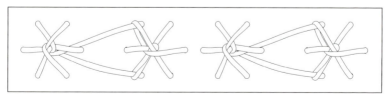

SHOOTING STAR

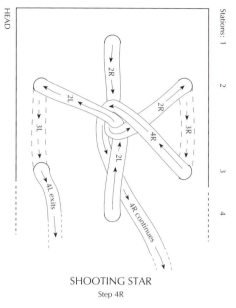

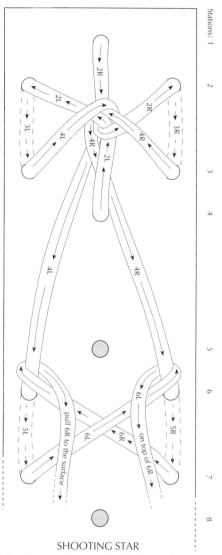

SHOOTING STAR
Step 4R

3R. Exit station 3.

4R. Angle backwards. Lap the intersecting threads. Link under the
two legs of the X which point to
10 o'clock. Continue under the
legs which point to 4:30 on the
clock. Angle forwards. Enter the
third section at station 6.

5R. Exit station 7.

4L. Angle backwards. Lap the intersecting threads. Link under the
two legs of the X which point to
2 o'clock. Continue under the
legs which point to 10:30, as
well as under the right thread.
Angle forwards. Enter the first
section at station 6.

5L. Exit station 7.

SHOOTING STAR
Step 6R angles to the outer side and links. 6L angles to
the outer side and links. Then ,pull 6R on top of the X
formed by 6R and 6L

6R. Angle backwards to the outer side, beyond the thread labeled 4L. Link
under 4L, and lap 6R.

6L. Angle backwards, under the dangling 6R, and over the stitch 6R, to
the outer side, beyond the thread labeled 4R. Link under 4R, and lap
6L and 6R.

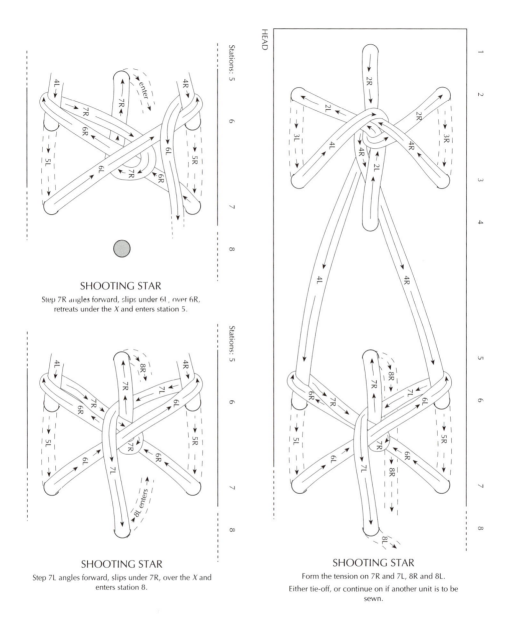

SHOOTING STAR

Step 7R angles forward, slips under 6L, over 6R, retreats under the X and enters station 5.

SHOOTING STAR

Step 7L angles forward, slips under 7R, over the X and enters station 8.

SHOOTING STAR

Form the tension on 7R and 7L, 8R and 8L. Either tie-off, or continue on if another unit is to be sewn.

Before step 7, make sure the dangling threads of 6R and 6L are out in front of the X formed by the stitches 6R and 6L.

7R. Angle forward, slips under 6L, then laps 6R, as you link under the intersection of the X. Adjust the tension. Enter station 5.

7L. Angle backwards over all threads to the outer side. Link under 4R.

Angle, slip under 7R at 10 o'clock. Enter station 8.

This completes one unit of the Shooting Star.

Remaining Stations: Form as many units of the Shooting Star as desired. To get to the next set of sewing stations, the right thread exits the middle section at station 9. This will be step 8R.

8L. Exit the middle section at station 12.

Repeat steps 2L through 7L and 2R through 7R to form the next unit. After completing the final unit, tie-off the two threads inside the middle section with a square knot.

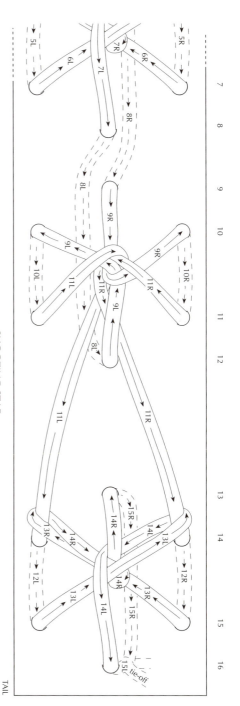

SHOOTING STAR

Repeat steps 1-8 for each shooting star.
After the final unit, tie-off on the inside with a square knot.

SPINE BRAID

Sewing three sections offers the possibility of braiding as part of the structure and design. You might follow up the possibilities. I will offer one. I
chose to double the threads. This gives a thicker braid. Secondly, it deco-
rates the head and the tail, reminiscent of endbands.

Sewing Stations: All three sections pierce all 10 stations.

Stations: 1   2   3   4   5   6   7   8   9   10

HEAD   Sewing stations for the SPINE BRAID   TAIL

SEWING PROCEDURE

A separate thread sews each section, with a needle at
both ends, for a total of three threads and six needles. Since the sewing wraps around the head and
the tail, the sections must be the exact height of the
paper cover, so that the thread will not crimp a taller
cover.

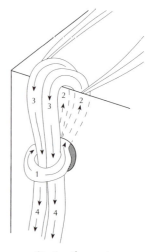

1. Start section 1 at the head. Enter station 1 from
    the outside of the spine to the inside of the sec-
    tion with both needles. Pull until a small loop of
    thread remains on the spine.
2. Both needles proceed on the inside to the head.
3. Wrap around the head to the spine.
4. Slip both needles through the loop at station 1.
    Pull to tighten. Start separate sewings for second
    and third sections, following the same procedure.

Starting the sewing

Prototype sewing for the SPINE BRAID

Grasp all three sets of threads on the spine, and braid them until you approach stations 2 and 3. With one set of threads, enter the first section, one thread entering station 2, the other, into station 3. Take another set of threads and enter stations 2 and 3 of the second section. The remaining set of threads on the spine enters the third section at the same stations. It does not matter if the sets originated with the same section as they now enter. Whichever direction to which the threads point in the process of braiding will determine which section is more directly entered. If you start with a different color thread for each section, you may wish to keep the same color always in the same section. If so, control the number and tightness of the twists in the braiding so that as you approach the stations to enter, you will be lined up properly.

5. Exit station 4 in each section with one of the threads. Exit station 5 with the other.

6-8. Repeat steps 4 and 5 to finish the braiding.

9. After the final braid, do not enter, but proceed to the tail with each set of threads.

10. Wrap around the tail to the inside of each section. With one needle, exit each section at station 10.

11 Loop the set of threads and re-enter station 10 into the same section. Step 11 forms a horizontal bead, similar to the initial loop at the head. Tie-off on the inside.

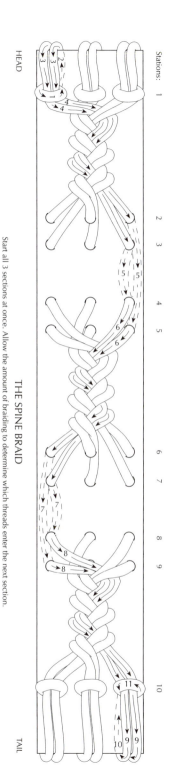

Start all 3 sections at once. Allow the amount of braiding to determine which threads enter the next section. (Threads starting in the first section may end up in the third section.)

THE SPINE BRAID

HEAD

TAIL

Stations: 1   2   3   4   5   6   7   8   9   10

THE COIL SPRING

Packing supports is a major part of the sewings in Volume III of *Non-Adhesive Binding,* sub-titled *Exposed Spine Sewings.* In that volume, it is generally cords which are packed. In this final sewing of Volume II, the support which is packed is the thread down the center of the spine, created by the first sewing, a running stitch.

After sewing the second section as a running stitch, a separate sewing starts in the first section, packs the running stitch to form the "coils", then enters the third section.

Sewing Stations: The second section pierces all 10 stations. The first section pierces stations 1, 4, 5, 8 and 9. The third section pierces stations 2, 3, 6, 7 and 10.

SEWING PROCEDURE

FIRST SEWING:

1. Start inside the second section. Exit station 1.
2. Enter station 2. Tie-off.
3-11. Continue a running stitch to the tail. Exit station 3, enter 4, exit 5, enter 6, exit 7, enter 8, exit 9 and enter 10. Proceed inside to station 9. Tie-off with a half hitch.

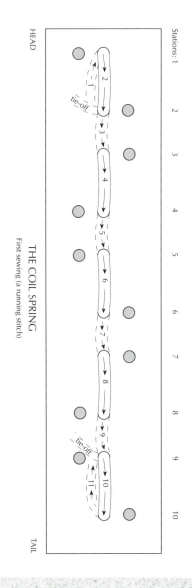

Prototype of THE COIL SPRING

SECOND SEWING:

The second sewing might be of a different color.

1. Start inside the first section. Exit station 1.
2. Span to station 1 of the second section. Slip under the running stitch.
3. Pack tightly, clockwise to the end of the running stitch.
4. Set on the third section. Proceed from under the running stitch, span, and enter station 2 of the third section.
5. Exit station 3.
6. Span to station 3 of the second section. Slip under the running stitch.
7. Pack tightly, counter-clockwise to the end of the running stitch.
8. Proceed from under the running stitch, span, and enter station 4 of the first section. Tie-off on the inside at station 4 with the dangling thread.
9. Exit station 5.
10-16. Repeat steps 2 through 8, entering the first section at station 8 with step 16.
17-20. Repeat steps 9 through 12, entering the third section at station 10 with step 20.
21. Proceed on the inside to station 7. Tie-off.

THE COIL SPRING
Second sewing

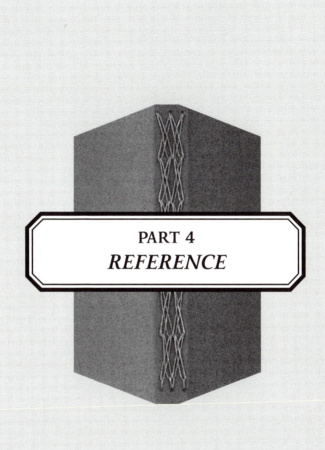

PART 4
REFERENCE

CONCLUSION

The most difficult task in writing Volume II is the Conclusion. This is because there isn't any.

Parts of Volumes II and III were started in March 1993, as a single book. As I evolved the sewings, I found it was too thick to be published as a paperback. I had to split the project in half.

The first half was easy to determine. All the continuous support sewings on limp paper covers made a nice size book. Actually, the same number of pages as in Volume I. These sewings became Volume II, and the title was changed to fit: *1– 2– & 3–Section Sewings.*

The remainder of the project was continued, and became Volume III. I worked back and forth on these two volumes, so there was not a serial progression from one to the other—therefore, this book did not conclude, but both volumes ended simultaneously. There was need for only one Conclusion, and it comes at the end of Volume III.

Generally, I love writing Conclusions. It allows me to sum up several thousand hours of work. I have logged over 7,000 hours on my computer for these two volumes. It has not been work, but a joy.

I wake up each morning, jump out of bed so that I can begin. Averaging ten hours a day, seven days a week, I must again say thank you to my partner, Scott McCarney, for his understanding.

Now, it is all coming to a close. It is not a sad thing, for I can look forward to how this all translates on the published page. It will look little differently than what I see on the computer, for even the photographs were scanned. But holding a book, turning pages, has an influence on *how* it is read, and, yes, even *what* is understood.

It is a comforting feeling to offer it to my reader. I hope that this book gives you even a fraction of the pleasure I have had constructing the sewing prototypes, then writing and drawing my descriptions directly on the computer, onto the formatted page. Even if I had not been able to publish, it would have been worth the effort.

Keith A. Smith
1 March 1995

GLOSSARY of TERMS

accordion pleat 1. Several parallel, alternating, and closely placed folds. Pleats are usually not pages, but an additional hinging device between the backbone and the attached folios or sections. Very often the pleat *is* the backbone, with separate side-covers, rather than a flat back. Pleats also expand the depth of the backbone to accommodate additions to the book block. 2. Also known as the *concertina fold.*

across 1. Perpendicular to the folds, cover to cover.† 2. Sewing which proceeds from section to section, generally in two or more separate sewings, using paired stations. Examples are Blanket Stitch with Slit Strap, 2–Needle Coptic Sewing and the Celtic Weave. Sewing across the spine is always more secure than sewing along the spine. If a thread breaks, only the sewing at those paired stations is affected. If the thread breaks sewing along the spine, the entire binding is compromised.

adhesive Generic for glue and paste. Glues used for binding remain pliable, and are used on the backs over the sewing of most bindings. Glue on the backbone may be a heat glue, made from animals. It is archival, in that it may be easily removed, but not in the sense it attracts insects which eat it. Another pliable glue is a poly-vinyl-acetate.Plastic based, it does not attract animals, but is not archival, inasmuch as it is not removable, and thwarts attempts at book restoration. Pastes are used to adhere leather to spines, paper to paper, and paper to boards. Wheat or rice paste are commonly used.

adhesive binding single leaf binding without sewing using a synthetic adhesive consolidation on the back.* Referred to as *perfect binding.*

against the grain Folding paper at right angles to the grain.

along Parallel to the folds, head to tail.†

angle To move diagonally.†

Asa-No-Ha Toji Japanese name for the stab binding also known as the Hemp-Leaf Binding.

back or backbone 1.The binding edge of a text prior to sewing or adhesive consolidation.* Note: The *back* differs from the *spine,* which is part of the cover which overlays this.

back saw Moulding saw or tenon saw used to cut the sewing stations when the book block is held in a finishing press.

backward (reverse) Counter to the direction of the sewing.†

bead 1. Top edge of the book (when viewing the book upright). 2. The little roll formed by the knot of an endband (see: *spine-bead* and *inside bead*).

beeswax Cake of wax purchased in a small block from a binder's supply. It is used for waxing all unwaxed thread, prior to sewing.

---

* *A VOCABULARY of TERMS for BOOK CONSERVATION PRACTICE,* by Gary Frost

† *"GLOSSARY of TERMS,* based on the work of Pamela Spitzmueller and Gary Frost," a handout in a workshop by Betsy Palmer Eldridge

blind A type of book (see: *venetian blind*).

blind embossing Stamping type into leather, without gold or foil.

board or **book board** A layered stock specifically for side-covers.

bodkin A sewing tool which is a type of awl. Unlike an awl which has a shaft which graduates in thickness, a bodkin has a thin metal shaft which remains constant in diameter except for narrowing at the point. It is similar to a *bradawl,* which is a carpenter's tool. An awl is inferior for piercing sewing stations, as it is difficult to obtain proper size of the opening in the paper. Choose a bradawl or bodkin which will give a hole slightly less than the diameter of the needle which will be used in the sewing.

book block or **text block** Total of the collated signatures, sections, folios, or sheets, constituting the body of a book.

book block pleat See: *concertina guard.*

booklet 1. A one-section binding. 2. A pamphlet. 3. A magazine.

bostrophedon A Germanic term meaning *as the ox plows.* In a single word, it graphically describes moving across a field, back and forth in a continuing *S* fashion. It is as if a page of text were read, the first line from left to right, the second from right to left, and continued in this alternating manner. This movement, and thus his term, describes the Scott McCarney binding. He also calls this the *snake format.*

bone or **bone folder** A flat, polished tool, made of bone or plastic. Paper is folded by hand to a temporary fold. The bone is used to score the fold to a permanent position, and to flatten the fold. This is done in a single stroke, as burnishing the paper will scar or make it shiny.

bradawl A straight shafted awl with chisel edge used to make holes for brads or screws. Like the bodkin, a bradawl is ideal for piercing sewing stations in paper in bookbinding. Either tool is superior to an awl for piercing sewing stations.

butterfly sewing An across the spine sewing which utilizes paired stations. Each needle spans, enters the next section, then cross inside to exit the other station. It is also called the Japanese 4–Needle Sewing, not to be confused with the stab binding called the Japanese 4–Hole Sewing. This 12th century binding is known as Yamato Toji.

catch-word In early printed books, the last word on a page was positioned at the foot. The same word was repeated at the top of the next page. Perhaps this served as a bridge in reading from page to page, but its purpose was a guide in collating signatures.

chain stitch "Chain stitch" is an embroidery term, not actually a stitch in bookbinding. In binding, the chain is a result of a succession of link stitches. *Link* is a stitch; *chain* is the resulting pattern.

to change over To continue sewing in the different section.†

clamshell A box for storing a book. It has a bottom and a lid, hinged to open like covers.

climb To move upward.†

codex (plural: **codices**) A book, bound along one edge. One of the four types of books, the others being the *fan, blind,* and *the fold book.* Note: Many binders do not agree with this definition.

compound binding A hybrid book structure of two of the same or differing *types of books.* There are 4 types of books: the fan, the blind, oriental fold book and the western codex. Creating a structure of two or more of these types of books is a compound binding. Examples: 1. Sewing sections onto an accordion pleat for a concertina binding. 2. Including a fold book as a unit, along with sewing sections into a single spine.

concertina 1. A type of binding, utilizing the concertina fold. 2. The concertina fold is also called an *accordion pleat.*

concertina guard A form of construction securing sections to folded stubs with a pamphlet sewing and, in turn, sewing the stubs together to form a text block.*

content Statement within the book of text and/or pictures. In a no-picture book, it is the cast shadows, cut shapes, holes, et cetera. Note: To avoid confusion in this text, *content* is never used to mean *satisfied.*

continuous support sewing Use of a single support, as opposed to sewing onto cords or tapes. The paperback sewings in Volume II of *Non-Adhesive Binding* are examples. It is important to reinforce the spine on the cover. Folding or pasting a second ply of paper in this area strengthens the sewing.

to continue on To continue sewing in the same section.†

cover stock or **cover weight** Heavy paper used for covers as opposed to text weight used for book blocks. Commercial printing papers generally come in both cover weight and text weight.

crease A fold induced by pressure marking or die debossing, not cutting. * Other binders refer to this procedure as a *score.*

creep The successive protrusion from the outermost folio to the innermost within a section or signature.

crossbar The wooden dowel held above and parallel to the base of the sewing frame by threaded posts. The crossbar is often slotted to accept threaded hooks.

curl The distortion of a sheet due to differences in structure, coatings, or moisture from one side to the other.

deckle In papermaking, the width of the wet sheet as it comes off the wire of a paper machine.

deckled-edge The untrimmed feathery edges of paper formed where the pulp flows against the deckle.

display Presentation of the object, generally through turning pages. Books with one-sided display, the fan, blind, and fold book might be displayed fully extended on a table, or wall displayed. Books with unusual formatting may be presented in the round as sculpture, the pages not meant to be turned. Note: To avoid confusion in this text, *display* is never used as a verb.

dos-à-dos A specific traditional format of two connected codices which have a back cover in common.

drop To move downward.†

duodecimo aka **12mo** A sheet folded down to create a section of 12 sheets, or 24 pages (see: *folio, quarto, sexto, octavo,* and *z fold*).

end paper In tradition binding, the sheet which is glued down on the inside of the cover board, extending across the gutter as the first page.

endsheets The first (and last) folio or section of a book may be blank and perhaps a nice laid paper in a particular color different from the bulk of the book block. Endsheets function as a mat surrounding a drawing. It is blank space to clear the mind before the introduction of the content of the opus.

enter To pass from the spine side to the fold side.†

exit To pass from the fold side to the spine side.†

F&G's (Folded and Gathered) The F&G's are the assembled signatures ready for sewing.

fan A book, bound at one point. One of the four types of books, the others being the *blind, codex,* and the *fold book.* Fans and blinds are used by South Sea Island cultures.

first section In the sewing procedures, the term first does not necessarily mean the beginning of the book. On the bench, you may very well start sewing from the back, towards the front of the book. In that instance, the "first" section to be sewn is the final section of the book.

flap An single extension on each side of the spine at the hinge-fold. The flap is usually one piece, crossing the spine, and included in the sewing. Covers are attach to the flap.

flatback cover Paper cover with two folds which delineate the spine from the side-covers. These folds create the hinging action of the cover, and are called *hinge-folds.*

flush cover 1. A cover whose front and back panels are the same dimensions as the pages. 2. In commercial binding, a cover that has been trimmed with the text block, so that cover and text block are the same size (see: *overhang cover*).

fold see: *accordion, hinge-fold, fold out, gate fold,* and *thrown out.*

fold book A book, whose binding is mechanical; the sheet is folded back and forth upon itself to create pages. One of the four types of books, the others being the *fan, blind,* and the *codex.*

fold-out See: *throw-out.*

folio aka **fo** A sheet folded in half to yield a section or signature of 4 pages, and two leaves (see: *quarto, sexto, octavo, duodecimo,* and *z-fold*).

foredge 1. The front edge of a book. (pronounced *forrej*). 2. The edge of the side-cover and book block opposite the spine.

format The size, style, type page, margins, page set-up, etc.

forward In the direction on the sewing.†

gate fold Two facing fold outs in a codex. Each fold out is hinged on the foredges of an opened folio. When the gate fold is opened, or thrown-out, there are four facing pages, the two at each extreme extend beyond the book block.

gathering Assembling the folded signatures into the proper order for binding (see: *F&G's*).

grain The direction in which most fibers lie which corresponds with the direction the paper is made in commercial production machinery. Note: To avoid confusion, this is the only definition of *grain* used in this text.

gutter 1. The blank space or inner margin, from printing area to binding. Note: To avoid confusion, this is the only definition of *gutter* used in this text.

head and **tail** The top and bottom of a book when stood upright. They are at right angles to the backbone and foredge. Note: Only definition of *head* or *tail* used in this text.

head band/tail band Wrapping and beading decorative thread, usually of colored silk or cotton, at the head and tail of codices. Thread is wrapped around a core and periodically stitched into the book block. "Imitation" machine-made head bands are sold by the yard and pasted onto the backbone of commercial hard cover books.

hinge-fold The folds on either side of the spine, delineating the side-covers from the spine-cover (see: *flatback cover*).

horizontal wrapper See: *wrapper*

implied compound binding A inventive folding of pages or itinerary through a book that suggests a hybrid book structure of two of the same or differing *types of books*.

imposition The laying out of pages on a sheet, so that they will be in numerical order after the sheet is folded down as a folio or section or signature.

inner Between paired sewing stations. The approach to a station which is towards the center of the spine, rather than to the outer, which is near the spine-hinge. Inner should not be confused with the term inside.

inside The position on the valley side of a section, as opposed to the mountain peak, which is called the outside.

to the inside Toward the head or tail.†

inside bead In sewing Endbands as Change-Over, the sewing procedure results in beads on both sides of the packing. The bead on the spine side is referred to as the *spine-bead*. The bead facing the foredge is called the *inside bead* (see: *Two-Sided Beading*, page 139, Volume III).

Japanese 4–Needle Sewing See: *butterfly sewing*.

jog To knock up and level to an edge, preferably at the head to keep text in registration.

Kangxi Binding Japanese name for the stab binding known as the Noble. This binding is also referred to as Koki.

kerf cuts made with a back saw across the section folds of an unsewn text. *

kettle stitch sewing procedure of ending one section, changing direction of movement in adding the next. The sewing drops backwards and links, slips and climbs.

key a 2-pronged metal unit, about the size of a key. A key for each cord rests under the slot in the base of a sewing frame temporarily tying the cord while the sewing proceeds.

Kikko Japanese name for the stab binding also known as the Tortoise-Shell Binding.

Koki Japanese name for the stab binding known as the Noble Binding. This binding is also referred to as Kangxi Binding, after its reputed originator.

lap To pass over a support or sewing thread.†

leaf 1. A sheet. 2. Two pages, back to back; a recto/verso.

link To pass under another thread.†

loop To circle around a support or sewing thread.†

moulding saw Backsaw or tenon saw used to cut the sewing stations when the book block is held in a finishing press.

octavo aka **8vo** A sheet folded in half three times, to yield a section or signature of 16 pages, with 8 leaves. A *sextodecimo,* or *16mo,* has 32 pages with 16 leaves (see: *folio, sexto, octavo, duodecimo* and *z-fold).*

one-of-a-kind A book conceived and executed as a single copy. I do not use the word *unique,* meaning "special" to define a single copy item, as the term applies to production work as well. Note: Some librarians define a book as an item which must have more than one copy. Consequently, they do not recognize or purchase one-of-a-kinds.

open ended Open ended stations refer to the use of the head and the tail as sewing stations. The support is not pierced. It is a *passive station,* that is, the thread wraps around the head or tail, marking the change-over.

opened folio The two facing pages at any point to which the codex is opened.

Oriental fold book See: *fold book.*

outer Towards the outside of paired sewing stations, rather than centrally, between. Outer should not be confused with the term outside.

outside The position on the mountain peak of a section, as opposed to the valley, which is called the inside.

to the outside Away from the head or tail.†

overhand knot Half a square knot. For instructions how to tie, see: *Knots,* page 50 in Volume I.

overhang cover A cover larger in size than the pages it encloses. The amount of the side-cover that extends beyond the book block, bordering the head, foredge and tail is called the *square.* (see: *flush cover).*

pack To loop several times around.†

page 1. One side of an unfolded sheet. 2.That portion of a folio or section or signature bordered by folds and/or the edge of the sheet.

paired stations Sewing directly across the spine employs two sewing stations. Other paired stations along the spine are sewn independently. Each paired station uses one thread and two needles.

pamphlet   1. A one-section text. 2. A booklet. 3. Type of sewing for a booklet.

pamphlet sewing   Type of sewing used to bind a booklet (see: page 57, Volume I, and, page 16, Volume II). The term *pamphlet stitch* should be avoided, as it is a sewing. *Pamphlet stitch sewing* is correct, but awkward. The pamphlet sewing is a *"b"* stitch, as opposed to a *figure 8* stitch (see: page 132-135, Volume II).

paste   See: *adhesive.*

perfect bound   1. Adhesive binding. 2. Binding of a book which has no sewing, and no folds on the backbone. The book therefore has no sections, signatures or folios, only a stack of sheets. The back is glued. Commercial paperbacks are generally (imperfectly) *perfect bound.* Thus, unfortunately there is a general low esteem for any book with paper covers. In the past, the main difference between trade books which were paperback and hard cover, was the latter was sewn. Now, many publishers are reducing the quality of their hard covers, and are using perfect binding, rather than sewing them.

pleat   An Oriental fold used to attach sections, rather than as a complete book in itself. Also known as a concertina, concertina guard, or accordion fold (see: *accordion pleat).*

ply   In this text, the term is used as one piece of paper, rather than the process of making paper in layers. *Two-ply* is only used in this text to mean a sheet folded back upon itself for reinforcement. This fold could optionally be sewn down. The term is never used to mean *duplex,* a type of commercially made paper with a different color on each side of the sheet.

production books   A book made in an edition, whether by hand, or published (printed).

punch   Metal cylindrical tool with sharpened hollow shaped end for cutting, and solid head for striking with a hammer to cut through paper. Shapes are usually various diameters of circles, and, rarely, squares, diamonds, oblongs.

quarto aka **4to**   A sheet folded in half twice, first against the grain, then with the grain, to yield a section or signature of 4 leaves, or 8 pages (see: *folio, sexto, octavo, duodecimo,* and *z-fold).*

ream   Five hundred sheets of paper.

recto/verso   Two pages, back to back; a leaf. *Recto* is a right hand page. *Verso* is the back of that leaf, not the page facing the recto in the opened folio. Note: Recto does not mean *front;* verso does not mean *back.* A recto or a verso is a front side when it is viewed. Each becomes a back when the page is turned, and it is not in view. Recto/verso is convenient terminology for folding and collating signatures.

saddle wire or **saddle stitch**   In commercial binding, to fasten a booklet by wiring it through the fold or the side of the single section. The machine is adjusted to the thickness of the opened section, and uses a spool of wire. It is looped through the section, cut and crimped, similar to stapling.

score   1. To indent with a bone folder. 2. A light surface cut made to facilitate folding or flexing in card or board (see: *crease).*

section   1. A sheet folded down to yield eight or more pages, such as an octavo, sexto, or duodecimo. 2. Two or more loose folios compiled. NOTE 1: To avoid confusion, *section* is never used to mean a *portion.* NOTE 2: If the sheet has been printed, then folded down, it is referred to in printers' terminology as a *signature.* Any signature can be called a section, but only a section which has been printed is technically a signature (see: *signature).*

self cover   A cover of the same paper as the text block.

sew a set   To sew one more than one section on at a time.†

sewing stations   1. The mark, or the pierce along the spine-fold of the cover, and the backbone of the section, or folio showing the positions of the sewing. 2. Path of the needle through paper to create the sewing on the spine. If made with a saw, they are called *kerf stations* (see: *sewn vs stitched).*

sewn vs **stitched**   Sewing refers to the thread path along the valley and mountain peak, as opposed to set in from the fold. That is *stabbing.* Stabbing is *stitching*, not sewing. Path of the needle limited to the gutter is not "stitching", but sewing. *Stitches* is appropriate to sewing in the fold, but *stitching* equals *stabbing.*

slip   To pass under itself.†

span   To climb and change over to another section.†

sexto aka **6to**   A sheet folded down to create a section of 6 leaves, or 12 pages. The sheet is first folded against the grain with a Z-fold, dividing the sheet into thirds. That is then folded in half with the grain (see: *folio, quarto, octavo, duodecimo,* and *z-fold).*

sheet   1. An unfolded piece of paper. 2. A leaf. 3. The full size of the paper before being folded down into a folio or section. 4. In single sheet bindings, a sheet is two pages back to back; a recto/verso.

side-cover   Front and back cover, as opposed to the spine.

signature   A specific type of a *section,* differing from the general term of section, in that a signature is a sheet that first has been printed, then folded to a section. *Signature* is a printer's term for the binder's word *section.*

simple/compound   Terms used only to differentiate basic bindings from hybrids constructed by combining two or more basic *types of books.*

slips   The ends of tapes, cords, or supporting straps that are attached to the covers.

slit   Slit is a severing with a knife. It has length, but no width (see: *slot).*

slot   A slot is an opening, constructed by two slits, parallel, and no more than about 1/8" apart. Slots, rather than slits, are needed to accommodate the thickness of the inserted photographs, or weaving a strap or flap, to help prevent buckling of the sheet.

Smythe-sewn   Commercial method of machine-*stitching* a book (see: *sewn vs stitched* in the Glossary).

spine or **spine-cover**   1. The depth of a bound book, connecting the two side-covers. The spine-covers the back, or backbone. 2. That part of the book that is visible when it is on the shelf. It is sometimes referred to as the *backstrip.*

spine-bead In sewing Endbands as Change-Over, the sewing procedure results in beads on both sides of the packing. The bead on the spine side is referred to as the *spine-bead*. The bead facing the foredge is called the *inside bead* (see: *Two-Sided Beading*, page 139, Volume III).

spine tab A strip woven onto the spine.

square or **square of the book** 1. The projection of the side-cover beyond the book block. 2. Only the part of the cover that extends beyond the book block and borders the head, foredge, and tail. (The total surface of the cover is referred to as an *overhang cover*.)

square knot Reef knot (see: *Knots*, page 50, Volume I for instructions how to tie).

a station 1. A place where the sewing stops to attach a section to other sections or to a common support or to both.† 2. *Passive sewing stations* is the use of the head and tail as change-over. This is referred to as *open ended*. In diagramming sewings with endbands as change-cover, I assign the support, usually cords, at the head and the tail a sewing station number. They are not pierced sewing stations, but *passive,* that is, *open ended*. This makes for easy reference in the drawn illustrations (see: *paired stations)*.

stitching See: *sewn vs stitched* in the Glossary.

strap Horizontal supports across the spine onto which supported sewings are made. The strap is usually separate from the cover, and attached after the sewing. In the Buttonhole binding, the straps are sections of the spine.

supported sewings Sections sewn together around common straps, tapes or cords, which go across the back, perpendicular to it. The supports are generally attached to side-covers.

swelling Thickness added to the backbone by the accumulation of sewing threads or any guards (see: *swelling the backbone*, page 47, Volume I and *expanding the spine pleat*, page 226 and 272, Volume I).

tab A narrow strip woven as means of attachment.

tail 1. The bottom edge of a book when standing upright. 2. The edge opposite the head, and perpendicular to the spine and foredge.

tapes Woven fabric supports, usually linen, onto which the sewing occurs. They are usually 1/4" wide, and always are non-adhesive.

tenon saw Moulding saw or backsaw used to cut the sewing stations when the book block is held in a finishing press.

tension Regulation of tautness. Uniform shape and tautness is desired. Betsy Palmer Eldridge says that the tension varies with each sewer. It varies even if one person stops for a break. It is best to start and sew the entire book at once. The operative word is snug. Tension should not be loose, but neither should it be tight. I find that men tend to sew too tightly. Link stitches lose their teardrop shape when pulled tightly.

text block See: *book block*.

throw-out A fold-out. The action of unfolding of a fold-out or throw-out is referred to as *thrown-out*. A throw-out might be a single fold, gate fold, or any other page which is larger than the book block, and folded down for storage. Traditionally refers to a fold-out at the end of a book containing a map. The map is *thrown-out*, so that it remains visible while any other page in the book can be read and turned.

types of books   There are four basic types of books, determined by how they are bound:

1. at one point is called a fan.
2. at two points is the venetian blind. The fan and blind are used by South Sea Island cultures.
3. across one edge, is the western codex.
4. alternate folds back and forth upon itself is the Oriental fold book. The other three types of books are sewn. The fold book's binding is mechanical.

unsupported sewings   Sections sewn directly together, without common straps, tapes or cords.

venetian blind   A book, bound at two points. One of the four types of books, the others being the *fan, codex,* and the *fold book.* Fans and blinds are used by South Sea Island cultures.

verso   See: *recto/verso.*

vertical wrapper   See: *wrapper.*

with the grain   Folding paper parallel to the grain of the paper.

wrapped stations   Head and tail of the sections used as sewing stations. Passive, as opposed to a pierced or slit stations. Open ended.

wrapper   Paper covering board covers without the use of adhesives (see *Flat Back with Boards,* page 244, Volume I and *Separately Wrapped Boards,* page 246, Volume I).

Yamato Toji   Japanese name for the 4–needle sewing, across the spine (see: *butterfly sewing).*

Yotsume Toji   Japanese name for the 4–hole stab binding.

Z-Fold   Procedure to create a 6, and a 12 page section. The sheet is first folded in thirds, against the grain (the Z-fold). Folding the Z-fold in half once, with the grain, gives a sexto. Folding the sexto in half with the grain gives 12 leaves, or 24 pages. It is called a duodecimo (see: *folio, quarto,sexto, octavo,* and *duodecimo).*

REFERENCE of PHOTOGRAPHIC ILLUSTRATIONS

PHOTO CREDITS

All digital scans by Scott McCarney. All photographs by Keith Smith, except for the following: Page 32, Paul Warchol; 33, Wilber H. Schilling; 40-41, D. James Dee; bottom 41, Daniel Kelm; 44-48, Jeroen van Westen; bottom 109, D. James Dee; 125, D. James Dee; 126, Emily Erb Hartzell; top 127, Daniel Kelm; bottom 127, D. James Dee; 128, D. James Dee; 130, D. James Dee; 148, Daniel Kelm; 152-153, Paul Warchol; 154, D. James Dee; 156, Kathryn Leonard; 175, D. James Dee; 176, Daniel Kelm; 256-257, Daniel Kelm; 267, Gisela Reschke; 272 courtesy of Granary Books; 288-289, Daniel Kelm.

BOOKS-on-BOOKS

CONCEPT
Structure of the Visual Book, keith a smith BOOKS, Third Edition 1994, discusses concepts of ordering a book of pictures by means of a group, series, or sequence. Pacing is stressed by composing the pages as well as the individual pictures. Utilizing the space between pictures is part of the awareness of time in books. 240 pages with 198 photographic illustrations by 53 book artists. $25   ISBN 0-9637682-1-2

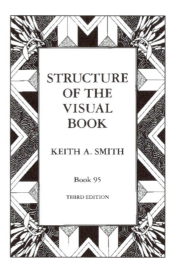

STRUCTURE
OF THE
VISUAL
BOOK

KEITH A. SMITH

Book 95

THIRD EDITION

CONCEPT
Text in the Book Format, Second Edition, 1995, is a concern for conceiving text as a book experience. This differs from writing a running manuscript or the single sheet format. A book experience cannot be fully revealed in a recitation but demands holding the physical object and turning pages conceived as part of the content. This approach does not treat the book format as a vessel, but allows writing to emanate *from* the inherent properties of the book—the opposite of sticking words *into* the object. 128 pages. $17.50   ISBN 0-9637682-3-9

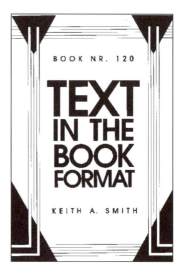

BOOK NR. 120

TEXT
IN THE
BOOK
FORMAT

KEITH A. SMITH

All the books are printed on archival paper. Available either as Smythe sewn paperback, or, in sheets, folded and gathered sections, if you wish to hand bind your own copy.

How To Bind
*Non-Adhesive Binding, Volume I:
Books without Paste or Glue,* keith a
smith BOOKS, Third Edition,
1994. Introduction covers binding, paper, sewing, knots and
tools. This is followed by detailed
written instructions for 32 simple
to complex sewings. The procedures are also presented in 250
drawings, diagrammed step by
step. 50 photographic reproduc-
tions of bindings by 22 binders.
Source section contains over 650
addresses of suppliers of papers,
tools and equipment; workshops;
guilds; dealers, book stores and
periodicals. 320 pages. $30
ISBN 0-9637682-0-4

How To Bind
*Non-Adhesive Binding, Volume III:
Exposed Spine Sewings,* keith a
smith BOOKS, First Edition,
1995. Variations on raised support sewings with pack cords, or
endbands as change-over, rather
than using kettle stitches.
Descriptions of sewing across the
spine include 2–Needle Coptic,
Greek Binding, Celtic Weave and
Caterpillar. Most of the sewings
were devised by Smith as the
book was written. Photographic
illustrations by contemporary
binders are shown. 320 pages.
$30
ISBN 0-9637682-4-7

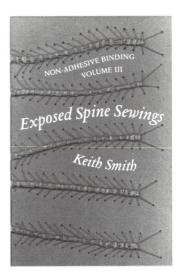

To order books or for a free brochure on all titles, contact:
Keith Smith, 22 Cayuga Street, Rochester, NY 14620-2153
Telephone or FAX: 716/473-6776

COLOPHON

Book 169
was begun in March 1993 on a Macintosh IIcx, and completed on a
Power Mac 7100/66. There was no running manuscript. Text was formatted *as* it was written, using Quark XPress. Drawn illustrations were
imported from Aldus Freehand, and, later, Macromedia Freehand.

1- 2- & 3-Section Sewings
was periodically proofed on an Apple Laserwriter II NT, and later, on a
Hewlett Packard LaserJet 4MV. The book was sent to the printer on-disk,
postscript, using SyQuest 44 megabyte removable cartridges, for negative
output: 1200 dots per inch for the type and 150 line screen for the drawings and digital scans.

Typeface is Columbus MT and Columbus Expert MT, with captions in
Optima. Drawn and photographic illustrations are by the author, except
for the Photo Credits listed on page 313.

Non-Adhesive Binding, VOLUME II
cover design and digital scans of the sewings and photographs are by
Scott McCarney.

This second printing of the First Edition is offset in 2000 copies on
Mohawk Superfine 80 lb. text and cover with matte film lamination. The
book is Smythe sewn, paperback.

Additional copies are available unbound, folded and gathered, for those
who might wish to hand bind their own copy.

Keith A. Smith
August 1995

KE◎TH